e-tailing

BERNADETTE TIERNAN

DEARBORN™
A **Kaplan Professional** Company

This publication is designed to provide accurate and authoritative information in regard to the subject matter covered. It is sold with the understanding that the publisher is not engaged in rendering legal, accounting, or other professional service. If legal advice or other expert assistance is required, the services of a competent professional should be sought.

Acquistions Editor: Jean Iversen
Managing Editor: Jack Kiburz
Interior Design: Lucy Jenkins
Cover Design: DePinto Studios
Typesetting: the dotted i

Library of Congress Cataloging-in-Publication Data

Tiernan, Bernadette, 1951–
   e-tailing / Bernadette Tiernan.
      p.   cm.
   Includes bibliographical references (p.).
   ISBN 1-57410-129-3
   1. Electronic commerce. 2. Retail trade—Automation. I. Title.
HF5548.32.T53 1999
658.8'7'00285—dc21   99-36561
                                      CIP

■ Dedication

To my parents Regina and Bill Brunhuber with love and gratitude

CONTENTS

ACKNOWLEDGMENTS

I am deeply grateful for the encouragement and support I have received from my family, friends, and professional colleagues while working on this book. First of all, I could never have completed this book without the support and encouragement of my husband, Bill Tiernan, who helped me with research and news updates in the constantly changing environment of e-commerce as corporations reconfigure at Internet speed. Thanks also to our children, Katherine, Bill, and Caroline, who reinforced how powerful a tool e-tailing is as they evolve into the consummate online consumers.

Thanks to Vicki Quigley for her research into the legal aspects of e-commerce security, and to Kathleen Appleton for assisting in the compilation of resource and reference materials. Alyson Miller-Greenfield at the Rutgers University Small Business Development Center has been a great source of advice and referrals, for which I am very grateful. Thank you to John Burke for taking the time to carefully review my early manuscripts for technical accuracy. I am very grateful to Jean Iversen at Dearborn for the opportunity to write *e-tailing*, and for guiding the focus of this book. Finally, thanks to Regina Burke for having Faith.

INTRODUCTION

What is the new paradigm for e-tailing, the electronic aspect of retail commerce? Business owners and managers who require the precision of an established business model to operate comfortably in this new world undoubtedly will need to stock up on some heavy-duty headache remedies in the months to come. E-tail is evolving as fast as this sentence is composed—at Internet speed.

The 1999 National Retail Federation Survey projects that over 9 percent of total retail sales in North America will be made over the Internet by the year 2001. That doesn't seem like a very high percentage until you realize that this could translate into an e-commerce market of $2.1 trillion worldwide in the near future.

Barry Diller, chairman and CEO of USA Networks, Inc., says that the Internet is stabilizing as a convergence of entertainment, information, and e-commerce. As the popularity of the Internet increases in households and in businesses for entertainment and information, users easily integrate it as a shopping tool and research assistant for product and price comparisons. In fact, saving money, along with convenience and selection, are key factors that influence a consumer's decision to buy online. Online shoppers are now rapidly becoming repeat customers, and the anticipation of new information adds to their enjoyment.

Just as a fascinating storefront grabs your attention, lures you back, and creates a local buzz, successful e-commerce sites attract repeat visitors and buyers. These sites combine energy, ingenuity, economics, the latest technology, and a good old-fashioned sense of security. Add consumer consciousness and marketplace savvy and designs that catch your eye but don't bog down transmission time, and before you know it you are replicating a successful sales transaction of any type. Except that on the Internet, you can conduct business *all over the world,* regardless of your size. You can enter the e-commerce explosion, with online retail revenues reaching $18.1 billion today and growing exponentially.

Peter Levitan, the first Internet news professional in the country to be selected for the Small Business Administration (SBA) Media Advocate of the Year Award, is ready to harness this energy. "It's important to understand the retail spectrum," he says. "At one extreme, we have businesses that are only online, such as Amazon.com. At the other extreme are those that are totally offline, which are Main Street. The rest will be some combination of online and offline." As president of New Jersey Online (NJO), a company that handles 480,000 pages of information a day, Levitan tracks trends closely. NJO expects its growth to come in the joint online-and-offline markets. "We tell local retailers that 35 percent of their market went online last week," Levitan says.

New Jersey is a snapshot of the nation's potential e-commerce picture. For huge numbers of people nationwide, shopping is a way of life, offering a legitimate rainy-day alternative to outdoor exercise. Retailers consider e-commerce nirvana because of high disposable incomes. In New Jersey alone where more than 1,131 shopping centers offer 154.6 million square feet of leasable retail space, shoppers spend almost $77 billion in a given shopping year. The state boasts more than 20,000 retailers operating about 50,000 shops, including megamalls. Mall shoppers are ripe for conversion to e-tail outlets, because shopping in malls or brick-and-mortar stores generates major stress. We possess minuscule patience and minute amounts of time. Our extraordinary stamina for trekking across parking lot terrain (unless, of course, we opt for valet service) and rigorous endurance of long checkout lines are exhausted by intolerable traffic congestion. Online shopping provides a logical solution to the cognitive dissonance we experience when we need to shop but can't tolerate the mall experience. And when shoppers collectively switch their intensity to cybermalls, retailers had better watch out.

Business organizations and associations provide insight about the grass-roots impact of e-commerce. Small Business Development Centers (SBDCs), which provide local services for small business owners and budding entrepreneurs, have established special technology help services to train, support, and jump-start technology-based companies and businesses that want to incorporate technological advantages into their plans for growth. Alyson Miller-Greenfield, associate director of the Rutgers University SBDC, meets regularly with business owners who are assessing their online future. "I strongly believe that the role of online communities will become increasingly important," she says. Bob Sepolen, manager of an SBA Business Information Center, estimates that more than 250 clients per month seek information about electronic business in his local office alone.

Diahann Lassus, president of the National Association of Women Business Owners (NAWBO), believes that e-commerce will open opportunities for expansion that small businesses were never aware of. Lassus says, "E-commerce is taking companies global that never thought of it before. It's the new frontier for small businesses."

Curt Macysyn, a director of the 60,000-member National Federation of Independent Businesses (NFIB), said recent survey data from his organization indicates that 38 percent of their membership are doing business online, 58 percent are using e-mail regularly, and 68 percent are using the Internet to some extent. He anticipates dramatic growth in online business in the very near future.

E-tailing provides a step-by-step guide for consumer retailers wishing to enter the e-commerce explosion, which will bring businesses of all sizes to levels of phenomenal national and international growth. Successful Web sites strike a delicate balance between the mesmerizing effects of bleeding-edge technology and the most traditional customer connections. *E-tailing* addresses both technological and customer concerns.

Successful e-tail efforts incorporate up-to-the-moment trend analyses, comprehensive project management, propitious technical design and implementation, perceptive customer responsiveness, astute marketing and sales, impenetrable security, and more. Because of the rapidly evolving nature of the Web, *E-tailing* emphasizes principles and concepts that can be applied even as hardware and software change.

Every attempt has been made to present technical information in a practical, easy-to-follow manner. Although this book is not intended to serve as a programmers' guide, *E-tailing* can be used by technicians to gain insight regarding the dynamic interaction of sales, marketing, advertising, layout, and customer relations. Checklists, charts, table, graphs, and printouts of Web sites have been included for ease of understanding. Case studies are used to show real-world application of theory.

E-tailing features current information about major corporations and small businesses that provide relevant tools, equipment, and support services. Associations and organizations that provide information, consulting services, and networking opportunities for e-tailers are also described. Magazines, newsletters, Web sites, and resources that feature the most up-to-the-minute news and reviews of electronic commerce strategies, techniques, and concerns are listed in the reference chapter.

As online business increases, so too does the need for timely and comprehensive information. *E-tailing* addresses a complete range of business categories and individual merchants, including the following:

- Managers and owners of businesses of all sizes, from major corporations to sole proprietorships, who need to learn about electronic commerce to oversee development efforts in their own organizations
- All levels of employees, from executives to staff personnel, who may be part of a business' transition to electronic commerce
- Home-based business owners and consumers who have made purchases online and are now considering e-commerce for their own products or services
- Teachers (from high school through graduate levels, as well as continuing education) and workshop leaders in business or computer curriculums who are running courses or programs on electronic commerce
- Entrepreneurs who need to jump-start their ventures through e-commerce
- Consultants who are engaged in helping companies establish a strong online presence

While *E-tailing* is directed to the general reader, it is structured to allow easy use in an academic or workshop environment. After more than 25 years in and out of classrooms, I know how important it is to be able to explain complex issues in straightforward terms. For almost 12 years, I worked in the engineering department of AT&T, most of the time in the field of human engineering. I had the privilege of working with some of the brightest thinkers in the corporation, before and during the transformation of antiquated processes into streamlined computer systems, and throughout the conception and refinement of ISDN (integrated services data network). It was a hands-on opportunity to witness that even monolithic mega-structures and vast global networks could be humbled in the hands of a solitary individual seated before a computer screen. And so it is today—the power of e-commerce rests in the hands of each individual consumer, pointing and clicking on a personal computer.

Comments, questions, or case studies? I'd love to hear from you.

Bernadette Tiernan
Tiernan Associates
P.O. Box 1382
Ridgewood, NJ 07451
E-mail: Btiernan@aol.com
Phone: 201-447-5625
Web site: etailing4profit.com

"Click Here" Economics

■ The E-Commerce Big Picture Today

"The real movers and shakers are pointers and clickers," proclaimed an ad for the *Wall Street Journal* Interactive Edition. We're on our way from an Internet dominated by business-to-business specialists to a power shift. Consumers, get ready to rule.

Shopping has assumed a brand-new look as online retail blasts off and Internet sales skyrocket. Convenience, ease of purchase, simplified comparison shopping, and enhanced security contribute to the wave of shopping binges at today's new online shopping malls. The Internet also presents an entirely distinct mode of establishing customer rapport. At the major department store Web sites, holiday shopping seasons alone have demonstrated online sales increases of 200 to 500 percent. Welcome to the world of electronic commerce, the fastest growing facet of the Internet.

U.S. businesses have more than tripled the amount of goods and services exchanged on the Internet annually, now spending hundreds of billions of dollars. By 2002, the front-runner—business-to-business electronic commerce—will reach $327 billion, while business-to-consumer electronic commerce quickly catches up. Businesses of all types are feeling the force of the Internet, from stockbrokers and travel agents to retail merchants. Companies that have already launched e-commerce enterprises attest to the incredible power and potential for growth. Jeff Bezos, chief executive of Web bookseller Amazon.com, says, "This is the Kitty Hawk era of electronic commerce."

■ Who's Buying and Who's Selling?

1998 will go down in history as the year e-commerce mainstreamed. As e-commerce grew in popularity, online retailers were able to buck sluggish seasons in brick-and-mortar stores. Online book and music retailer Amazon.com broke through all slow retail periods and continued to grow at an amazing rate. When Amazon.com expanded to Amazon-almost-everything with the confidence of a true market leader, the company began the slow but steady ascension to a leadership position in more than one niche.

Traditional retail establishments like the Gap, Sears, Macy's, Kmart, and Toys 'R' Us joined catalog companies like Lands' End with promotional attractions and creative Web sites to lure new Internet consumers and convince shoppers to return and spend even more of their holiday budgets online. With a record-breaking $13 billion in sales for the year 1998, both multi-channel merchants (who own brick-and-mortar stores, catalogs, and Internet sites) and Internet-only businesses thrived. At that point, multichannel merchants more than doubled their sales volume over the previous year, reaching $2.3 billion. Internet-only companies generated over $5.3 billion.

Today, more than 50 percent of all U.S. households shop over the Internet, and online sales more than triple each year. It is safe to predict near-future revenue increases of over 200 percent annually. The most popular sites continue to include books, music, and movies, with major jumps in toy sites and specialty clothing stores during holiday shopping seasons.

Consumer confidence in the interactive media marketplace has surged since 1998. Online retail has taken on a life of its own and shapes the direction of e-commerce. While new mainstream retailers go online every year, major players like Amazon.com fine-tune their strategies and increase their market share.

In 1998, record numbers of first-time online shoppers caused cyberspace sales to soar. The single most powerful influence in the transition to online retail shopping is the consumer. Buoyed by increased confidence in Internet security, optimistic about the concurrent resurgence of the stock market, or simply more willing to try something bold and different, consumers translated their new point of view into solid sales through electronic commerce.

Statistics that delineate the breakdown of online sales by major industry reveal a wide range of success stories. Top online shopping sites traditionally have included books and music, computers, travel, and ticket event sales. The huge increase in demand for online sales has caused its fair share of problems. Promoted and perceived as a way to avoid long lines, cranky crowds, and unbearable traffic, virtual shopping has offered its own version of congestion during peak volume periods. The combination of heavy traffic and e-mail correspondence about supply shortages has led to crashes and clogged lines at some sites. A sharp rise in dropped calls unfortunately has characterized several of the top Internet service providers (ISPs). Heavy holiday shopping traffic caused delays and occasional crashes for such sites as Amazon.com, Barnesandnoble.com, and the auction site Ebay.

■ Past Growth and Future Projections

To compete in the new millennium, businesses will need to become fluent in electronic commerce today. Online sales are projected to continue to soar in every industry, according to data from Jupiter Communications and Forrester Research, Inc., the two primary research companies that track online spending. They differ in their precise projections of growth but concur in explosive rates. Jupiter Communications has estimated $41 billion as their best bet for business to consumer online sales by 2002. They break out dollars to computer hardware at 30.1 percent, travel at 29.6 percent, books at 9.2 percent, and 31.1 percent for all other sales. Figure 1.1 illustrates several significant markets.

Most experts agree that business-to-business transaction volumes will continue to outrank business-to-consumer transactions in the immediate future, but that trend is expected to shift. Consumers will need to see value added to their traditional ways of shopping in order to change their behavior patterns consistently.

■ Perspectives of the Cybersavvy

The notion of "cybergeek" has changed shape from pocket-protected programmer to savvy connoisseur of information. A June 1998 article in

Figure 1.1   Online Sales Growth Projections

Product/Service Category	1997	2001 Estimate
Business-to-business sales	$8 billion	$183 billion
Financial services	1.2 billion	5 billion
PC hardware and software	863 million	3.8 billion
Travel	654 million	7.4 billion
Entertainment	286 million	2.7 billion
Books and music	156 million	1.1 billion
Apparel and footwear	92 million	514 million
Ticket event sales	79 million	2 billion

Business Week stated that ". . . the Net has gone from a playground for nerds into a vast communications and trading center where some 90 million people swap information or do deals around the world."

The innovative seller knows that being on the Internet means he or she can sell virtually everywhere. Some traditional storeowners still eye the Internet with suspicion, however, fearful their total sales will decline if they offer products online. They worry that fewer people hanging around the malls and buying on impulse will kill their brick-and-mortar stores, and many are not confident that they can make it with online sales alone. Those who have been most successful have learned not to cannibalize different segments of their business, but to design a marketing strategy that maximizes the strengths of each element of their business, including their brick-and-mortar store, mail-order catalogs, television shopping, and Web site orders.

Other retailers are uncomfortable moving into an area of selling in which they are not fluent. If they have minimal experience working with the Web, their lack of expertise may inhibit their marketing strategy. The Web-impaired are forced to face an additional element of fear. Retailers who realize that manufacturers have begun selling directly on the Web, undercutting the retailers' prices, are more receptive to exploring their online potential and creating new partnerships.

Online consumers cherish the simple advantages of shopping in their pajamas, avoiding crowds, and comparing prices with a few clicks of a mouse. Electronic commerce, or e-tailing, is like a set of interactive catalogs with the enhancements of TV shopping. Medical research indicates that there may be more to this phenomenon than meets the eye. One recent AMA study that examined the physical effects of shopping for men and women found mall shopping elevated blood pressure and increased heart rate to a disturbing degree in men, but had little or no effect on women. These men experienced the physical manifestations of stress that were equivalent to those of individuals in a wartime situation.

What are the Web's advantages over the catalog-and-call method of shopping? Some, particularly those individuals who put off their holiday shopping until the week before Christmas, might dispute the timeliness of online shopping. Invariably they faced traffic conditions on the Internet that were almost as maddening as those in mall parking lots. What's more aggravating: a 40-minute wait to exit a shopping mall parking ramp or enduring 40 minutes of busy signals on America Online? Frustration is in the eye of the beholder.

When you know what you want and where to find it, the Web is at its best, even when busy. If you want to browse, your patience may be tested as you click here then sit and wait. Even if you are using a 56K modem, you may feel like pictures and graphics take forever to appear if your ISP transmits data at a slower rate (more on site strategies later).

■ Web Demographics

If it seems as though almost everyone is talking about the Internet, recent statistics indicate that this perception is a reality. Internet use has jumped to over 53.5 million, with more than 72 million Americans, 37 percent of the U.S. adult population, having access to the Internet. At least 40 percent of Americans have Internet access either at home or at work, with 34 percent using it at least one hour per week. Internet usage is becoming mainstream.

At-home Internet usage, which once lagged behind work use, now exceeds work use by more than 28 percent. About 25.5 million people have accessed the Internet from work, while 35.3 million have accessed it from home. Men use the Internet at a rate of 52.5 percent; women, at 47.5 percent, are steadily increasing their rates of usage while male usage has declined. Women business owners skew the statistics in a different direction, however. Women business owners have used the Internet at a far greater rate (83 percent), and 43 percent have a home page on the Web, according to research by the National Foundation for Women Business Owners (NFWBO).

A typical online household has 1.5 adults online at home, spending 8.2 hours online per adult per week. The median age of Web users is 38, and mean income has been determined at $60,850, with 43.8 percent college graduates or more. So while the computer-savvy Generation X population would seem to be great targets for e-commerce, it appears that the older population—with higher incomes—are online the most. Most researchers agree, however, that these figures are shifting rapidly. The mean income is decreasing, the number of noncollege graduates is increasing, and the male/female usage pattern is even or shifting in favor of women. Total online shoppers for 1998 were estimated at 16 million, growing to 23.1 million in 1999; 33.4 million in 2000; 45.2 million in 2001; and 61.1 million in 2002, according to research by the National Retail Federation and Media Metrix, a leading provider of statistics on Web usage patterns.

Small businesses are also making big moves onto the Internet. About 2.6 million small businesses are online now, of which at least 30 percent now allow secure credit card transactions. Access Media International (AMI) estimates that the number of Web sites hosted by small businesses should approach 5 million by 2002. Forrester Research predicts that 45 percent of small businesses (fewer than 100 employees), 85 percent of medium-size companies, and 98 percent of large businesses (over 1,000 employees) will do business online by 2002.

Trust in the Internet, however, has not escalated in direct proportion to usage. Ogilvy Public Relations Worldwide found that most Americans never trust a sponsored Internet site as a reliable source of information, and only 45 percent indicated they could sometimes trust the Web.

The downside of Internet usage has been described by some analysts as the "digital divide" between those who have access to information and those who do not. In the United States, about 50 percent of urban households with annual incomes of $75,000 or more have Internet access. Fewer than 10 percent of the rural poor do.

■ Major Players Today

About 39 percent of retailers currently sell online, up from 12 percent in 1997. The number of retailers who plan to sell online in the near future continues to increase exponentially. But in order to reach a company's Web site, most of us pass through one of the major players. America Online still holds the lead, but other companies are following in hot pursuit. Popularity in usage is paralleled in huge stock market gains for these players as well. A breakdown of the major Web properties is shown in Figure 1.2.

The single most visited site on the Web has been AOL.com, accessed by almost one-half of all Web users, but there are challengers to their domain reign. May 1999 domain ranks appear in Figure 1.3.

Figure 1.2   Top Web Properties

Rank	Property	Number of Unique Visitors
1.	AOL network—proprietary and WWW	46.2 million
2.	Microsoft sites	32.4 million
3.	Yahoo! sites	31.3 million
4.	Lycos	30.1 million
5.	Go Network	20.9 million
6.	GeoCities	20.0 million
7.	The Excite Network	17.2 million
8.	Time Warner Online	13.1 million
9.	Amazon	10.8 million
10.	Alta Vista sites	10.6 million

Source: Reprinted with permission of Media Metrix, New York, May 1999. "Properties" include the largest single Web site brands as well as consolidations of multiple domains that fall under one brand or common ownership. "Unique visitors" are unduplicated (counted only once).

Figure 1.3   Top Web Domains

Rank	Domain	Number of Unique Visitors
1.	Yahoo.com	31.1 million
2.	AOL.com	28.9 million
3.	MSN.com	22.2 million
4.	Geocities.com	19.5 million
5.	Go.com	18.9 million
6.	Netscape.com	18.5 million
7.	Microsoft.com	16.0 million
8.	Excite.com	15.2 million
9.	Lycos.com	14.9 million
10.	Angelfire.com	12.6 million

Source: Reprinted with permission of Media Metrix, New York, May 1999. "Unique visitors" are unduplicated (counted only once).

In December 1998, America Online closed a $4.2 billion deal to buy Netscape, shifting the balance of power in electronic retail to three dominant companies: AOL, Yahoo!, and Microsoft. As these major sites become larger and draw more visitors, they also increase their potential to draw new stores ready to go online. As their respective collection of stores increases, "malls," or bundling of groups of retail stores, become more interesting and enhance benefits to the consumer.

■ Who's Who of Market Leaders

Explosive growth in online shopping has characterized all the major online retail players. Initially only certain goods sold well on the Web. Books, CDs and personal computers were among the first to find their niche in electronic commerce, and subsequently the first to achieve major sales. On the other hand, companies that quietly, behind the scenes, helped other businesses move into the limelight of electronic commerce also grew.

Highlights of many of the major players—those who made headlines and those that discreetly made millions—follow. This list includes major corporations who have created successful Web sites, as well as portals, search sites, and search engines. The companies listed below have each been credited by at least three major reviewers as key players.

Major Corporations

IBM. IBM's worldwide electronic business revenues were $27 billion, one-third of their $78.5 billion total. AOL and Microsoft made headlines more often, but IBM's Net.Commerce rules. IBM has put an incredible collection of prominent e-commerce retail stores on the Internet. IBM's list includes Macy's (www.macys.com), Nordstrom (www.nordstrom.com), and L.L.Bean (www.llbean.com), to name a few. IBM's major advantage is that they can put together a complete package for any type of business: software, hardware, networks, and professional services (including Web site design, managing and storing data, project advice). IBM can offer a start-to-finish solution. The only feature IBM lacks is a cybermall.

AOL. America Online's December 1998 deal to buy Netscape Communications for $4.2 billion provided the groundwork to construct the world's largest shopping mall online. AOL hosts J. Crew (www.jcrew.com) and J&R

Computer World (www.jandr.com), and intends to strengthen its lead as the first-ranking cybermall with Netscape. Netscape earned its reputation based on its Internet browser, but the Netcenter portal and e-commerce software are features that enrich AOL's position in both the home and work environments. In a third piece of AOL's deal, Sun Microsystems began to license Netscape's e-commerce software to sell with computer systems geared to industry.

Amazon.com (www.amazon.com). Amazon.com gained fame as the largest online bookseller. When Amazon.com added compact discs to its product list, it quickly became the leading online music retailer. Amazon.com has managed to increase the distance between themselves and Barnes & Noble by miles. It also acquired the Junglee service for comparison shopping.

CDnow, Inc. (www.cdnow.com). The strategic merger that occurred when CDnow bought N2K created a combined company with approximately 1.2 million customers, offering about 500,000 items, the largest selection of music products. This merger placed CDnow in a better position to challenge Amazon.com. The new company has the potential to become a leader among Internet companies. CDnow offers a collection of music-related items ten times the size of the average music store. N2K's Music Boulevard was the world's largest online superstore as measured by number of titles (see Figure 1.4).

Dell Computer Corporation (www.dell.com). Dell Computer Corporation estimates $500 million in annualized sales over the Web to consumers and small businesses. Online sales tripled over one year to $10 million a day. Dell began its strategy of providing customized computer models with telephone orders, keeping in constant communication with parts suppliers to maintain the best control over inventory. With the Internet, Dell keeps in contact with suppliers on an hourly basis, keeping inventory on hand down to record lows. Dell's home page is shown in Figure 1.5.

Cisco Connection Online (www.cisco.com). Cisco Systems, Inc. is described as the worldwide leader in networking for the Internet, selling over $22 million in products every day. Their products include routers, LAN and ATM switches, dial-up access servers and network management software. Cisco provides end-to-end networking solutions for customers to build their own information infrastructure. Their products connect people, computing devices, and computer networks.

Figure 1.4 CDnow, Inc. offers a collection of music-related items ten times the size of the average music store.

Figure 1.5 Dell Computer Corporation sells over $10 million every day.

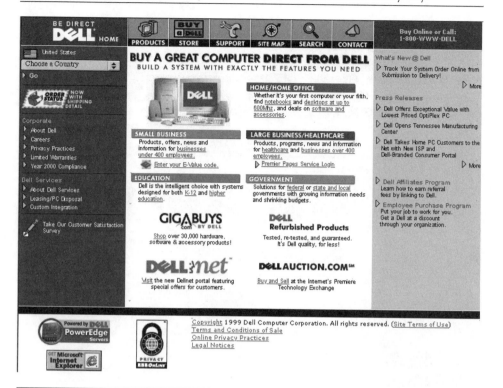

Cyberian Outpost (www.outpost.com). Cyberian Outpost (Figure 1.6) is one of the leading online retailers of computer products, selling hardware and software, peripherals, and accessories. Cyberian Outpost promises to be competitively priced, usually delivers within 24 hours, and offers downloadable software for 100,000 titles. Web-related news and computer product information are timely and extensive.

eBay (www.ebay.com). Ebay (Figure 1.7) is the Internet's leading flea market. Officially named eBay, Inc., they are a San Jose, California–based company that sells just about anything on earth via their Web site. They held 13.6 million auctions last year, justification for their self-proclaimed status as the world's largest personal online trading community. Ebay runs about 400,000 online auctions every day, bringing buyers and sellers together. This vast collection of participants will buy and sell virtually anything (more on eBay in Chapter 8).

Figure 1.6 Cyberian Outpost revenues have exceeded $26 million.

Figure 1.7   Ebay attracts over 6 million visitors to their online auction site during holiday shopping seasons.

iMall (www.imall.com). The largest online shopping mall, or collection of online stores, is iMall (Figure 1.8), which has about 1,500 merchants selling video, music, and gifts of all types. Imall promises quality and bargains, and keeps the shopping experience simple. Customers can comparison shop with ease.

eToys (www.etoys.com). Etoys (Figure 1.9) is a Santa Monica, California start-up that took off like wildfire in late '98. It now offers 2,200 toys, covering the gamut from mass-market to elite. Their goal is to make mincemeat of Toys 'R' Us by growing to 4,500 items. They expected revenues to reach $10 to $15 million in 1999, and will be profitable when sales hit $75 to $100 million.

Broadcast.com (www.broadcast.com). Broadcast.com (Figure 1.10) serves over 800,000 users daily and broadcasts on the Internet 24 hours a day, seven days a week. They claim to be the leading aggregator and broadcaster of streaming media programming on the Web. Their first live broadcast was in September 1995. Since then, they have broadcast over 16,000 live events of every type, including radio programs, sporting events, annual meetings, and the Academy Awards. The company can deliver hundreds of live and on-demand audio and video programs over the Internet.

Portals, Search Sites, and Search Engines

Yahoo! (biz.yahoo.com). Yahoo!, the most popular Internet search index, was created in 1994 by Jerry Yang and David Filo, Stanford University doctoral candidates, whose original program indexed Web sites in a library catalog format. Advertisers generated revenues, and the program was free to Web users. Today Yahoo!, the corporation, offers not only search capabilities, but also more than 2 million products from more than 2,700 online stores, including JC Penney and Cigars-R-Us.

AltaVista. AltaVista, a widely used search engine, also offers news, shopping services, and stock quotes. Last year, company revenues reached $40 million. Compaq Computer Corp. announced in January 1998 that it wanted to sell off AltaVista into a separate publicly owned company. This spin-off will allow AltaVista to enter agreements with Compaq rivals and give them an opportunity to grow more rapidly.

Figure 1.8   Imall, the largest cybermall, promises quality, bargains, and easy shopping.

Figure 1.9   Etoys reaches a peak in visitors during holiday shopping times.

Figure 1.10   Broadcast.com offers a state-of-the art way to view live events.

2

Exploring Technological Frontiers

■ The Pioneers of E-Commerce

Larry Downes and Chunka Mui identify e-commerce as a "killer app," defined as "a new good or service that establishes an entirely new category and, by being first, dominates it, returning several hundred percent on the initial investment" (*Unleashing the Killer App,* Harvard Business School Press, 1998). Many of the pioneers of e-commerce still dominate the scene. But *pioneer* doesn't mean the same thing as *explorer.* The e-pioneers rode in behind scouting parties of banks and brokers.

Banks were among the earliest users of electronic information exchanges, passing data along before we knew enough to question them. Our paychecks were automatically deposited, our money was moved from one account to another electronically by the 1970s, before we had even heard of encryption. We were delighted that our money was managed quickly and efficiently; most of us never thought to interrogate a bank officer about the security of the procedure. Less than a decade later we made the transition from tellers to ATM machines with equal aplomb.

The consumer adjustment to e-commerce was not as smooth. While we trusted our banks to safeguard our money and confidentiality, the consumer perspective on retail establishments was somewhat reserved. Transferring money electronically from a business to personal bank account might not faze us; applying for a car loan online and waiting for the auto to be delivered may be a different story. If you bare your financial soul online, does this exposition have the privacy guarantee of confessional secrecy?

Many consumers are still concerned that online information is not secure. While security issues may not faze professional online shoppers, it is still a deterrent to the uninitiated. Deb Zeyen, vice president of CBS New Media, has a positive outlook. She buys books and does her banking online, and says both e-commerce outlets work phenomenally well. Does security concern her? "The privacy and security issues are being addressed by the whole industry," she said, "with the understanding that if security isn't addressed, there won't be a business. The excellent e-commerce sites and banking sites have handled security." The pioneers of electronic commerce—banks, books, travel, CDs—have instilled consumer confidence in confidentiality and remain excellent sites today.

Internet pioneers cannot afford to be complacent. If they don't keep moving and changing, they will be destroyed by their competitors within moments. Following are ways in which pioneers work to stay in the lead:

America Online. This pioneer built its name as an easy-to-learn household tool that was full of features that appealed to all ages. Still a formidable force in the cyberworld, AOL now faces the challenge of retaining a leadership position. America Online's announcement of its intention to become involved in e-commerce raised the eyebrows of executives who would now have to take them seriously in the office as well as at the home PC. AOL will help businesses set up online stores, offering software and consulting services, providing end-to-end solutions for e-tailers. By purchasing Netscape Communications Corporation, AOL gained an edge with software to make this support possible. Not resting in a dormant position, AOL has chosen to keep moving and changing.

Dell Computer Corporation. This pioneer's business strategy, which worked well before the company's move online, exploded with success in the transition to e-commerce. Letting consumers take control over the design of their purchases, offering some guidance and advice, and giving inventory status information for a shopper's computer components made Dell an early leader in customer connections.

Amazon.com. This online pioneer started selling books in 1995, offering 30 percent discounts on bestsellers, and expanding to the sale of mega-quantities of books. It's a good thing they didn't stop there. Barnes & Noble jumped in with 40 percent discounts online, and Wal-Mart offered 45 percent. But before you could say "rainforest," Amazon.com added CDs to their inventory. Then in December 1998, "Shop the Web" was launched. With Shop the Web, e-tailers can be featured on Amazon.com's site. Will this work? If so, what's next?

Ebay. This pioneer made auctions a 24-hour-a-day possibility, turning shopping into a hobby for insomniacs and treasure-seekers of all ages and geographic locations. Ebay created something that not only works, but also is fun.

Broadcast.com. This site brings live events to the Internet, giving us a feel for what the future holds when media intermingle. With the computer terminal serving as a vehicle for live broadcasts, it's easier to imagine the television set becoming interactive. Watch for Broadcast.com to maintain a leading role as the scope and depth of their events continues to expand.

Netrepreneurs' Secrets of Success

Internet entrepreneurs, or *netrepreneurs,* have made headlines for advancing new and exciting technologies, creating and promoting innovative products, and earning billions of dollars in the stock market while actually making no profits at all. Headlines come in all forms. In an amazing leap away from technological proficiency, a bold move by Victoria's Secret earned more than just sound bites for their online business. Victoria's Secret decided to feature a simulcast of their annual fashion show on their Web site. The event was advertised during the Super Bowl, at a rate of about $1.6 million for a 30-second spot. When the event aired, Victoria's Secret landed more hits on their Web site than ever before. The site, which was designed to handle a maximum of 500,000 viewers, attracted over one million. The Web site was sluggish, the video jagged, and the sound cut out. But while the Victoria's Secret effort failed technically, it drew more publicity for the company than an advertising campaign alone could have accomplished. Every major television network covered the fashion show and Web site problems in the following morning's news broadcasts. Did they highlight fuzzy images from the Web site? Hardly. Footage from the live fashion show, which may not have been a newsworthy event on its own, gained prominent coverage—mostly because the Web site fizzled. Go figure.

A potential failure turned into a success story for Victoria's Secret, with a format that was by no means leading edge. Broadcast.com has broadcast live events on the Internet with the most sophisticated technology and highest quality for years, without nearly as much media hype. But the Victoria's Secret event combined major advertising dollars to promote their Web site show on a nationally prominent event with a target market that had a high probability of response. The combined package turned into a winning blend. They were willing to invest in success.

For Internet leaders, the Web site is simply one component of an overall integrated strategy. Dell, for example, had already streamlined communication with its vendors and had refined the concept of personalized computers before beginning to sell on the Web. Selling computers online enhanced a system that was working well to begin with, making it easier to purchase products that were already in demand.

Net.B@ank (www.netbank.com), the largest FDIC-insured bank operating solely on the Internet, became the world's first profitable Internet bank. In February 1999, Net.B@nk announced that its overall business plan for rapid growth included a dramatic increase in marketing initiatives. The company's strategic marketing push for expansion included extensive public relations, online and offline advertising, and a branding campaign. The company's goal clearly is to become the dominant brand name in Internet banking by increasing their customer base and deposits. They have set the ambitious goal of achieving strong growth and profit simultaneously.

The success of netrepreneurs is truly multidimensional. Their stories convey a common theme: a leadership role in their field. Michael Treacy and Fred Wiersema describe the tension that this leadership role—specifically product leadership—generates, in their book, *The Discipline of Market Leaders* (Addison-Wesley, 1995). Treacy and Wiersema say that the dual responsibility of striving to upgrade existing products while simultaneously creating the next generation makes companies vibrant. They say that this responsibility serves the purpose of keeping market leaders preoccupied while they take charge of orchestrating the dynamic balance. The balance is "between the defense of existing products and the introduction of new ones; between unbounded creativity and the concerns of fiscal practicality; between getting the product right and getting it to market; between betting on a few big ideas and nurturing a broader range of maybes." High-tech companies outnumber all other companies cited as market leaders by Treacy and Wiersema.

Leaders are described as those who evaluate their products and services, customer base, staff, and available resources (including time and money, besides people) before jumping into development of any new venture. Can they handle the potential increase in sales from online orders? With the world at their fingertips, can they meet the demands of the world? Successful netrepreneurs incorporated many of the following elements into their earliest initiatives:

- *Take a long-range view.* If these companies needed to make a profit immediately, they would have abandoned their e-commerce strategy in their first year.
- *Sell products that are easy to identify.* Products that can be described, illustrated, or photographed simply were the first to do well on the Internet. You don't have to touch or feel a book or CD to buy it. Commodities that can be illustrated effectively generate faster sales.
- *Capitalize on the value of product extensions.* When consumers know your brand, you have a better opportunity to continue the line with online sales.
- *Provide services that are understandable.* You can't touch or feel a service, but if it can be described in simple terminology comprehensible to the shopper, you have a better chance of selling the service. Priceline.com will find the best price on airline tickets for you. That's pretty simple.
- *Recognize the potential in niche markets.* Niche markets include experts in some area and know the value of the goods they are seeking. To the right shopper, antiques, coins, and stock trades are worth searching for, and paying for.
- *Acquire prominent listing in the big-scale portals.* Get known fast, big-time, using delivery vehicles that are well-known for achieving results.
- *Install high-profile security systems.* Remove all traces of doubt about confidentiality and dependability, eliminating this huge obstacle to consumer confidence.

Figure 2.1   Seven Secrets of Successful Netrepreneurs

---

1. Take a long-range view.
2. Sell products that are easy to identify.
3. Capitalize on the value of product extensions.
4. Provide services that are understandable.
5. Recognize the potential in niche markets.
6. Acquire prominent listing in the big-scale portals.
7. Install high-profile security systems.

■ Lessons from Other Market Leaders

Perhaps the true sign of success on the Internet is to be imitated. As Amazon.com became recognized as the online market leader, other companies aspired to become "the Amazon.com of. . . ." Fill in the blank: toys, wine, travel, information. But as the company advanced so far ahead of the herd that it seemed no one (even the mighty Barnes & Noble) could catch up, Amazon.com became a verb. A Web site that is "Amazoned," or "Amazon.commed" can no longer compete because the market leader has become so strong as to be untouchable. Whether used as a noun or a verb, Amazon.com was first. Etoys was first. First is best, according to *The 22 Immutable Laws of Marketing.*

To summarize, successful businesses have the following characteristics in common:

- *Innovation is a high priority.* Being first isn't good enough if a company does not maintain its leadership position by striving to *stay* first. Treacy and Wiersema's research confirms that market leaders are their own fiercest competitors. They are working on their next product while they are rolling out their latest innovations. Look at how quickly Amazon.com reached the top with online book sales, then moved right into selling CDs.
- *Strategic decisions support business planning.* In 1999, Net.B@nk rolled out a marketing plan that reinforced its decision to keep building its customer base as quickly as possible. Net.B@nk's services allow customers convenient access to checking, money market accounts, and certificates of deposit with excellent interest rates, brokerage services, mortgage lending, business equipment leasing services, and more. They are not planning to sell music CDs or create customer confusion about their mission.
- *Produce an excellent product.* Dell produced an excellent product before moving onto the Internet. Their emphasis on value extends to pricing and delivery, and has resulted in sales of over $10 million worth of computers daily.

In an article in *NetCommerce* magazine, a leading resource for e-commerce companies, Gerry Gottlieb wrote that the success of an online enterprise involves "developing a brand identity, building site traffic and retaining customer loyalty." Seven points synthesize many of the critical characteristics of companies who retain their leadership positions (see also Figure 2.2):

1. *Make the shopping experience a good one to differentiate your brand.* If a shopper can navigate the site quickly and easily, he or she is more likely to return. Return visits reinforce brand identity.

2. *Strongly differentiate yourself from less-experienced Internet retailers.* Companies that know the retail business of order fulfillment have an edge. If you are new to the Internet but you know how to pick, pack and ship, you have an advantage.

3. *Develop an innovative leadership position.* Know your strengths and communicate them strongly.

4. *Use a multitiered approach to build activity on the site.* Reinforce your brand image through multiple media outlets, including a traditional marketing approach and Internet advertising.

5. *Form a business alliance with an established advertising or marketing firm.* Companies that specialize in Internet advertising (banner services, etc.) help to create a name quickly and maximize results from any marketing campaign.

6. *Establish links with a network of affiliate sites.* Then these sites help sell your products and services, like a virtual sales force.

7. *Ensure that your site is helpful, informative, and functional.* The site should support product sales; no matter how good the product is, if the site is difficult to navigate, visitors won't return.

In the following chapters, additional questions about e-tailing will be answered:

- How can you design a site that keeps customers coming back?
- What really turns visitors from browsers to buyers?
- How can you market your Web site to increase "eyeballs" (a Web measure of visits to a site)?
- Can consumers' fears about security really be calmed?
- How do strategic partnerships enable exponential expansion?
- What have the experts found will work and will not work online?
- What's sticky? (You may already be wondering, "What *is* sticky?" *Sticky* refers to the ability of a Web site to hold on to visitors, to make them return over and over again, and eventually to buy something.)

There is almost unanimous agreement that e-tailing is better suited to some products and services than others. While the door is open to virtually all businesses, some have a higher probability of success based on customer demands and purchase patterns. Products that need to be touched and felt to be purchased still seem to be problematic, but this is changing. Products that are

Figure 2.2   Successful Site Secrets

25

Exploring
Technological
Frontiers

1. Offer a great shopping experience.
2. Differentiate from nouveau Net retailers.
3. Innovative in a leadership position.
4. Promote the site in multitiers.
5. Form alliances with advertising/marketing firms.
6. Link with affiliate sites.
7. Create a helpful, informative, and functional site.

unwieldy and therefore costly to ship also deter shoppers. Cases that work and may not work are discussed in further detail in Chapter 8.

ASE STUDY:
CBS New Media—A New Strategy

CBS.com, the Web site of CBS television, was the first network to provide visitors to the site with direct access to their local CBS affiliate station by simply entering a zip code. "We felt it was a huge improvement over anything that existed before," said Deb Zeyen, vice president of CBS New Media. The difference? Other networks only provided a link to their local stations. CBS brought the sites together, so that the CBS and affiliate sites would be one and the same, acting as a single source of information. A visitor to the Web site of Pittsburgh's local CBS station will be presented with a page that looks and feels like Pittsburgh but also provides immediate access to the national CBS database. "The page is branded KDK.com," said Zeyen, "but you have the extra added benefit of national information."

To make this work on a grand scale, CBS needed agreement from the local stations. According to Zeyen, they expected to launch with only 50 stations, but actually launched with 157 sites. "The scalability issue became enormous," she said. "We had a very intense service and a very heavy usage converging. We had to react quickly." They responded by adding new servers and new equipment, and by looking for ways to make the system work more efficiently. At first, the highest priority was to just get the site up, but as usage continued to grow, it became critical to be sure that everything was designed in the best way possible. "We had to get into the coding to see how to make changes. It seemed that every time we made one change, ten other things would need to be addressed. As we changed our navigation, we changed even more." In true new media style, nine months' worth of work was completed in one month, according to Zeyen.

Today CBS.com handles more than 27 million pages a month. "For every page you present to a Web site visitor, you may dip into your database 40 times," said Zeyen, emphasizing the complexity of the work behind even the simplest transaction. CBS.com expects to triple capacity in the next year. And CBS New Media is forming new strategic alliances that will expand the scope of the site exponentially. For more on this, see Chapter 13.

3

Digital Middlemen

■ Supply Chains Revisited

For every business that moves to electronic commerce traditional patterns shift dramatically. The most significant change occurs in supply-chain management where improvements have a direct effect on overall business performance. With electronic commerce, customers, distributors, factories, and suppliers can connect instantly. Before you know it, the respective parties begin to question old methods of indirect routing and look for ways to streamline their communication. There is every incentive to improve their transactions, because time and cost savings can be realized immediately.

Retail e-commerce provides one of the best opportunities for drastically changing supply chains. Suppliers who suddenly have the potential to reach out directly to customers can establish logical, direct links between the manufacturer and the consumer that save time and money. This gives new meaning to the phrase, "If you build it, they will come." If manufacturers make it, why not have consumers go directly to them to buy it? Why add another step, another body, more paperwork, more time, more overhead, more inventory, another headache?

The communication channels made available by intranets make it possible to deliver timely information to manufacturers. These capabilities were once prohibitively expensive for all but the largest companies. In addition to intranets, advances in electronic data interchange (EDI) technology and extranets enable even small businesses to realize these advantages (more on this in Chapter 6).

■ Supplier-Manufacturer Relationship Shifts

The role of middlemen (including resellers, vendors, distributors, and other intermediaries) is redefined when businesses establish direct sales links between suppliers and customers. The bad news is that jobs (and in some cases, whole companies) are eliminated in the process.

The death of the middleman, or "disintermediation," has been proclaimed the most dramatic change in supply chains. With direct communication between suppliers and customers the supply chain is streamlined. Manufacturers in a variety of industries can sell online quickly, cost-effectively, and to the satisfaction of their customers. Direct selling online by manufacturers has been estimated to cut sales costs by about 15 percent through paperwork reductions and elimination of sales commissions. The role of sales representatives has been disrupted more than ever before.

In the short term, the Internet does eliminate some jobs for middlemen as buyers and sellers are empowered with direct contact. Microsoft's Expedia Web site (www.expedia.msn.com), for example, disintermediates the role of travel agents by making it possible to browse through prices and conditions of tickets from several airlines, and to buy these tickets online. Expedia receives a small fee for each ticket sold. For airlines, this is a drastic reduction from the traditional travel agent fees. The challenge will be to find new ways to enhance value and provide extraordinary services.

Travel agents, real estate agents, insurance brokers, and book dealers have already felt the immediate impact of disintermediation. Without value-added service, e-commerce could reduce instead of enhance these professionals' positions with the consumer. Travel agents are at a disadvantage: they don't sell things you must test and touch to buy. Book dealers can be another easy target: not everyone needs to physically flip through the pages of a book, sip a latte, snuggle into a comfy chair, or secure a date for the following weekend every time he or she buys a book. Books can be depicted through vivid visuals of their covers, a list of the contents, a summary of reviews by the "average reader," and a synopsis by an objective reviewer. A Starbucks latte is optional.

For many industries, the role of intermediaries will be redefined rather than eliminated. Some middlemen will shift roles, and others will evolve into new roles. To survive, many middlemen will need to "go digital," becoming "cybermediaries."

Cybermediaries bring buyers and sellers together. They provide personal services, expert advice, or benefits such as personal consultations. The role of cybermediaries is to decipher huge amounts of information stored in thousands of Web sites. They act as gurus of information flow.

Microsoft's HomeAdvisor (www.homeadvisor.msn.com) acts as an efficient middleman by providing a referral service for homebuyers. Buyers can receive a list of homes available in any given area that meet their specifications. There's no real estate fee for the service, since Microsoft makes money on ad revenue and related services.

Portals can act as cybermediaries, as Yahoo! has chosen to do. So can new online businesses, formed specifically to provide this function. Etoys, for example, seeks a perfect match between people and toys, even promising to track down limited supplies of the hottest seasonal items. Ebay facilitates the exchange of information between hundreds of thousands of buyers and sellers each day in online auctions regardless of their location, time zone, or language.

Existing businesses tend to use e-commerce for retail products along with traditional distributor channels for wholesale items. This approach keeps the relationship with distributors intact and still provides a more efficient way of doing business. It works when a business can provide an electronic catalog for only their distributors, not the general consumer. Distributors are still responsible for taking orders as they did in the past; however, ordering information is passed back to the manufacturer electronically, using an extranet.

Fruit of the Loom is an example of a company that decided not to sell directly to consumers. Instead they worked to develop closer relationships with their distributors by improving the speed and accuracy of the information flow between them. Fruit of the Loom distributors have access to the company's electronic catalog, and they communicate orders, inventory, customer service, and pricing information through the company's extranet. When prices change or inventory is low, distributors are informed as soon as the manufacturer knows.

Minnesota Mining & Manufacturing (3M) has also been concerned about preserving their distribution channel structure. They provide an electronic catalog of hundreds of products online, but consumers still need to contact a distributor to purchase anything. For now, 3M is convinced that it is more profitable for distributors to handle their many low-cost, small items than it is for the company to start packing and shipping the items themselves.

The more direct approach is for a business to take on the role of both supplier and distributor. The music and computer industries have opted to implement this strategy, with huge success. Dell has eliminated the middleman; customers order their computers directly from Dell's Web site. Ranking communication with suppliers as a high priority, Dell kept profits high and inventories low even before e-commerce. With the transition to online sales, Dell shared even more information with their suppliers, including company inventories, production plans, and feedback about shipping deadlines.

Levi Strauss & Co. is another example of initial success with direct sales, although overall sales dropped from 1997 to 1998 (more on this later in this chapter). Levi Strauss launched their Levi's® Online store (www.levistrauss.com) in November 1998, selling direct to consumers. Clinique initiated direct online customer sales with dramatic results (www.clinique.com). Customers were eager to bypass department stores for a brand they already knew, armed with specifics about ounces and formulas they had already become acquainted with from their long history of physical shopping.

Car dealers have had considerable leeway in the past with the prices they charged, going above cost and keeping anywhere from about 3 to 15 percent of the final sale price. Today Internet car-buying services simply gather prices online and send prospective buyers to a dealer for their purchase. Microsoft's CarPoint.com and autobytel.com serve as research tools for car buyers to find the best deals when shopping online. General Motors recently entered the ranks with a new site, GMBuyPower (www.gmbuypower.com). Shoppers can use this Web site to browse through the inventories of individual GM dealers and compare prices.

The next step in online car buys will be far more dramatic, according to some experts. Autoweb.com cofounder and executive vice president Iayam Zamaric believes his company will assume more of the relationship with the buyer. Consolidation among car dealers will be the next step, because sites will offer a more economical way to reach car buyers. Zamaric describes car dealers of the future as "virtual dealerships." "It will be more cost effective to send cars to homes to test drive than to have 300 cars sitting in a lot," says Zamaric.

Purchasing departments can have better control with electronic commerce. Relationships with suppliers can actually be improved when purchasing managers have a better understanding of their buying patterns and their company's needs. With more precise control over orders, a better understanding of buying patterns, and timely information exchange, companies have a better chance of implementing JIT (just-in-time) inventory systems. There is no longer a need to stock up in advance to meet unexpected demands. Projections are more accurate, so the quantity of goods manufactured can be adjusted as needed to meet seasonal or peak demands. Cost reductions are immediately evident when there are fewer warehouses overloaded with goods that aren't selling.

E-commerce can enhance businesses' purchasing power, giving them access to a wide range of suppliers. If a supplier cannot meet price and schedule requirements, e-commerce makes it easier than ever before to shop around for a replacement. The power is in the hands of buyers, who can always look elsewhere if they don't like the terms being offered.

Customer-driven manufacturing, or manufacturing on demand, advances the precision of production to its height. With customer input directly to the manufacturer, the manufacturer has an instant view of what is needed and when. Customers will expect products to be custom-manufactured—like the computers they can now assemble through Dell—and manufacturers will need to improve production and delivery systems to meet these expectations.

■ Economies of Consolidation

In spite of the complexities of the Internet, the intricacies of establishing a Web site, and the minutiae involved in managing any online business, the results of this investment can be beautifully simple. Business should ultimately become less complicated and more efficient with electronic commerce. When suppliers and customers communicate directly, the supply chain is streamlined. Relevant information for the manufacturing process can be transmitted directly.

Electronic commerce can make a catalog come alive for consumers. Merchants, on the other hand, have to reevaluate the value of their brick-and-mortar stores. To draw traffic, these stores have to assume a new role, like that of the digital middleman. For many multimedia merchants, the physical store will have a greater value if it functions as a hands-on demonstration site, a showroom, or checkpoint for direct home delivery.

Electronic commerce creates faster and more efficient business transactions through a synchronized mix of consumer, technological, financial, marketing, legal, and policy issues. E-commerce should increase the speed of businesses, enhance customer service, increase competitiveness, and eventually reduce prices for products and services, with savings passed along to the consumer.

The authors of *Electronic Commerce: Technical, Business and Legal Issues* (Prentice Hall, 1999) indicate that e-commerce empowers businesses by creating a wider scope of clients (without geographic boundaries), analyzing products (from customer and supplier feedback), doing market research (from customer databases), obtaining expert advice, acquiring information rapidly, providing faster customer communications, facilitating payments, and using cost-effective document transfers. What a list! Dr. Nabil Adam and coauthors present a technician's guide to handle the details of design and the tough technical questions, formulas, and algorithms that are part of the implementation of an e-commerce Web site.

■ Impact on Existing Business

Retail establishments have two different perceptions of how the Internet can impact their existing offline and catalog business. First, they fear Web site sales could drive traffic away from their brick-and-mortar stores and catalogs. Others may believe that a Web site will serve as a positive shot of energy for lagging sales. Both expectations can be wrong. Publishers have shared the same concerns, but were also quick to embrace the expanded audience of their online markets.

Publishing

Andy Cohen, publisher of *NetCommerce* magazine (www.netcommercemag.com), says there will always be room for printed publications as well as online publications. "The look and feel is different," he said. "Printed publications will not be eliminated by online publications. The Internet is great for instant access to current information." NetCommerce uses its Web site as a way to draw traffic to the publication, and to take subscriptions online.

Reader's Digest Association, Inc., announced recently that it planned to move beyond its traditional magazine business into Internet promotion and sales of vitamins, pharmaceuticals, credit cards, and insurance. The Internet will play a major role in this expansion. To achieve these goals, the company expects to spend $100 million or more to overhaul existing Web sites and start new ones. Magazine and book publication, and direct marketing through sweepstakes mailing were the hallmark of *Reader's Digest* in its glory days, but readership has diminished. Will consumers respond to the new-and-improved version of this traditional company? Will shoppers make a connection between their B-12 vitamins and *Reader's Digest*? An attractive and well-designed Web site may not be enough to draw consumers.

Retail Shops

When the Gap reported a 46 percent rise in earnings for fourth quarter of 1998, earnings were up to $313.9 million, from $215.6 million in 1997. Sales totaled $3 billion, up from $2.2 billion the previous year. Was this increase due to their move to the Internet? No single factor put them in this positive position. As a popular retailer, the Gap covers several consumer price ranges among its Gap, Banana Republic, and Old Navy stores and keeps pace with what appeals to customers. The company's brand image is strong, and it markets aggressively through television, radio, and print.

The Gap didn't report growth only in Internet sales, although the Gap Web site operates with healthy efficiency. Gap also reported an increase from 2,130 stores in 1997 to 2,428 stores by the end of January 1999. Gap retail space grew 22 percent. The overall impact was terrific. Andy Cohen says that stores like the Gap offer the blueprint of e-commerce marketing. "Every Gap store shows their URL," he pointed out. "They rely on their stores to drive the site. If you're in Oshkosh and you want to order from the Gap, you can."

Morgan Stanley reports that there are five key points to consider when moving into the Internet retail market:

1. Online shopping will not eliminate traditional shopping, but will provide opportunities to expand marketing opportunities for particular products.
2. Developments in EDE (electronic data exchange) offer greater potential than ever for interorganizational retail applications to succeed.
3. The mail-order catalog business should lose some market share to the online business.
4. As the demographics of the Internet change, the business model will be influenced.
5. Key areas for e-commerce success are brand name recognition, low cost structure, legacy systems integration, leverage of applicable technology, and ease of use.

Management of the online and offline sales efforts can be enhanced by the use of intranets to quickly communicate with sales teams about products, forecasts, and reports. To minimize the impact on existing business during the transition to online selling, it is wise to exercise caution in upsetting the balance of partnerships with distributors and retailers. Think through the following issues, which will directly concern the income and job responsibilities of others:

- *Commission structures.* Should anyone receive a commission for online sales, or should commissions be eliminated? Some businesses opt to extend a commission to the sales representative in the physical territory in which the online sale originated. Others feel that is unrealistic, and try to work out new formulas.
- *Discount offerings.* Should you offer the opportunity for distributors or outlets to discount more than the prices you offer online, or vice versa? Will you permit more price flexibility and negotiation for in-person deals?
- *Personal contact.* Should sales personnel be encouraged to extend face-to-face contact or phone follow-up to online sales customers to cement relationships? If so, how can compensation be handled?

The hardest adjustment will be for businesses that have concentrated on personal contact, face-to-face meetings, socializing, and in-person product demonstrations to sell. These irreplaceable customer relationships have generated millions of sales dollars for some of the world's largest corporations. If sales are just a click away, what does the future hold?

When a Main Street store builds a Web site (Figure 3.1, Model B), they open up opportunities to expand their market beyond geographic boundaries. Their chances of losing sales from the physical shop are slight, but the potential to increase sales through their Web site could be enormous if they market well.

Catalog Sales

Some experts claim that the catalog portion of existing businesses will suffer the most from the introduction of e-commerce. Others believe that catalogs are safe and sound, for there is a time and purpose for all different methods of selling. According to Jessica Neville, director of strategic planning and circulation for the Haggin Group in the San Francisco Bay area, catalogs have their own niche. "I think the Internet adds another channel, and won't take away from catalogs or retail," she says. "Perhaps the overall outcome will be to drive all sales up." That would be good news for everyone. After the 1998 holiday season, a number of established retail companies supported this position. The Sharper Image, for example, reported a 492 percent increase in online sales in December, but the specialty retail catalog and physical stores also experienced increases of 27 percent and 9 percent respectively. Clothing

Figure 3.1   Net Predictions

Will online sales impact traditional offline sales?

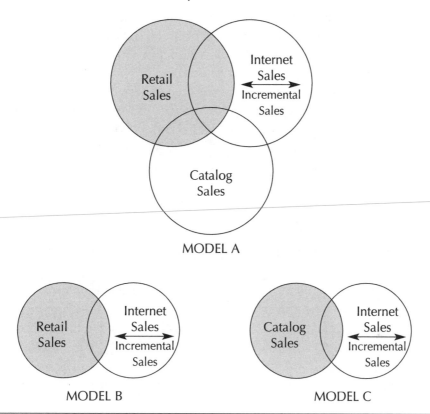

retailer Eddie Bauer, with shops, catalogs, and a Web site, also reported over-all sales increases. Nearly 60 percent of online customers were new to Eddie Bauer, and thousands of site visitors ask to be sent a catalog every month.

Neville described this effect as a set of interconnected circles (Figure 3.1). Retail companies with a catalog (Model A) are in the best position to begin to sell online. "If you have a profitable business, I'd encourage you to go on-line because you can achieve incremental sales," says Neville. "I'd encourage them not to drop their print catalog because there will always be people who prefer print." After all, this is a customer base you already know. "You *know* they like catalogs because they've stayed on your list."

Catalog-only companies (Model C) can also make a smooth transition to online sales. "Catalog companies already have the structure in place to pick, pack and ship," said Neville. "They've already invested in the back-end processing." In fact, their transition to online sales will be easier than for an online-only start-up business. "It's very expensive to start a catalog business," says Neville, "and you can't break even for three years." Once you have a catalog, however, you can find inexpensive ways to move onto the Web. Your major costs have already been incurred: Your products are photographed or illustrated, described, and organized; you have a pricing structure in place; you know how to exhibit your products most favorably.

Will the Internet ever completely replace catalogs? Neville doesn't think so. "Print catalogs are so portable. And they offer you flexibility. You can be doing two things at once," she says. "It can distract you, hold your attention, and inspire a spontaneous purchase."

CASE STUDY: ■
Example of a "Relationship Shift"—Levi Strauss & Co.

In the same week that the Gap announced their successful increase in 1998 sales, Levi Strauss & Co. broke the news that it would close 11 plants and lay off 30 percent (a total of 5,900 workers) of its work force in the United States and Canada. Levi Strauss & Co. employs about 30,000 people worldwide, with offices in over 30 countries. Fiscal 1998 sales of $6 billion represented a 13 percent decline from their 1997 sales of $6.9 billion. Since then, the company has made serious efforts to regroup.

One of the world's largest brand-name apparel marketers, Levi Strauss makes jeans and sportswear under the Levi's®, Dockers®, and Slates® brands. They sell exclusively to approved retail stores globally. There is no catalog, unless a European branch office produces one for its region, although their products are sometimes listed in other retail catalogs in the United States.

Sales in the original Levi's brand took the 1998 hit; Dockers and Slates each had a great year. The five-pocket jeans of baby boomers' youth have stayed the same for so long that trendier Tommy Hilfiger, Old Navy, and the Gap left them in the dust. Slow to catch on to fashion shifts and even slower to change, Levi's had never been big with men in their 20s and 30s (who identify them as their fathers' pants).

Levi Strauss was a textbook case of good Web site planning (www.levistrauss.com). The initial Web sites for Levi's and Dockers have been up since 1994, but the real action started with the launch of their e-commerce site in November 1998 (Figure 3.2). Jeff Beckman, senior manager of communications for Levi Strauss & Co., explained, "Traditional retail will continue to be our primary method of sales. Retailers can take on the mix of products that are best suited for their customers." But the e-commerce site offered a dynamic new opportunity to grab onto the younger market. If a young consumer goes to a department store that features only specific products, that reinforces their perception of the brand. The Web site is the place to feature product depth and breadth for the complete line of Levi's and Dockers accessories, shirts, jackets, and more. "Consumer expectations are high when they visit a manufacturer's site," according to Beckman. "They expect to see a wide variety of choices." On the other hand, it was important not to let technology drive the process. "You can build a temple to your product, but if it doesn't resonate with the consumer you're talking to yourself," says Beckman.

The goal of the Web site is to be completely customer-driven and customer-focused. According to Beckman, "We set consumers up as the architects." They thoroughly researched their customers before designing the site. They sought feedback from expert to novice Internet shoppers to make online

Figure 3.2   Levi Strauss & Co. Home Page

shopping easy. As a result, the site now contains features that are unique and appealing:

- Style Finder gives a series of questions about fashion, music, and miscellaneous items, responding with recommendations for the shopper about the Levi's styles that should fit their personal preferences. This feature was tested with focus groups who rated it more than 74 percent accurate. Beckman describes Style Finder as a "virtual sales assistant" working with the online shopper in the same way that a good sales associate would help you in person.

- Product descriptions let the shopper see front and rear views.

- Fit Detail slips a body into the pants so that shoppers can visualize the difference between different fits such as boot-cut and flared.

- My Collection let shoppers identify gift hints for themselves by assembling holiday "wish lists" for distribution to family and friends. (This feature could have obnoxious results if it reduces holiday distress for the person who has created the wish list but increases it for family and friends. What if you were only going to give him a pair of socks and he wants Silver Tab pants? On the other hand, this feature can also be used to get a second opinion on something before you buy it, just like bringing a friend in with you to shop.)

But even a shift to more customer-efficient ordering methods on the Internet cannot save a company that has lost touch with its customers. Direct contact with the customer through a Web site isn't enough; the customer has to want the product in the first place. It just doesn't work to have a state-of-the-art technological approach when your marketing arm appears to be asleep at the wheel. Focus group results revealed that many younger people had no idea what products Levi Strauss & Co. really produced. Typical comments among these shoppers included, "You mean you make products in *yellow?*"

So behind the scenes, Levi Strauss & Co. was also hustling to introduce a new strategy, increasing marketing efforts substantially and raising its advertising budget by 13 percent. The challenge was to hold on to the loyal 35-and-older crowd and also attract the 25-to-34 age group that they had missed. As a bonus, they hoped to draw in 15- to 24-year-olds as a primary market. Dockers were rebranded Dockers Khakis, to capitalize on the everybody-loves-cotton theme. And there was a deliberate effort to rebrand with a new image. The Dockers Khakis image was drastically changed from the collegiate "Nice pants" to a blatantly sensual "Nice bod" in a new series of television ads. Foote, Cone San Francisco senior vice president Chris Shipman told *New York Times* reporter Stuart Elliott, "You've got to do it right. A brand trying to be cool and failing is worse than an uncool brand." Foote, Cone San Francisco created the new campaign, an enormous change in attitude for Levi Strauss. According to Shipman, the image must shift in order for the brand to shift.

Besides the new advertising campaign, Levi Strauss & Co. began concert and film sponsorships, product placement in movies and television, and niche marketing. Can this attempt expand the target market? Will Levi Strauss successfully shift its image and build a broader base of customers? The plan to sell directly to customers on the Web has worked well. Loyal customers who had trouble finding their styles and sizes in local stores no longer had to shop around. Not only is the base of customers growing rapidly, but customers are returning to the site. Retail stores still carry their brands and the manufacturer-retailer relationship has been preserved.

And they have avoided being perceived as uncool.

4

Facets of Electronic Markets

■ Economics

We are in the midst of an era that has been described as "frictionless capitalism," with a total exchange of goods and services over the Internet of about $17 billion in 1998, growing to $327 billion by the year 2002. Internet commerce has the potential to change the way we buy and sell almost every product and service.

Experts estimate the Internet could add $10 billion to $20 billion to the gross domestic product in four years.

Gains are expected to increase exponentially as more businesses catch on to the benefits of connecting globally. Is it possible that Ernst & Young's projection of a $350 billion savings in inventory is achievable if companies take advantage of intranets and extranets? Experts seem confident that these numbers are realistic.

Today the greatest percentage of Internet commerce is business-to-business. Business-to-consumer markets are young and blossoming. Fortunately, some of the realities of business-to-business models will transfer to the consumer, so we'll be able to benefit from the experience of others. One fundamental truth is already quite clear: Electronic commerce fosters competition. It is so easy for buyers to shop around, and so simple to locate an intermediary service if you're having trouble bargain-hunting on your own that discount prices probably will win out. Early signals of this pattern of consumer choice are apparent in the quest for the least expensive car deals, airline tickets, books, compact discs, and stockbrokers. Greed is not a vice to be tolerated for long on the Internet.

The yet-to-be-officially-defined economic indicators of e-tailing show that the opportunities of the next millennium will expand into frontiers beyond today's paradigms. The creation of new wealth is expedited through the growth of e-commerce. New markets can be explored, new geographic territories opened up, and greater savings achieved through implementation of direct and simplified supply chains. These opportunities will render obsolete any prejudices against home-based businesses. To some extent, the Internet ensures that all businesses are created equal. Companies will rise and fall on the basis of their own marketing strategy—not only on the design of a Web site.

◼ Finance

The financial dimension of electronic commerce is changing just as quickly as technology. Four dynamics of electronic commerce, and the Internet in general, are stock market activity, return on investment, taxation, and access fees.

Stock Market Activity

Internet stocks have risen at a rate that has exceeded the most optimistic predictions. It has become a cliché to say that anything with dot.com after its name not only will sell, but will double in value instantaneously. Valuations of high-tech stocks have never been higher. Prices of Internet stocks rose so high so fast in 1998 that there were no signs of the bubble bursting. Established Internet companies Yahoo! and Amazon.com doubled their value in one three-month interval. Newly public companies including Marketwatch.com, a company that provides financial data to Internet sites, saw a fourfold rise.

So far there seems to be no direct connection between how well the Internet stock is doing and the profitability of a given company. Take the example of Broadcast.com, which provides audio and video from 345 radio stations and 17 television stations, plus its own coverage, over the Internet. In a snapshot of 1998, Broadcast.com lost $10.5 million on revenues of $11.4 million.

The market value of the company at the same time was $2.33 billion. Many Internet companies are in the same position—awesomely valued on the stock market, while years away from a profit. Even the highly acclaimed Amazon.com has yet to realize a profit. But Amazon.com confidently predicted the days of future profit are around the corner. They have built a solid loyal customer base that they believe will grow as they grow. In January 1999, after reporting that fourth quarter 1998 sales exceeded expectations, Amazon.com stock skyrocketed to 125⅜—the seventh most active stock in U.S. markets. Amazon's market value grew to five times the combined value of competitors Barnes & Noble, Inc., and Borders Group, Inc. Microsoft and Intel announced healthy profits and solid projections of continued growth, indicating that if you can stay in the game, it's yours to win.

The Internet auction site Ebay has consistently high market value. Ebay's market value rose to eight times that of Sotheby's Holdings, Inc., the auctioneer and art dealer. The market value of Ebay soared to $12.2 billion since it first sold stock in September 1998, and it announced a three-for-one stock split. When the venerable Sotheby's announced that they, too, would begin to use the Internet for some auctions, their shares rose 50 percent.

Early in 1999 the frenzied pace began to slow down. Will this trigger a panic or have a negative overall impact on Internet stocks for the future? Experts don't seem to think so, but only time will tell.

The roles of the major players shift just enough to keep the average observer a little off-balance. Who's really buying all this stock? *Everyone.* Major corporations and your next-door neighbor. When Microsoft split in late January 1999, who became wealthy? Possibly your next-door neighbor.

Unfortunately just as soon as you think you've begun to grasp the scenario, the players shift position. Mergers and buyouts run rampant. In every case, the shareholders initially benefit—on paper. And even more multibillion ventures are being formed. Today the big keep getting bigger.

Return on Investment

It can be extremely difficult for a business to calculate the return on investment (ROI) for the use of electronic commerce. The traditional use of ROI to determine costs versus benefits changes with electronic commerce, according to Nabil Adam et al in *Electronic Commerce: Technical, Business and Legal Issues* (Prentice Hall, 1999). The cost and complexity of the technology involved to create a new sales environment is not well understood by many organizations; as a result, they don't attempt to measure it. While hardware and software investments in new technology can be quantified (i.e., the cost to set up a Web site, install security measures, etc.), other investments are not as simple to compute (i.e., the cost to train staff on the new procedures, learning curves until they reach proficiency, potential loss if the system crashes, and more). Savings, both intangible and tangible, also are difficult to quantify (e.g., cost-cutting from eliminating middlemen, time savings from more efficient order-entry processes, and so on).

Some larger corporations have made the decision not to try to put a direct price tag on electronic commerce and consider it a strategic investment in their future. Once, in a conference panel discussion, Intel CEO Andy Grove said, "What's my ROI on e-commerce? Are you crazy? This is Columbus in the New World. What was his ROI?" So while the traditional cost-benefit analysis may be worth running for a company's e-commerce initiatives, it should not be the single overriding criterion for decision-making. The e-commerce industry is too young, too volatile, and too all-encompassing in impact to pin down. Goldman Sachs warns that because of high start-up costs, electronic commerce retail ventures should expect to wait two to three years to see a profit.

Here's the bottom line: In the final analysis, your decisions about whether to venture into e-tailing will be more than a simple mathematical calculation of costs, or a spreadsheet summary of revenues versus expenses. The cost-effectiveness of implementing electronic commerce in your business is only one consideration. A cost analysis will not immediately show the real value that e-commerce will contribute. Unfortunately, e-tailing may involve temporary suspension of the traditional pro forma cash flow analysis as a key component of your decision. The value of a strong online sales presence is still part tangible and part intangible benefits. Your decision about your investment in a Web site will need to take into consideration both intangible current benefits and future benefits (such as the value of being a market leader). The most visible intangible benefit today is the "dot.com stock effect," the stock market value of the company. And of course, there is the nebulous but potent factor of your perception of the significance of *your* role as Columbus in the New World.

Taxation

While there is an adrenaline rush on the stock market, there is a government-imposed moratorium on taxation. At the most simplistic level, a fundamental fact about selling online is that until the year 2001, almost every Internet purchase is tax-free. Congress passed the Internet Tax Freedom Act in October 1998, placing a hold on taxes for Internet transactions for three years. The purpose of this law is to protect fledgling businesses until an equitable method of taxation could be worked out. Only states that beat the federal legislative agenda and instituted their own tax plans first are protected from the tax moratorium. Electronic commerce clearly demonstrates that there will have to be a new way to streamline tax issues. The present, albeit temporary solution, is not likely to become the long-term resolution. Sales taxes fund too many state and government programs to be taken lightly. A loss of sales tax revenue can directly impact how police and fire departments, transportation systems, schools, and roads are supported. How do you tax purchases that cross state lines?

Access Fees

In February 1998, the Federal Communications Commission (FCC) declared that a computer user's calls to access the Internet are interstate communications subject to federal jurisdiction. Consumer groups protested this action, stating that it inadvertently opened the door to future increases in charges for Internet access. The prevailing fear is that this declaration will move us in the direction of per-minute access charges, like long-distance phone calls. Consumers are used to dialing a local phone number to access the Internet, and paying for that access as a local call. Internet service providers are exempt from paying fees to local phone companies. Long-distance companies pay the fee and pass the charges along to the consumer. The FCC stated that their action should make no difference to the consumer, and proposed that states and companies decide how carriers should compensate each other in the future.

■ Marketing

Early in 1999, Toys 'R' Us announced that it had started a free Internet service in Britain. The British market for Internet retail sales is predicted to increase to $5 billion by 2003. Toys 'R' Us hopes that as more people in Britain shop online, the company can increase their sales and make money from advertising.

The decision to sell a product, product line, or service on the Internet should not diminish the quality of an integrated marketing strategy for any company regardless of size. Components of a comprehensive marketing plan are covered later in this book. Marketing strategies are discussed in further detail in Chapter 7; online selling in Chapter 8; and customer relations in Chapter 9.

Following are highlights of four major components: market research, target markets, advertising, and public relations.

Market Research

The Internet serves as a valuable market research tool for any company, but in electronic commerce the role is indispensable. Now businesses have the opportunity to study niche markets and refine strategic decisions about marketing. It is possible to examine buying patterns (Who buys specific products? What other items do they purchase?), and identify the geographic locations you are reaching. The data collection potential of the Internet is invaluable. In addition to tracking their target niche, companies have a quick and anonymous means to track their competitors' pricing and advertising schemes. It is as easy for a business to compare prices of their competitors as it is for their customers to comparison-shop. The same techniques that appeal to consumers also benefit sellers.

Target Markets

Perhaps the most indisputable and awesome advantage of Internet selling is that you have access to markets you might never have dreamed of. Within hours of the "grand opening" of your online store, the world is at your doorstep. You can customize your Web site to appeal to one or more market niches. As long as you can meet supply requirements and deliver a quality product in a reasonable time frame, you have the potential to reach your target market. Your prospects are limited by your own capacity to produce. Your most important question up-front will be, "Can you handle the truth?" The truth is that you could be overwhelmed by the volume of orders in a very short time.

Advertising

Advertising works in at least three different ways. A business can use its Web site (1) to attract browsers and retain them as buyers, (2) to attract advertisers and provide a new source of revenue, and (3) to link to other Web sites with strategic partners. While Web revenues are still lower than other forms of advertising, they are increasing. The Internet Advertising Bureau (IAB) estimated that Web advertising revenues totaled $343.9 million in the first half of 1997, 322 percent over the same period the year before. But ad banners have already become overused, and savvy Web shoppers tend to find them annoying. Ad pricing has fluctuated, as there are few clear-cut guidelines. The current rule of thumb is that if a Web site is popular, the ad price is outrageous.

Public Relations

Company press releases and news announcements can be published on the Web site for faster communication. Suppliers, manufacturers, vendors, and strategic partners can be kept up-to-date about critical and interesting business developments. These updates can work through a company's intranet, extranet, and Internet (more on these components in Chapter 6). A Web site can serve as a place to post good news about your business, or to provide information at no cost to the shopper, generating goodwill.

One of the best illustrations of the power of positive public relations is Blue Mountain Arts. Formed in 1971, Blue Mountain Arts acquired the enviable status of the Web's most popular shopping site—without selling anything. This small greeting card and publishing company started their Web site (www.bluemountainarts.com) in September 1996. Cleverly designed and empathetically sentimental electronic greeting cards (e-cards) were offered free and were successful instantly. Before long, Blue Mountain Arts surpassed Hallmark and American Greetings, who charge a fee for e-cards. The core publishing business of Blue Mountain Arts has grown 20 percent per year with the addition of their Web site. The publishing business supports the online greeting card business and has incurred a healthy profit on its own, before the creation of the Web site. Owners Stephen and Susan Polis Schutz emphasize the importance of their goal to become an "emotional center" of Web communications. They have established an enviable relationship with their customers. Both owners are hesitant to turn their Web site into a profit center, but potential investors and second-generation son Jared are urging them to make this transformation soon. Who will win? It remains to be seen. In the meantime, the feel-good sentiments of the Schutz poetry continue to elicit warm thank-you notes from satisfied "customers."

■ Production

Behind the scenes, the marketing dynamics and customer interface with your company are supported by a highly complex set of interrelated functions operating within the overall context of legal and government policy considerations. Electronic commerce encompasses a wide range of major functions, including acquiring and storing information, providing an electronic catalog, handling money for products and services, providing security against theft, interfacing with strategic partners, and managing the site itself. Chapter 6 covers the steps to implement your electronic commerce strategy. A brief description of major functions follows.

Information Acquisitions and Storage

Information available today in different levels of quality and in all different formats (such as books, catalogs, film, audio) needs to be converted or digitized for even the simplest case scenario. Vast quantities of information coming from different providers (e.g., your customers, your suppliers, your vendors, your staff) must be retrieved quickly and modified easily.

Electronic Catalogs

An electronic catalog, which is usually a series of Web pages, presents information about your products and services graphically. E-catalogs run the gamut from digitized photos of products to electronic models that demonstrate the items. To bring added value to the online mode, the e-catalog should be more than the Internet version of a printed catalog. At the more advanced level, electronic catalogs access information from a number of sources and present the results under one location. For more on e-catalogs, see Chapter 6.

Payments

Electronic commerce payment methods include credit card payments, electronic checks, and digital currencies (smart cards and electronic money, or "e-cash"). Credit card information is transmitted as encrypted data over the computer network, but still raises some concerns about privacy and safety. Electronic checks (e-checks), more convenient than conventional check payments, use digital signatures that are transmitted between your company, the consumer, and the bank. Smart cards not only access financial accounts, but can also store information about a purchaser's preferences and buying patterns. Electronic money, or digital cash, is stored in the consumer's computer and is transmitted to you directly or through a third-party payment service. E-money requires some sort of bank certification to avoid fraud or insufficient funds in the account. Some start-up electronic commerce companies (like CyberCash, DigiCash, and Mondex) have sprung up to handle electronic payments for e-tail companies. Methods of payment are discussed in further detail in Chapter 6.

Security

Security issues are among the greatest concerns of online shoppers. In fact, some analysts have described security as the primary barrier to an even greater explosion of e-commerce. In the electronic commerce environment, security is addressed from two dimensions: the security of the Web site itself and your company's systems, and the security and privacy of individuals who interact with you. You will be equally concerned with the potential for sabotage by a competitor as with the possibility of paranoia by a customer. When considering security ask whether the information you send (credit card numbers and expiration dates, personal and financial information) is private and safe, or will other people or systems have access to it? Business controls, user perception, and confidence are critical. Security considerations are covered in greater detail in Chapter 10.

Communicating with Strategic Partners

Intranets and extranets can keep you and your business allies in tune with the latest information about one another (inventories, sales figures, marketing data, customer service issues, new policies, or organization changes) as they occur. You will need to factor these patterns of communication into the early design of your system, allowing for the most efficient flow of data from one business to another, considering frequency, volume, destination, and type of information transmitted.

Up and Running

Web page design, while the most popularly discussed component of an integrated process, is only one small step. Web site design, development, implementation, and monitoring require the skills of experts. Do-it-yourself kits, such as the templates available from America Online, may be helpful for designing a single Web page. But real electronic commerce weaves an intricate web of supportive services. Chapter 11 covers the cast of characters needed to support electronic commerce activity and provides guidelines on how to find the best support team for your business.

■ Project Management

Project management techniques have come in and out of fashion over the past two decades. Considering the urgency and competitiveness that accompanies the creation of many e-commerce sites, it makes sense to start off with a positive attitude toward project management techniques and a plan to use them to control implementation of your electronic commerce program.

Most e-commerce projects operate under time and cost constraints, yet must pull together highly complex and interrelated system functions, sensitive user interfaces, and a team of different system experts. Tracking people and functions is a task that grows exponentially in complexity with each additional feature or person. Project management of highly complex e-commerce projects may best be handled through a software package. Bruce Taylor, principal at Bluewater Management Services, found software-aided project management to be the most effective solution. His experience indicates that project management software is now so easy to learn and to use that it can save time and money. Microsoft Project 98, for example, includes Gantt charts, PERT charts, task completion estimates, cost tracking, and resource utilization reports. A PERT (Program Evaluation and Review Technique) chart is similar to a flowchart, and provides a clear visual of how a whole project comes together. Project team members can track progress and share reports quickly. When your team incorporates different specialists (discussed in Chapter 11) and different technology (discussed in Chapter 12), project management is a critical function. You or a designated project manager will need to oversee all components.

Regardless of whether you use a software package like Microsoft Project 98, project management should cover four steps:

1. *Setting specific goals.* What should this project accomplish? Clearly defined goals help you manage all the interrelated components of electronic commerce more efficiently. In Chapter 6 you will find further details about goal-setting from a business plan and a project plan perspective.

2. *Defining project plans.* Unless you use a template from your server to set up a very simple Web site, you will be working with a contingent of professionals, all with their own set of functions to accomplish. Each member of your team will have tasks, time requirements, due dates, resource needs, and contingencies that have an impact on the whole project. Information about the complex interrelationships of tasks and due dates needs to be shared with all project team members.

3. *Reporting on progress.* Is everyone on time and within cost constraints? To avoid last-minute surprises, the project manager's role is to track tasks and deadlines daily. If one or more tasks are out of line, dependent tasks can be readjusted right away. Is there an impact on your final deadline? What are the risks? When you're all working in the same

office, regularly scheduled face-to-face meetings are the preferred method of gathering information to accomplish your objectives. But when you are not co-located, e-mail and shared data bases have to keep the work and communication among team members moving.

4. *Tracking final results.* Did everyone deliver what was expected of them? Did your actual time and costs come within your targets? Does the final product accomplish what you expected? After implementation, when you're ready to enter your growth phase, your actual development time and costs will help you project new schedule and resource requirements more accurately.

SELF-ASSESSMENT:
Can Your Business Profit from the E-Commerce Explosion?

It won't be long before every business will have a presence on the Web. Does your business need to go online today? Will ".com" after your company name increase your value? Will your product or service sell online? We've already seen that some products and services have made an easy transition to online sales. Others are slowly and steadily entering the race. The front-runners have already begun to expand their territory into wider ranges of products and services, increasing not only their scope but also their visibility. As a newcomer, are you ready for this? Answer the following questions honestly:

1. Do you have *time* to focus on this Web site? (Even if you outsource the work, you'll still need to dedicate time to managing the project.)

2. Do you have *money* to invest in this Web site? (Even though there are low cost bootstrap ways to get an e-commerce site up and running, there aren't any *no*-cost options.)

3. Do you know *what to sell* online? (Can you sell some of your products/ services, gradually increasing selection, or should you jump in with everything?)

4. Can your products be made to look visually appealing online? Will positive attributes be visible? Or can a combination of words and images convey your message and enhance the products' features? (This can influence how well your products sell online.)

5. If you are selling a service, can you create a visual image or a catchy narrative that grabs attention and accurately portrays your capabilities?

6. For both questions 4 and 5, if *you* can't write about, draw, or photograph what you are selling, do you have the resources to hire someone to do it for you?

7. Can you be ready to ship your product in 24 hours or less?

8. Can you ensure that your product will arrive fresh (if it's perishable) and safe (if it's breakable)?

9. Can you arrange for efficient product shipping? (If your shipping costs will seem outrageous to the consumer, no matter how hard you try to seek out low-cost mailing options, this could inhibit sales.)

10. Do you have the resources (in-house staff or personal patience, if you are starting solo) to handle customer service and other sales follow-up activities with customers?

11. Can you handle unexpected sharp increases (or decreases) in volume of orders? (Your production capability, your relationships with vendors, or both, must be firmly in place *before* you start to sell online.)

12. Can you match or beat your competition on price? On quality? On uniqueness? Remember that Web shoppers comparison-shop shamelessly. You'll now be in competition with more than your local retail mall; your competition will be global.

Scoring your results. If you answered yes to every question, you're in great shape to get started now. If you are hesitant on some questions, start working on addressing those elements. Soon you'll have a game plan for entering the e-commerce explosion.

5

The Psychology of Internet Usage

■ Web Addiction

There are already early warning signals that the Internet has bred a new kind of addict. Perhaps the number of individuals who spend all their leisure time surfing the Web is relatively small, but there is evidence of a growing population who spend as much as nine hours a day locked behind a computer terminal surfing. What is the tremendous psychological appeal? Does this attraction differ when seeking information, or connecting with people, or transacting business, or shopping? Is it the freedom and relaxation of being able to carry on the pursuit of higher learning or commerce donned in a bathrobe? Or the potential anonymity while engaging in intellectual—or silly—debates with people from all over the country—or world—whom you've never met? Is it the relief of having your questions answered swiftly and succinctly without the tedium of dealing with a librarian? Or is it the incredible feeling of becoming totally absorbed in a task, having time fly while you are intensely focused on tracking down a topic or a product, following an online stream of consciousness? Perhaps *this* is the top of Maslow's hierarchy of needs, self-actualization. For some dedicated surfers, this is as good as it gets.

■ The Appeal of Online Shopping

The appeal of shopping online encompasses behavior we're just beginning to understand. For disorganized people, it doesn't matter if they kept the most recent copy of their favorite retailer's catalog. They can track it online. For impatient people, there's no need to wait for an available salesperson or cashier—you're in the queue without the annoyance of standing in a line. For shy individuals, online shopping offers an opportunity to bid wildly at auctions and act assertively, while avoiding personal confrontations and unpleasant disagreements. For dominant individuals who prefer to skip sales small talk and negotiate directly to the bottom line, it is far easier to click "order now" than to slip past a gregarious sales clerk.

But the truly extroverted types—who thrive on social interaction and hang on every bit of small talk that accompanies a visit to the mall—are far less likely to be spending excessive time on the Internet in the first place, according to early research. They also are less likely to be shopping online. We have data to support the fact that extroverted individuals with a wide range of social contacts spend the least amount of time on the Internet. Data about online shoppers is still in the embryonic stages. There are some indications, however, that people who need people are the luckiest online shoppers in the world. They are the least likely to become addicted to the Internet and abuse their shopping privileges.

Perhaps the most interesting piece of scientific research is a recent study conducted by members of the American Psychological Association at Carnegie Mellon University. The report concludes that Internet use led to less social engagement and poorer psychological well-being. This longitudinal study measured the connection between Internet use, social relationships, and psychological consequences over two years for 169 participants in Pittsburgh. All participants were new Internet users. The indicators used to measure social involvement were family communication, size of local social network, size of distant social network, and social support. Psychological well-being was measured by loneliness, stress, and depression.

The important finding is that depression increased with greater use of the Internet during the study period. Researchers concluded that the use of the Internet caused an increase in depression, increases in loneliness, and decreases in social interaction. Yes, the people in the study who used the Internet most frequently connected with family and friends least frequently. The final conclusion was that heavy Internet usage adversely affected social involvement and psychological well-being. Can these findings be generalized to the population at large?

The paradox of this study is that the Internet is a technology that is designed to enhance social connections with individuals and groups, yet the opposite was achieved in this study. In spite of the expansion of interpersonal connections to widespread locations around the country, the long-range contacts were not of the quality that could substitute for close personal relationships, imperfections and all.

An interesting sidebar about this study is that the research at Carnegie Mellon was supported by grants from about 20 different public and private sector resources, including many of the major players in the field of online communications systems. The degree of interest in the capacity of the Internet to influence human behavior in previously unanticipated dimensions is huge. We recognize the impact of the telephone and television on our ability to communicate personally and publicly; the Internet has already made its mark, and we have not even begun to scratch the surface of quantified measurement of the human implications.

■ Implications of Psychological Research

Has increased use of the Internet changed us for the better or worse? Are we allowing ourselves to be cut off as we become more and more attached to our computers, socializing with anonymous strangers? Are we then substituting weak ties for strong ties, as the Carnegie Mellon study suggests? For some individuals, using the Internet reduces the level of physical activity and decreases their face-to-face social interactions. While the Carnegie Mellon study found that interpersonal communication is the dominant use of the Internet at home, the type of social interactions and relationships on the Internet are not the same as traditional in-person contact. Many early studies found that while people do form social relationships online, the number of strong ties is low. The implications for e-commerce are more complex. While a merchant may not feel that every consumer needs to be a personal friend, there is something to be said about forming strong bonds—and securing repeat sales. The benefits are less psychological than financial in this case. However, all indicators seem to point in the direction that strong personal ties with customers via the Internet will translate into brand loyalty. There's something to be said for a coherent psycho-financial sales strategy.

The Carnegie Mellon research calls for the extended study of the Internet as a communication device, not just for gathering information but also to enhance the quality of social interactions. The study team called for more intense development of services that support communities and build strong relationships. "As a nation," the researchers recommend, "we must balance the value of the Internet for information, communication, and commerce with its costs. Use of the Internet can be both highly entertaining and useful, but if it causes too much disengagement from real life, it can also be harmful."

Isolation and Integration

Some researchers have found that the Internet not only removes constraints of geography, but also constraints of isolation due to illness, handicap, or schedule. In breaking through these barriers, the Internet enables communities of individuals with similar interests to find one another and to communicate more easily. It also brings information, education, and entertainment right into the home. The use of technology to enhance social contact for the home-bound or schedule-constricted through e-mail, chat groups, distribution lists, and other applications works in a positive way. Electronic commerce enables those who are mall-impaired to achieve equity when comparison shopping, equality in the search for the greatest discount, liberty when circumventing inclement weather conditions, and justice for all when avoiding taxes from state to shining state.

Abbreviated Attention Span

While some unique individuals may tolerate extended periods of computer wait-time, most people have a low tolerance for verbosity, too many screens to get what you want, too many clicks in the process, complicated photos and graphics that take too long to load, too many links to other sites, long download times (unless you are forewarned), too many instructions, information that is too vague, and information that is already available in a million other places.

What are shoppers looking for? To start, fast-paced, novel, entertaining, upbeat, timely information. If your site opens with anything that looks like last month's data hasn't been updated, you'll lose attention. People tend to return to sites that are fresh. Niche markets seek depth without being tedious or boring.

Instant Gratification

How patient are we when we are sitting at our computer? How long does it take for us to lose interest in a single attraction? We are, in general, not very patient. Once we have experienced fast response time—as in the first moment working with a 56K modem, then the experience of using a T1 line—we're never the same. This simple fact goes way back to the primitive days of computer usage. In a 1976 study at AT&T, a colleague and I measured the effects of computer response time on operator perception. In a Cincinnati study group of more than 80 full-time computer operators, we found that user attitudes towards system reliability, accuracy, and effectiveness improved with reductions in response time. When response time increased or varied significantly, operators experienced increased stress, leading to an increase in fatigue and error rate, reduced typing speeds and productivity. We found that users noticed even minor changes in response times, and were frustrated by what was described as a "waste of time" waiting for a response. So even when full-time computer operation was relatively new, people hated to wait. And if they had to wait, they became impatient. When impatient, they decided that the system they were using was unreliable, and they messed up. Productivity declined.

In today's high-speed environment, where instantaneous response time is possible, businesses need to be wary of the user's basis of comparison. Once you've seen how fast response time can be, anything less can feel intolerable.

■ Cognitive Computing

Behavioral psychologists now assess how the psychology of Internet usage can influence the design of Web sites and the structure of electronic commerce transactions. The emerging field of cognitive computing is a blend of computer science and the behavioral sciences. With a combination of the skills of a software engineer and human engineering, using a blend of psychology, sociology, and cultural anthropology, it is possible to maximize your impact consciously— or subconsciously.

Consumer behavior patterns can be analyzed in order to create Web sites that meet not only different customer needs and wants, but also unique personality characteristics. Cognitive computing is used to make the whole shopping experience more intuitive, not just provide the incentive for the consumer to click and buy. Color, screen positioning, format of text-oriented material, and number of clicks to accomplish a task have all been analyzed and enough data gathered to positively influence the design of the human-computer interaction. In Chapter 7, these considerations will be incorporated into recommendations for online store design.

6

Implementing E-Commerce Strategies

■ Steps to Move from Storefront to Online Sales

It seems as if so many steps in the process of selling online need to be handled concurrently that it is difficult to force the process into a straight-line logical sequence. In fact, many aspects of the design of your Web site and your method of handling customers will need to be considered while you are trying to figure out security systems and how people will pay you. This chapter pulls the pieces together in a step-by-step overview. Further details on technical design, security, sales strategies, and customer service are covered in later chapters.

Your own sequence of going online may involve circumventing one step to get to another, then a little backtracking. In the end, your decision-making and design process—by whatever sequence of steps you pursue—will yield a Web site that simulates the best aspects of a physical shopping trip, without the hassles of parking. To begin, a brief overview of commonly used terminology follows.

Buzzwords 101

Two words often used interchangeably, although technically they are not synonyms, are *Internet* and *Web*. Paul Weidner of the University of Scranton Electronic Commerce Resource Center (ECRC) describes the differences in a simple but clear way: "Think of the Internet as the hardware system that carries information; think of the World Wide Web as the information itself, or the software."

Technically, anytime you connect two networks together, allowing computers to communicate and share resources, you have an *internet*. The *Internet* (capital I) is a vast worldwide collection of interconnected networks, all using TCP/IP (Transmission Control Protocol/Internet Protocol), the suite of protocols, or instructions, that define the Internet. Originally developed in the late 1960s for the UNIX operating system, TCP/IP is now available for every major kind of computer operating system. Your computer must have TCP/IP software to be on the Internet.

The *World Wide Web* (WWW) is the user-friendly Internet utility comprised of graphics, text, sound, and electronic data interchange (EDI) capability. The Web is made up of sites, or "home pages," with links to information. *Home page* commonly refers to the main Web page of a collection of pages, which could be for a business, organization, or person—anyone or any place. The links may be to files maintained by the creator of the page, or to pages maintained by other businesses or individuals. *Hypertext* is any text that contains links to other documents, words, or phrases in a document that cause another document to be retrieved and displayed. The coding language used to create hypertext documents, or Web pages, is called *HTML* (HyperText Markup Language). The codes specify words or blocks of text that are linked to other files on the Internet.

HyperText Transport Protocol, or *HTTP,* is the most important protocol used in the Web, for it moves hypertext files across the Internet. For HTTP to work, a *client* program must be on one end, and a *server* program must be at the other end. Each client program (software) is designed to work with one or more specific kinds of server programs, and each server requires a specific kind of client. Web *browsers* are client programs that are used to look at various kinds of Internet resources, acting as a way to view the Internet while not actually connecting you to the Internet. Netscape and Microsoft Internet Explorer are examples of browsers.

The World Wide Web is just one utility, or function of the Internet. Other utilities include the following:

- *E-mail* (electronic mail)—Messages, usually text, sent from one person to another almost instantaneously via computer
- *Usenet*—A world-wide system of subject-centered discussion groups known as newsgroups
- *FTP* (file transfer protocol)—A common method for storing and retrieving files between two Internet sites
- *Telnet*—The command and program that allows the user to log in to a remote computer system
- *IRC* (internet relay chat)—multiuser, live chat facility for real-time discussions.

Subsequent chapters will discuss peripheral considerations and technical service providers in more detail. This chapter identifies key points in the overall process.

Figure 6.1 is summary of the ten steps to follow when implementing electronic commerce in your business.

■ Step 1: Set Your Goals

Electronic commerce is a technology that exists to support the goals of your business. It is not technology for the sake of technology. Electronic commerce should help you accomplish the following:

- Make your business processes simpler, faster, and more efficient.
- Cut overall costs (eventually).
- Make your business more competitive.
- Enable your business to serve consumers and other businesses globally, as if they were local.
- Help you create new products and services to meet customer needs.
- Level the playing field for large and small businesses.
- Expand your view of future possibilities.

If you want e-commerce to enhance your business rather than weigh you down with another set of monthly expenses and migraines, take this first step very seriously. If you do this right, you will do more than just create a multi-page Web site. You can create a window into your business for customers everywhere, at any time of day, who might never have been accessible to you. You will create a convenient, secure environment in which to handle purchases.

Figure 6.1   Ten Steps to E-tailing

1. *Set your goals.*
   - Be consistent with your business plan.
   - Address potential problems right from the start.
   - Reinforce your marketing strategy.
2. *Access the Internet.*
   - Assess computer components and upgrade them as necessary.
   - Assess network connections and implement changes (Internet service provider (ISP), transmission speed, etc.) as needed.
3. *Promote your Web site.*
   - Establish your presence on the Internet (register domain name, establish keywords; link to and from other sites that serve your target market).
4. *Design your Web site.*
   - Project a professional image.
   - Consider electronic commerce components, such as EDI compliance, digital currency, and electronic catalogs.
   - Consider intranets and extranets.
5. *Create an electronic catalog.*
   - Determine if you want a stand-alone catalog, or if cybermalls are for you.
   - Invigorate presentation of your products and services.
   - Achieve the best balance of graphics and text.
6. *Identify your distribution channel.*
   - Determine your supply chain and create appropriate links.
7. *Develop a method of order processing.*
   - Have electronic funds transfer capability.
   - Offer real-time payment solutions (credit cards, e-cash, smart cards, e-checks).
   - Work out arrangements for product delivery.
8. *Select security systems.*
   - Safeguard your customers' privacy.
   - Protect your confidential company records and data.
9. *Develop inventory tracking procedures.*
   - Cut your costs by tracking and controlling.
   - Link to suppliers, customers, and others as needed.
10. *Refine your customer interface.*
    - Encourage feedback from your customers.
    - Communicate with your customers.
    - Track customer purchase patterns.

You must create a meaningful connection with your customers if you ever want them to return, and if you want them to spread the good news about you. The Web site is part of a process that adds value to your business.

What is the actual value added by e-commerce? Initially, the value will be apparent in the exposure your company achieves within the Web marketplace. In addition to exposure, consider your image. There is still a sense of being "cutting edge" for businesses that launch online shopping sites. E-tail holds a certain mystique for less-jaded Internet users.

Be Consistent with Your Business Plan

It is vital that you integrate electronic commerce with the rest of your business. Your business plan provides the structure to support your goals for marketing and financing your company.

Because e-commerce is still relatively new—probably not even in Microsoft's business plan four years ago—the financial analysis of your investment in e-commerce most likely will not show an instant profit. But remember that you are in good company; Amazon.com didn't show instant profits, either. The expenses incurred to get your Web site up and running may take time to recoup. The impact on your pro forma break-even analysis could make the decision to implement online sales appear risky. A pro forma cash flow analysis could reveal a sluggish pattern when you start, gaining momentum only as your Web site becomes more popular. So determine your costs and the return on your investment, but also consider *tangible* and *intangible benefits*.

Address Potential Problems from the Start

In your goals for setting up your e-tail system, delineate specific ways to minimize the risk of your investment of time, effort and money. For example, it's a sure thing that your potential customers will shop around before they make a purchase. After all, comparison shopping is half the fun of online shopping. Address this potential problem. Check out your competition and guarantee that the prices you are charging keep you in the game. A few additional problems to address from the start are included in Figure 6.2.

Reinforce Your Marketing Strategy

A comprehensive marketing strategy integrates all you have learned about your target market (demographics, psychographics, niche needs, etc.) through your market research (price, quantity, seasonality, etc.) with an effective approach

Figure 6.2   Potential Problem Areas to Consider When Introducing E-commerce

You Know . . .	Therefore you should . . .
Customers often get nervous about security.	Address security issues up front.
During peak usage periods, shoppers experience delayed responses.	Ensure you can handle high volume.
Downtime occurs at some sites.	Have backup system protection.
Potential customers comparison shop.	Price your products competitively.
Competition can develop quickly.	Keep on top of other Web sites.
Shoppers can lose interest if nothing is new.	Update your site frequently.

to getting your message out through your marketing materials (brochures, booklets, letters), sales, advertising, public relations, promotions, and networking. Your online sales strategy will succeed most quickly if it is wrapped in a total package that grabs consumer attention. Position your products and services with strength and conviction.

Set goals for your electronic commerce strategy, and set goals for your Web site. Be specific about what you expect to do with your Web site. Consider the following:

- What is your mission? Who are you and what makes your business better than your competition?
- What do you want your Web site to accomplish? How will your Web site help your business achieve its goals?
- Will you provide information about your company? Your history? Your major clients? Will this serve as an online "brochure"?
- How will you provide information about your products, services, features and benefits, prices, and ordering information?
- To what extent will your Web site mimic offline materials and catalogs or offer fresh new information and features? Will you introduce new products and services, or provide a more vivid depiction of the same inventory?
- How detailed should your electronic catalog be?
- How will you use this Web site to establish a relationship with your customers, provide customer support, and gather information and ideas from your customers?
- What level of interactivity will you provide for your customers? How many different links should be offered?

Online marketing strategies are addressed in further detail in Chapters 7 and 8. Web dynamics require a proactive approach to dealing with customers and competitors—the marketplace changes very quickly. You won't have time to get bogged down in planning. Just be sure that you know what your business is trying to accomplish and how your Web site will help your business accomplish these goals.

■ Step 2: Access the Internet

What do you need to get connected to the Internet? If you already have experience using the Internet to gather information, or to shop, you are off to a good start. On the other hand, what works for you as an information-gatherer won't be enough power for you as an e-tailer with a Web site. How can you support your electronic commerce goals? Consider your core components, shown in Figure 6.3.

Figure 6.3 Access the Internet

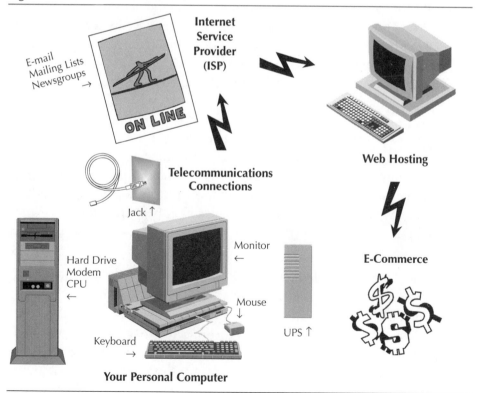

Assess Computer Components and Upgrade Them as Necessary

Your computer configuration is the complete set of equipment (i.e., computer hardware) that you will use to access the Internet for your business. It includes your PC (personal computer), CPU (Central Processing Unit), RAM (random access memory), hard drive, UPS (uninterrupted power supply), modem, and a monitor.

Get the best configuration you can afford, with an eye to the future, regardless of whether your system is located in your basement home office or a prestigious corporate headquarters. Products change so quickly that to specify models and speeds in this text would instantly date the material. New products come out almost daily. The bottom line is this: If you do not have the latest hardware, get it. Your old equipment can be sold or donated to a start-up company or a nonprofit organization that doesn't need to be bleeding edge of high tech. Shop with a professional (more on this in Chapter 11) if this is not your area of expertise.

For electronic commerce, you will need the most sophisticated capabilities to support multimedia programming. Your hardware should have dedicated support, so if you order your components from an online computer company be sure you know how to contact the manufacturer's technical support center. Better yet, find a local technical support company or person who knows your equipment and is available 24 hours, seven days a week—or close to it.

The larger your operation, the more critical round-the-clock support is. When the volume of orders coming into your business begins to increase, you will need to consider handling noncritical functions during nonpeak hours. Some processing functions can be scheduled for the evening hours to keep the PC free for other interactions during peak volume periods.

If your business is (or will be) using EDI to transfer information such as inventory or billing data from manufacturers or distributors to your work location, you may still be able to operate using a basic personal computer. When you use EDI, three different options are available to configure your computer system hardware:

1. Your hardware could be a personal computer (DOS or Windows based)
2. It could be a minicomputer and a mainframe computer (i.e., a *maxi-computer*)
3. It could be a PC at the front end connected to a mainframe. (This is *not* the type of computer configuration that you would handle on your own. This calls for professional assistance from design through implementation and maintenance.)

Your CPU (central processing unit) should have the fastest microchip (or simply, "chip") available to handle multimedia. Intel introduced their Pentium III processing chip in February 1999. The Pentium III works at speeds of 450 and 500 MHz for PCs. Later in 1999, Intel planned the introduction of a Pentium III processor at 550 MHz. A fast brain will make a big difference in your total system efficiency, so this is a key component of your system. The new powerful processors are well suited for networking functions, too, as your business grows.

Random access memory (RAM) capacity should be able to handle large space-eating software programs and run several programs concurrently. At least 128 megabytes or more of RAM will help you run many software applications, but additional RAM will make a visible difference in your speed of operation. Get as much as your computer can hold.

Your hard drive should have disk space for long-term storage of programs and documents of ever-increasing magnitude. At least an eight-gigabyte drive will work, but a 16-gigabyte drive is better, and costs only a few hundred dollars more. Be sure to include UPS (uninterrupted power supply) for your computer and your phone line.

Because your modem controls the speed at which you can interact over telephone lines, the fastest modem available is the one you'll need, while watching your service provider for their speed as well. Standard packaging with most computers sold as this book goes to press are 56K modems, which send 56,000 bits of data per second.

Last of all, remember you may be sitting behind a monitor for extended periods of time if you interact with your business, customers, and other Web sites, so comfort and clarity are critical to enable you to endure longer work sessions. Also consider the fact that the larger the monitor, the more you can display on the screen at one time. A 17-inch monitor will enable you to view several open windows at once. A 19-inch model will be slightly more expensive, but a worthwhile investment if you will spend a lot of time examining detailed lists of data or if you do a lot of switching back and forth between different Web sites.

Assess Network Connections and Implement Changes as Needed

Computer network. A computer network is a data communications system that connects computer systems at different sites. Your network may be any combination of local area networks (LANs) or wide area networks (WANs). A LAN is used to connect computers when you are covering only a small area (that is, a few computers located within a few square kilometers), usually within the same building or floor of a building. A WAN connects computer systems across a large geographic area, using serial lines, telephone circuits, or cables to interconnect.

Internet connections. You can connect to the Internet by modems connected to standard telephone lines or special lines, cable access (same as cable television), digital subscriber lines, or satellite. Dial-up modems connected to standard telephone lines are used by 90 percent of all Internet users at a cost of about $20 monthly. Most of us use phone lines when we first connect to the Internet for personal use. While this method is the least expensive, it is more appropriate for personal Internet use than for business use. For one thing, you tie up phone lines interminably. But worst of all, data transmission is slow compared to other alternatives. Speed affects the length of each and every transaction. If you download data via phone lines, it will occur very slowly. Can you use this arrangement for your business? Probably not. Speed is essential. Check out Figure 6.4 for a comparison of speed.

Cable and telephone companies nationwide are in competition to deliver high-speed Internet access to as large a customer base as possible, as quickly as possible. We are in the midst of a broadband war, waged to the benefit of the consumer as cable and telephone companies battle to roll out their upgraded services nationwide faster. Following are descriptions of today's alternatives to connect to the Internet for business:

Figure 6.4   A Comparison of Speed of Access to the Web

The time it takes to download a 10-megabyte file by alternative methods:

Method	Time
Dial-up modem (56K)	25 minutes
ISDN	10.5 minutes
Home satellite dish	3.3 minutes
DSL	2.5 minutes
Cable modem	1.3 minutes
T1 line	56 seconds

Source: Bell Atlantic

- *Cable access.* This provides high-speed broadband access through cable modems, providing access at rates roughly 50 times faster than telephone modems. Cable access is handled by a cable modem that hooks up to your computer and works with service provided by your cable television company. You no longer need to "dial up" the Internet—you are always online. In addition, this technology makes video over the Internet look much like television, and audio sound like radio. Downloading is *fast.* Because not all cable television companies offer this service, cable access is now used by a limited number of all Internet users. Where it is available, monthly cable access costs roughly $35 to $70.

- *Digital subscriber lines (DSLs).* Available only from regional Bell phone companies, DSLs provide fast access but are also available on a limited basis for about $60 to $150 monthly. DSL is rapidly becoming the preferred method of connection, although it is also not available everywhere yet. Major telecommunications corporations are attempting to roll out the service regionally as fast as they can. The speed and low cost of DSL make it an attractive option for the growing business. Asynchronous digital subscriber lines (ADSLs) will be the best match for many e-commerce companies.

- *T1 phone lines.* T1 is a leased-line connection capable of carrying data at 1.5 million bits per second. At a cost of $350 to $3,000 monthly, these super-fast lines are great, only unavailable in remote areas. They are now the most widely used paths by businesses.

- *Integrated Services Digital Network (ISDN).* An ISDN offers the advantage of being able to move more data over existing regular phone lines, with pricing only slightly higher than regular phone service at $70 to $180 per month. ISDN lines will soon be available in many more locations.

- *Home satellite dish.* For locations that are difficult to reach by land lines, there are new-and-improved satellite services. Satellite services, however, are still minor players in the Internet marketplace, and are prohibitively expensive.

Internet service provider (ISP). The ideal option would be to acquire your own server and install your own high-speed communication lines. It is the most expensive but most effective choice requiring a high level of technical expertise and continuous support. On the other hand, simply owning your own server does not guarantee access. Your connections to the Internet still have a direct impact on access by your customers and download time.

Many small businesses opt to select an Internet service provider rather than acquire their own. Be careful about your choice. Your ISP helps you take full advantage of the capabilities of the Internet. ISPs maintain pools of Internet Protocol (IP) addresses that enable each computer to reach every other computer. Every computer connected to the Internet must have an IP number, just as you must have a telephone number to receive phone calls. Web addresses or host names are translated into IP numbers through the domain name system, a part of the Internet. When we type in a name, like www.dell.com, our computer checks with a domain name server to translate this address into an IP address. The processes all take place behind the scenes.

Speed, capacity, and service are important to you. Providers that are focused on network service, such as the telecommunications companies, will better serve your business purposes than the larger portals, which may be difficult to access during peak periods (like 3 PM, when most kids get out of school).

Following are questions you should ask when selecting an ISP:

- *What speed lines does the ISP use to connect to its upstream provider?* When 56K modems became mainstream, service provider AOL still had not upgraded all their lines to the faster speed. If you've ever switched to a higher-speed modem only to find that your ISP was *not* up to your speed, you know how frustrating it feels to watch graphics and images slowly crawl onto a screen in spite of the upgrade you paid for.

- *Is the service provider filled to capacity?* You have goals for future growth; so do their other customers. Do they have room for growth, are they prepared to handle expansion, and can they stay ahead of you in technological gains? Downtime is frustrating to you as an Internet user—it is lost income to you as an e-tailer.

- *What is the ISP's track record for downtime?* Christmas 1998 took its toll on even some of the largest, most efficiently designed Web sites when traffic overload set in.

- *Do they have backup systems?* You want to know that there is redundancy built in to their systems: backup power generators, use of multiple phone companies for their network connectivity. Who are your local Internet service providers? www.thelist.com takes you to a Web site that lists all service providers by state. You can check out pricing and speed.

- *What other services can they provide?* Some Internet service providers will also act as your Webmaster, helping you with site development and site maintenance.

- *Do you have access to your local telephone exchange?* If not, every call that isn't local incurs a charge and is not covered under your regular monthly phone service charge.

- *Should you own or rent access to the Internet?* What if you are not satisfied with the responses to the preceding questions and the answers fail to satisfy your business goals? If you own your own server, you decrease access time for your customers and may have better quality control. While the cost is greater than renting, there are distinct advantages to achieving a high level of dependability.

E-mail. Electronic mail capability is a feature provided by your ISP, and could very well become your most significant source of information from customers and prospects. It's fast and easy. Because e-mail can be sent automatically to a large number of addresses simultaneously (via your electronic mailing list), this feature will enable you to easily send "hot flashes" like press releases or updated product information to your customers and vendors.

Browser. The software that enables you to view the Internet, although it does not actually connect you, should be user-friendly. For the security of your desktop PC transactions, your browser should also support 128-bit encryption. Netscape Navigator (www.netscape.com) and Microsoft Internet Explorer (www.microsoft.com/ie/) are still the most popular. In addition, be sure to download upgrades, which are generally free, to keep your browser state-of-the-art.

More software. Amazing new software packages to help you use the Internet more effectively, design your Web site, track your customers, and more are announced daily. It can be difficult to keep up with the latest developments. Paul Weidner, director of education and training at the University of Scranton Electronic Commerce Resource Center, suggests the site www.tucows.com for a list of software related to the Internet. "This is a good place to look for things that will help you design your Web page. You can try before you buy," he adds. This site provides listings by U.S. region and allows you to try some software packages for free. Another option is "shareware," which is software you can try out for a limited amount of time before buying it.

■ Step 3: Promote Your Web Site

Establish Your Presence

Establish your Internet presence early and definitively. If your Web site will take some time to be fully operational, create a Web page (a home page) in the interim to at least get your name out while you work on the bells and whistles of a comprehensive e-tail location. Avoid creating the online equivalent of "under construction," which is often associated with problems or unanticipated delays. Think of it as a "coming soon" sign in a brick-and-mortar Main Street window. Let people know how to reach you right away. Let potential customers know. A summary of actions appears in Figure 6.5.

Select your domain name. Your domain name is the unique name that identifies your Internet site. Domain names always have at least two parts: on the left of a dot is the specific name, and on the right of the dot is the general term (e.g., .com and .net for business, .gov for government, .edu for university or educational usage, etc.).

Can you use your own company name as your domain name? It's a good idea to try for easy recognition and memorization for your customers. If a brand name of your company is strong, that may be an even better choice. But possibly not. For example, someone snatched up "Tiernan" already, so a variation on my name will be needed to prevent confusion between this author and some heretofore-unknown branch of my husband's family tree. The gatekeeper for all this information is InterNIC, who guarantees that each domain name is unique and conforms to designated Internet standards for a fee of $100. Or you could log on to the U.S. government authorized registrar of domains, Network Solutions (www.networksolutions.com) to see if the name you have selected is available. An ISP can also register a domain name for you, but be certain that the name is yours and not the ISP's (just in case you switch providers). The new nonprofit Internet Corporation for Assigned Names and Numbers, or Icann, formed in early 1999, has been assigned the task of opening up competition to Network Solutions. Icann will also add new top level domains (like "use .com" for business) to meet the growing demands for new

---

Figure 6.5   Establish Your Internet Presence

---

1. *Select your domain name.* Dot.com your business with a recognizable name.
2. *Register with search engines.* Go for the most important first: Yahoo!, Excite, AltaVista, Infoseek, Hot Bot.
3. *Choose your keywords for indexing.* Select words that identify your products, services, and attract the right customers.
4. *Get the name out.* Dot.com or print your domain name on everything you produce: brochures, stationery, business cards, press releases, products, and more.
5. *Link to and from other sites that serve your target market.* Get in with the right crowd, passing information back and forth.

Internet addresses. Watch for new companies with which to register your domain name in the months to come.

Register with search engines. More than 300 search tools are available today. Search sites and engines help you find what you need on the Web; they'll also help potential customers locate your Web site. You are not really on the Web until you are listed in a directory that is accessible by a Web server program. "Until you register your domain name," says Paul Weidner, "it's like having an unlisted telephone number. No one will be able to reach you if they don't know you personally." Individual registration with each search engine is required. There are service companies that will register your domain name for you; however, by the time you follow up to insure they have done a thorough job, you might as well do it yourself. Go for the most important first: Yahoo!, Excite, Lycos, Snap, Alta Vista, Infoseek, Hot Bot. (See Chapter 12 for further information.)

Choose your keywords. Search sites like Yahoo! are directories sorted in categories and subcategories. Search engines, on the other hand, are computerized searches by keywords or phrases. Keywords can be any words you choose that have a connection to your product or service, and are not necessarily part of your product definition or service description. Keywords should make sense to your customer. Select keywords that quickly relate to your products and services to attract the right customers to your Web site. Keywords won't necessarily include the name of your company.

The only effective way to see if the keywords you have selected are working for you is to try out the search engines. Are you lost in the shuffle or does your site surface at the top of the list for the keywords you have selected? Change your keywords if you are not getting the results you need.

Get your name out. Reinforce your domain name on all of your printed materials. Dot.com everything you produce: brochures, stationery, business cards, flyers, press releases, advertisements. Your domain name should be as much a part of your work as your address, phone, and fax numbers have been in the past. If you use radio and television advertising, mention your Web site.

Link to and from other sites. Get in with the right crowd, passing information back and forth. This will increase traffic to your site. Which sites are most likely to increase your traffic? Companies that also serve your target market, even though their products and services are distinctly different from yours, can provide great connections for you. Businesses that offer products and services that can be used in conjunction with yours are also good resources for you. Links and strategic partnerships will be covered in greater detail in Chapter 13.

■ Step 4: Design Your Web Site

How complex should your Web site be? To determine complexity, consider the number of pages; the number of elements on a page (photos, articles, forms, headlines, etc.); site revisions (frequency of updates to the pages—daily, weekly, monthly, or less often); and interactivity. Interactivity refers to the dialogue between a user and your site. At the simplest level of interactivity, you will allow consumers to fill in forms and download files. More complicated links allow users to interact with your site and with one another in online conversations.

Plan the interface between your Web site and your customers, the interactivity between customer and Web pages; customers and you; and customers and one another before you get into the details of technically composing your Web site. Design of the human interchange should precede detail design of the computer interchange. Chapters 7, 8 and 9 address customer-oriented considerations of Web site design. Some ISPs, such as AOL, provide Web site design tools and space for your own Web home page free as part of your account. Remember that you will get what you pay for. Free packages generally work from templates that guide you through the design of your Web pages with the underlying assumption that most businesses are created equal. Templates do not offer much flexibility in layout and interactivity; on the other hand, you can't beat the price. For a low-cost start in simple e-tail, this option serves as a way to get your name out while you get your finances in order to invest in a more complex site. As more companies use these templates, however, you'll be able to spot them right away, which will signal lack of creativity and cheapness.

Project a Professional Image

The image you project online is just as important as your physical presence. In person, experts believe, it takes only a few seconds for us to form a first impression. The same is true of your Internet presence. You have only a few seconds to grab the attention of the shopper, and your introduction comes through your home page. You can create a pretty awesome introduction to your company using the technology available today, which becomes more powerful by the minute. Using small Java programs (called "applets"), Web pages can be designed to include animations, calculators, drop-down menus, scrolling text, moving graphics, and other more advanced features. Java is a programming language invented by Sun Microsystems that was specifically designed for writing programs that can be safely downloaded from the Internet and run immediately without fear of viruses or other harm to your computer or files. A Java program can be written to do almost anything a regular computer program can do, and can then be added to a Web page. Java allows for almost limitless possibilities for interactivity between user and Web site, consumer, and seller. Small business owners using HTML and Java have created their own sites and set up basic e-commerce transactions. For more sophisticated computer programs, and customized customer interactivity, Web site design should be assigned to experts. The cast of professional characters that can provide the necessary design and support are discussed in Chapter 11, and resources are described in Chapter 12. Following is a discussion of some of the technical elements that comprise electronic commerce.

Consider Electronic Commerce Components

Four main components of electronic commerce are: Electronic Data Interchange (EDI), electronic catalogs, digital currency, and intranets and extranets. Following are key points regarding each component.

EDI (Electronic Data Interchange). EDI is the interorganizational computer-to-computer exchange of structured information in a standard, machine-processable format, as defined by EC World Institute Resource Center (www.ecworld.org). EDI systems are private networks with dedicated software and limited access. Translated, EDI is the system that enables partnering companies or organizations to talk to one another electronically about dull stuff like purchase orders, inventory lists, bills of lading, bills of sale, etc. (lots of details, the type of information that leaves wide margins for error when done by a human). EDI lets any business send mundane, boring, tedious paperwork to another business with complete accuracy, even if the partner company has totally different computer equipment.

EDI is not used for business-to-consumer transactions. EDI has its most common use in business-to-business transactions. If your business begins to grow quickly, and if you decide to branch into business to business e-commerce, you will probably hear about EDI right away. If your company strictly sells to consumers, you can avoid it.

EDI becomes an issue when your trading partners are using EDI and expect to interact with you in the same mode. Who are your trading partners? Trading partners are virtually anyone you are doing business with.

If you ever want to sell your products and services to older, established corporations or the government, you will have to deal with EDI in one way or another. Before you say, "Not me!" note that the U.S. government buys just about everything, and when it buys, the purchases are *huge*. Local Small Business Development Centers (SBDCs) are ready and willing to assist small businesses in obtaining government contracts (referred to as procurement) and for many small businesses, this route can be the first step into the big leagues. The Electronic Commerce Resource Centers (ECRC) located all over the U.S. can help any small business make the transition to EDI transactions. (See the Appendix for a list of resources.)

Most Fortune 1000 companies have been online with suppliers and customers for more than a decade, long before e-commerce made headlines. Industry has used EDI for over 20 years to enable trading partners to exchange documents electronically. Today the companies who pioneered online transactions are left with a dilemma: Should they upgrade to Internet standards and go with state-of-the-art technology or stay put? Many companies with existing, older EDI systems have a considerable investment in their past way of doing business. What should they do? Should they incorporate the old systems into new systems and dive into Internet commerce or not?

Many "older" companies are finding that it isn't easy to add trading partners in different parts of the world to their old EDI systems. The Internet, however, provides tremendous flexibility. What types of companies face this problem? It seems that financial services and manufacturing companies are the most deeply into private networks. As a result, many manufacturers are likely to stay with their EDI networks for now. Others will wisely choose to use a combination of the Internet and EDI, using the Internet for catalogs of products for the public, and using EDI to order products from vendors.

Following are some of the advantages of EDI:

- Time required to process forms (such as purchase orders, invoices, receipts, and shipping orders) is significantly reduced with EDI because information only needs to be entered once. For example, information can be entered at a manufacturer's site, then transmitted directly to a seller. No further manual effort is required.
- Errors are reduced. Because there is no need for human intervention (such as transcribing notes from one form to another form), there are fewer opportunities for mistakes.

- EDI allows manufacturing on demand, because as a company automates procurement and order management, it is possible to use just-in-time (JIT) delivery.
- Customer and vender relations are improved, thanks to the transfer of accurate and complete information.

With EDI, trading partners with different hardware and software can still exchange information. EDI translation software handles everything. This software, which can be loaded onto a personal computer, converts information to a nationwide standard language referred to as ANSI X 12 (these standards cover minutiae beyond describing here).

Trading partners (such as you and the people with whom you want to do business) specify the information you will trade, what you must have at each end of the trade (or transmission), and precisely what details will be involved. A trading partner agreement is used to record all this information.

Internet EDI introduces the technology of EDI systems that once was available only to large organizations (like the government and major industries) and makes it affordable to smaller companies. In other words, small businesses can now become players in the world of older EDI companies. Because the cost of EDI transactions can be prohibitively expensive for a small business, many large corporations will absorb the cost of the transition to EDI so that they can work with smaller companies. In this case, small business owners can go directly to a corporate Web site, enter data about their products and services in a form provided by the corporation, and the corporation handles the translation to EDI.

Consider Intranets and Extranets

While an internet is a collection of networks (the Internet is the worldwide collection), an *intranet* is a private network using public Internet-based standards. Intranets are accessible only by members of a specific corporation or organization, for internal use and with authorization only. An *extranet,* or extended intranet, links two or more intranets together and makes information available to authorized members of the participating groups. Intranets commonly include four basic features:

1. E-mail, for improved employee or trading partner communication
2. Online publishing, for documents such as job listings, employee handbooks, phone directories, benefit information, internal news releases, and electronic forms
3. Online searches, for quick access to corporate data

4. Distribution of commonly used applications (like Excel), for brainstorming, collaboration on projects, and enhanced group tasks

Intranets can streamline business processes by disseminating information faster and making collaboration easier, regardless of geographic location. As businesses make more information universally available, there are greater opportunities to shorten development cycles and streamline operations through the collaborative efforts encouraged by intranets.

Almost every department in an organization can benefit from a combination of intranets and extranets. Marketing and sales can expedite orders. Research departments can access larger data bases for their studies. Customer service can track and examine input from customers and feed this information back to the sales and marketing staff. Human resources departments can disseminate personnel notices with ease. Manufacturing and operations functions can communicate better with the marketing department for more efficient supply chain management and elimination of the middleman.

■ Step 5: Create an Electronic Catalog

Stand-Alone Catalog or Cybermall?

Electronic catalogs, e-catalogs, can be used in two ways:

1. As a stand-alone catalog, to display your products and services in an innovative manner.
2. As an electronic mall, or cybermall, to list your products and services in the electronic catalogs of other companies to gain wider exposure.

Stand-alone catalog. This is a Web site put together to sell a product or service. More than an online version of a printed catalog, the stand-alone catalog should more closely represent an electronic storefront, bringing the shopper closer to the heart of your business. Amazon.com (www.amazon.com) sells books online this way. Peapod (www.peapod.com) uses this method to sell groceries for delivery to customers.

To attract customers, stand-alone electronic catalogs need to offer something different from their printed counterparts. Simplicity, lower prices, and extra information are just the beginning; audio, video, and animation can top it off. Invigorate presentation of your products and services in your catalog and you will offer an added value to your online package. Make your products and services come alive and shoppers are more likely to return—and buy. Further discussion of this topic, as well as examples, are in Chapter 8.

Cybermalls. An electronic mall, or cybermall, is a catalog of catalogs, a collection of catalogs from different merchants combined by an ISP. There are currently more than 4,000 malls on the Web. The largest online mall today is iMall (www.imall.com), with over 1,500 merchants. Another well-known mall is the Internet Shopping Network (www.internet.net). When you enter the "mall," you can access a classified directory to guide you to the merchant who offers what you are looking for. A listing of clothing stores on iMall is shown in Figure 6.6 and a sample of just a few of the many offerings available.

Presentation Is (Almost) Everything

Achieve the best balance of graphics and text. If it takes forever for your elaborately designed catalog to be fully displayed, beware. The same individuals who hate to wait on shopping lines in brick-and-mortar stores will lose interest in your online site, too.

Link to other electronic catalogs. You can decide to be part of an electronic mall in addition to having a stand-alone catalog. Some government agencies, for example, have electronic malls with catalogs for buyers to shop for commodities. You can be listed in their electronic catalog and linked to your Web site.

Cybermalls offer an opportunity to set up your Internet shopping site at minimal cost (virtually eliminating Step 4 of this process) by providing a package of services that make it easy to get on the Internet. As a merchant, you pay a monthly fee to a host who provides certain Web site services for you, including the following:

- *Space on the Internet.* Most hosts include site maintenance in their monthly fee, but charge a commission on sales and limit the number of site pages.
- *Templates for standard Web site pages.* Design help is offered by some hosts for an hourly rate.
- *A domain name.* Remember the earlier precautions about using someone else to do this for you—you still have to check up, and you want to ensure that you own the name even if they go out of business.
- Registration with search engines.
- Interactive site capability. Now you're getting somewhere. Handling forms, shopping, member discount programs—it is truly a cost-saver to have this covered by an experienced pro.
- 24/7 or twenty-four-hour/seven-day-a-week sales capability.
- Credit card payment processing including security.

Figure 6.6 iMall Stores and Products

Search results 1 - 10 of 79

Firefighter T-Shirts
We carry the best assortment of Hawaii Firefighter T-Shirts.

HiKids-Quality clothing, uniforms, dresses for children
Our store caters to children ages 0-18. Our beautiful inventory ranges from casual to exquisitely designed Dresses, Christening dresses, Wedding dresses, boy's suits, boy's clothing, shoes, ties, belts, bows, boy's and girl's socks, hats, boy's and girl's uniforms, colors white, blue, green, yellow WOW! We carry much, much, more...

DIXIE-Western Clothing, Boots, Jeans, Hats-Since 1914
Dixie II has been in the Western Clothing business since 1914 and our commitment to high standards and quality has never changed. Famous brands of boots and jeans are our specialty. Some of the famous names include Justin, Tony Lama, Nocona, Wrangler, Rocky Mountain, Montana Silversmiths, Panhandle Slim, Banjo, Circle T, Circle S, Bailey Hats and many others.

Fashion Clothing - Bags, Belts, Coats, Suits - Second Time Around
New and Used Designer Consignment Clothing and Accessories for Men and Women.

Lingerie Hangers -
Specialty Items Designed By Pam Foster

ABC Kids & Teens - Clothing TOP BRANDS AT UNBEATABLE PRICES!
Clothing, Accessories, and Shoes for children of all sizes. We carry apparel for all seasons, for all ages in The Hottest Styles and with The Coolest Prices!!

Luxor Online Catalog
Egyptian treasures, logo merchandise, clothing, souvenirs, and many more items are available through the Luxor Online Catalog. Great kid's stuff too!

Premium Quality Childrens Clothing at Affordable Prices
We offer only the finest in children's formal apparel, featuring stunning, frilly dresses, little boys' tuxedos, and combination outfits. Fashionablekids.com is dedicated to offering fine, distinctive, children's clothing with the closest attention to detail. Before we ship products to our customers, we inspect each button, zipper and hem. If it doesn't pass our strict inspection standards, we don't sell it. They deserve the best!

Webbster's General Mercantile
Come in and visit "The World's General Store." Fine Arts, Accessories, Holiday Gifts, Jerky, Pacific Northwest Specialties, Hand Crafts, Clothing, as well as other quality merchandise. Come on in for a visit. A FREE GIFT awaits you.

Skulldana
We sell all sorts of Bandana's

next 10

■ Step 6: Identify Your Distribution Channels

What functional flow will work your business? Your supply chain needs to be delineated in painful detail. Examine closely the tasks that will occur to get from the point where a customer places an order and the moment the order is shipped.

Determine Your Supply Chain and Create Appropriate Links

If you are completely self-contained (that is, your company manufactures every piece of your product), your communication links are internal but still need to be outlined. Each department's responsibilities should be clarified, as well as how departments should interrelate.

How should your teams work together to ensure the highest standards are met? If you are dependent on a conglomeration of vendors and suppliers who produce parts or goods for you, the flow of functions is more complex. In addition to defining the role of each company in the supply chain, responsibilities within each company must be clearly spelled out.

Consider the following questions in your analysis:

- What are the central lines of communication?
- Exactly who must you communicate with? When? How much advance notice is needed if a sudden increase or decrease in the volume of orders is anticipated?
- What information is passed back and forth, and in what format?
- If you need to expedite an order, what measures can be taken?
- If your primary supplier or vendor cannot meet your needs, do you have alternate companies that you can deal with?

When you clarify the functional flow of information within your company and among your business partners, you'll be in a good position to define the use of intranets and extranets. A combination of intranets (for interdepartmental communication) and extranets (for communication with vendors and suppliers) will enhance your capability to track information in a timely manner.

Companies that have been through the ISO 9000 process already know the drill (ISO, by the way, is the process of standardizing methods and procedures throughout a corporation to ensure that the highest standards of quality and excellence are being met in every aspect of operation. Then you document this to death.) As part of the ISO 9000 process, businesses go through function and task analysis in excruciating detail.

■ Step 7: Develop a Method of Order Processing

As soon as you develop an online sales presence, you have the capacity to sell 24 hours a day, 7 days a week, all around the world. Your clients and customers can have up-to-the-minute information about your products, services, prices, and availability. Steps to take to ensure that your customers can shop 24/7 include handling invoices, billing, processing payments, and transferring money.

Have Electronic Funds Transfer Capability

Your bank must be able to handle electronic funds transfers (EFTs). Small banks may not offer this capability, so be sure you check in advance. In addition, fees differ from bank to bank, so it may be in your best interest to shop around for lower fees.

Offer Real-Time Payment Solutions

The objective in selecting your method of payment is to minimize disruptions for you and your customers, while providing real-time solutions that are affordable and safe. Credit card payments, electronic money (e-cash), electronic checks, and smart cards are the most common methods of electronic commerce payments. Payment methods can be designed into your system or contracted out to a company that handles third-party payments as described below. The fundamental difference between these payment methods is that some are PC-based, while others are microchips embedded on a card. Methods of processing payments are summarized in Figure 6.7.

Credit cards. Jupiter Communications predicts that credit cards will be the preferred method of payment for online purchases 99 percent of the time until 2002. Credit card payment transactions are protected by encryption, which ensures that only the bank or credit card service provider, not the merchant, sees a number. MasterCard has been aggressively pushing the use of credit cards for online shopping through television ads, print ads in *USA Today*, and through promotions on Excite's site. In July 1998 MasterCard sponsored EZSpree, a Yoyodyne online promotion offering prizes up to $100,000 to spur credit usage online. Late in 1998, VISA USA jumped on board, accepting Secure Sockets Layer (SSL) security and backing off on its position that secure electronic transactions (SET) protocol should be adopted first. VISA had originally been strongly against any security protocol that did not include

Figure 6.7: Processing Payments

Type	Advantages	Disadvantages
Credit Cards	Traditional function, familiar	Difficult for micropurchases
	Most widely used method now	Usage limited to higher cost items (like CDs, books, PCs)
E-Cash	Very simple to use	Take extra precaution to eliminate fraud and security threats.
	Encourages impulse buying	
	Small payments are no problem	Account may not be backed up with actual funds
	Gaining popularity	
Smart Cards	Familiar (debit cards, phone cards)	
	Stored-value is easy to retrieve	If you lose it, it's gone.
	Stores extra information about customers	If it's gone, it can't be recreated.

SET. VISA now has a 51 percent market share of online purchases, according to Jupiter Communications' estimates. VISA has also been in the list of top ten Internet advertisers (for noncomputer ads), and is working to build solid connections with Yahoo.

To accept credit cards, contact your bank, a credit card service provider, or merchant service provider. Your costs will include several fees:

- Application fee ($50)
- Equipment lease ($30 per month)
- Software lease ($40 per month)
- Transaction fee (20 to 30 cents per transaction)
- Keyed-in charge (.25%)
- Discount (1.5% to 3% per transaction)

You could use an electronic commerce payment processing service like CyberCash to handle credit cards for you. CyberCash was first created in 1994 as a simple verification service to pacify customers who feared revealing credit card account numbers over the Web. Today they handle several types of payment services.

Credit card systems do not always respond well to large volumes of low-price transactions. Low value items, or intangibles such as information or on-line entertainment, with a cost of one cent to ten cents, are impossible for credit cards. Minipayments for items in the 25 cent to $10 range are also not well suited. On the other hand, if you ever intend to do business with the government you will need to be able to accept credit cards.

Electronic cash (e-cash). Electronic PC-based cash systems allow payments to be made by typing in an amount or clicking on "notes" or "coins" on the screen. E-cash is stored in the consumer's computer and is transmitted to the merchant directly or through a third-party payment service. E-cash requires some sort of bank certification to avoid fraud or insufficient funds in the account.

Electronic cash systems can indicate a running balance. The buyer and seller can be in any physically remote location, so e-cash works well for e-tailing. Electronic cash is not yet as popular as credit cards or smart cards, but Jupiter Communications predicts that the next three years will see a dramatic increase in usage. Experts predict that e-cash will grow in popularity and probably dominate as the number of small items and their corresponding micropayments increases.

Smart cards. An early popular use of smart cards were pre-paid phone cards, followed by an increasing use of prepaid "credit cards" that act like gift certificates in select retail stores. Electronic cash is stored on these "intelligent" credit cards that can be plugged into computers or given to merchants. Smart cards, or stored-value cards, not only access financial accounts, but also store information about a purchaser's preferences and buying patterns. Smart cards can be used to gather data, track products, and monitor purchasing decisions.

Electronic checks (e-checks). More convenient than conventional check payments, e-checks use digital signatures that are transmitted between your company, the consumer, and the bank.

Work Out Shipping Arrangements

Where is your merchandise? Is your stock stored at your location, or are you selling products from one or more manufacturers at various locations? Delivering your products to the consumer as quickly, and safely, as possible is as important as handling your financial transactions safely.

Work out your arrangements for regular and expedited shipment with the best carrier to suit your needs. Negotiate discount rates for frequent usage or take advantage of existing discounts offered through special deals for group memberships, whenever possible. UPS has generated software to integrate merchants' processes with theirs to provide a fast, efficient, and accurate approach to shipping merchandise.

■ Step 8: Select Security Systems

Safeguard Customer Privacy

Your security systems serve the dual purpose of safeguarding your customers' privacy and protecting all your confidential company records and data. Private information about inventory, suppliers, and clients cannot be accessible to unauthorized individuals. Security issues are discussed in detail in Chapter 10.

Protect Company Records

Security issues are a primary concern when implementing intranets and extranets. Because highly confidential information—including financial data, product specifications, and company projections—is passed back and forth, hackers target these networks. You can protect your networks from unauthorized access to confidential information by encryption, firewalls, and proxy servers. Encryption refers to the manipulation of data in order to prevent any but the intended recipient from reading it. Encryption forms the basis of network security. Firewalls separate a private network from an open network, screening access based on the owner's specifications. Firewalls can also include a proxy server, which handles communication between a private network client, and the open network server. Proxy servers provide user level authentication.

Passwords can be used to isolate specific sections of your server and allow only specific information to be accessible to authorized users. Firewalls can separate the intranet from the extranet and provide additional ways to delineate access to data by authorized personnel only.

Security precautions are critical in dealing with all forms of digital and electronic currency, particularly electronic cash. Merchants need system designs that reduce the possibility of fraud and security threats. As a very practical matter, you need to ensure that electronic cash is supported by actual funds.

■ Step 9: Develop Inventory Tracking Procedures

Tracking and Controlling Costs

Experienced e-commerce companies have found that it is possible to dramatically reduce overall costs by installing new procedures for inventory tracking and control. The Internet allows a vendor to build to demand, reducing inventory to the minimum. According to this strategy, manufacturers produce only as much as required by incoming orders. This eliminates the problem of overstocked warehouses, and as a result reduces debt for both merchants and manufacturers.

For this to work, there is no room for error. Every piece of order information must be accurate, and there can be no bottlenecks in the system. Dell Computer has operated in this mode even before selling online, so they have learned how to handle contingencies. Dell doesn't stock warehouses full of computer equipment. Dell allows customers to build computers to their own specifications; they also make sure that they know if a particular computer is low in stock. There are no surprises; the customer is informed of potential delays immediately.

Link to Suppliers, Customers, and Others

If your company is going to allow customer configuration, and that will be the way of the future for many of us, ensure that your mission is as well developed as Dell's. Decide who should have direct access to your inventory information: vendors, customers, salespeople, distributors? Just as important, decide who should not. Your security systems will be designed around blocks of information that will be accessible to some individuals or companies, and off-limits to others.

■ Step 10: Refine Your Customer Interface

Encourage Feedback

Your customers will need just as much attention in e-tailing as they would if you met with them personally or spoke with them over the phone. The fundamentals of nurturing relationships and building loyalty span the life of your business. Your system will need to be capable of receiving and monitoring feedback from your customers continuously. The best e-tail sites encourage feedback from their customers and work diligently to keep their customers coming back. Apprise your customers of "news" about your business. Set up ways for your customers to let you know how you're doing, what they need. Track their purchase patterns, and build on the information you have about their past orders to help them with future buys.

Listen to their suggestions for improvements and enhancements. If you find out that part of your Web site is inefficient, or your site is too difficult to navigate, fix it. Customer relations will be addressed in detail in Chapters 7 through 9.

7

Cybermerchants

■ Characteristics of Successful Cybermerchants

As online shopping gains popularity, the lines of demarcation are fading between stores, catalogs, and Internet sites. To assume a leadership position in the market, merchants need to excel in all three forums.

Consider three basic issues: (1) market trends, (2) customer service, and (3) profitability. Merchants face the constant challenge of keeping up with trends, yet they still need to be able to offer their customers something unique. Customer service assumes an equal level of importance on a Web site as it does in physical contact, but the cost to provide service—labor costs—is a big factor in most budgets. And while it may take some time to recoup the initial investment of the design of a Web site, there won't be enough demand to support the site at all if a merchant doesn't price products and services competitively.

In Chapters 1 and 2, it became clear that e-commerce companies under the direction of strong leaders have been able to maintain dominant positions in the marketplace. These companies have more than a simple recipe for success. They draw on the personality and character strengths of the founder, or the top decision maker, to start. A combination of winning personal characteristics and astute marketing techniques characterize merchants who master the art of cyberselling. In a large company, the president or CEO influences key managers and staff, often defining the corporate culture. In a microbusiness, where the founder serves as CEO and chief salesperson, personal characteristics of the owner and company mission are one and the same.

Successful cybermerchants are creative, insightful, collaborative, professional and dedicated, with well-honed leadership and negotiation skills. These characteristics are described in Figure 7.1.

Creativity

Original and imaginative powers of expression characterize successful cybermerchants. They have the ability to make the ordinary appear extraordinary. Personally, you will find they conceptualize in visual images, and can see in their mind's eyes what a display, or screen, should look like long before it is actually programmed. They can connect seemingly unrelated material and pull it all together coherently, generating new and fascinating forms of expression. Creative individuals also become bored with routine; they need change. They apply their creativity to the design of their Web site, and gratify their own need for novelty by constantly changing it.

Figure 7.1 Characteristics of Successful Cybermerchants

Creativity—They can make the ordinary appear magical.

Insight—They understand motivational factors.

Decisiveness—They are quick to respond to changing market demands.

Collaboration—They seek mutually beneficial interactions.

Professionalism—They master the task at hand.

Dedication—They sustain energy and enthusiasm for their work.

Leadership—They have a visionary perspective, and have no fear of being first.

Negotiation—They reach open and honest collaborative agreements.

Insight

With an ability to cut through superficial surface issues and see clearly to the heart of the matter, the successful cybermerchant is an individual who has strong intuition and perception. In general, they understand the motivational forces behind behavior. This characteristic gives them an edge when interpreting customer needs and wants. The timeless sales question "What's in it for me?" presents no challenge. Successful cybermerchants have already thought about the personality and needs of their customers.

Decisiveness

With little or no hesitation, successful cybermerchants react to changes in the marketplace and take swift action. They respond quickly to new demands, adjusting their strategy and implementing a new direction with strength of conviction. When something isn't working, they change it. Not a year later—right away.

Collaboration

A strong emphasis on cooperation versus competition drives most successful cybermerchants. They place a high priority on the establishment of mutually beneficial interactions. They will work jointly with customers, suppliers, and partners to define the most efficient processes to bring their products to market. Cooperative efforts characterize their dealings with all parties in their supply chain. How can they jointly make their transactions work more effectively and profitably?

Professionalism

A person who is an expert at his or her work can build a reputation as a professional in his or her field. The successful cybermerchant is a master of the task at hand. If the field is highly technical, for example, this individual is either recognized as an expert technician or as an excellent scout of highly talented personnel. As a professional, one can recognize what quality means and deliver flawless products and services.

Dedication

Successful cybermerchants are wholly committed to the task at hand. Their Web site is not an afterthought, but a high priority. These cybermerchants follow up on details and watch the process through from start to finish. This means that they have to stay on top of supply-chain demands, customer service requests, marketplace changes, product quality, and production and delivery issues. They sustain the energy and enthusiasm it takes to follow through the steps to refresh and update their Web site and all the integrated components of their marketing strategy.

Leadership

The formula for success includes a visionary perspective, the leadership factor. Successful cybermerchants assume a leadership role in reacting to market trends, initiating customer service, and ultimately achieving the goal of profitability. Personally, these individuals have an advantage over their competition because they have no fear of innovative initiatives, of being pioneers in their field. Successful cybermerchants are superior in one or more ways. They may have been first to market with a new product or service, first to provide their product on the Web, most cost-efficient, highest quality, most customer-service oriented, or most customized. They believe that if they stay the same, they are falling behind, so they constantly seek new ways to remain in a dominant position. They track economic, social, and market trends, with an eye to how trends can impact their future direction.

Negotiation Skills

In setting up collaborative agreements with suppliers and partners, successful cybermerchants exercise excellent negotiating skills. They can protect their own interests while ensuring a fair deal for others. They conduct open business discussions and carve out equitable deals. They arrange for open and honest settlement of the terms of their agreements.

Can you succeed without these characteristics? The secret is to know your own strengths and weaknesses, and hire or acquire what you lack.

- *Creativity* can be bought; graphic artists, designers, and writers can be hired to create the graphics and narrative that will draw shoppers to your site and keep them coming back.
- While you can't buy intuition, your personal *insight* can be enhanced through a better understanding of consumer psychology. Take advantage of studies and market research available through the Internet to expand your perception of buyers' needs and wants. Use market research to ex-

pand your frame of reference. Take advantage of the findings of cognitive computing.

- *Decisiveness* comes naturally when you have command of your subject and you feel confident that you have all the information you need to make a quality decision. Sometimes you won't have all the information you wish you could have. Learn to minimize risk by analyzing your options, weighing pros and cons.
- *Collaboration* with your customers, suppliers, and partners requires openness and honesty, but also a thorough understanding of your supply-chain possibilities. If you aren't clear on what these potential alliances are and how your transaction flow can be made more efficient, spend the time it takes to become familiar with the details of how your prospective partners operate. Learn how you impact one another and the customer.
- *Professional* expertise is yours to acquire or hire. Bring on the best possible staff and you build a reputation for quality.
- It is probably most easy to be *dedicated* in the early days of your Web sales—the novelty keeps you going. Dedication over the long-term, however, is the only way to keep customers coming back. Remember the fall-off in customer satisfaction ratings for e-commerce sales in Christmas 1998 versus 1997? Was quality taken for granted after a few years of success? Even some of the market leaders experience problems.
- As a *leader,* don't become so bogged down in managing minutiae that you miss the big picture: What business are you in? Shift your emphasis from doing things right to doing the right thing. Ensure that you act as a leader so that your business can assume a leadership position in your market.
- *Negotiating skills* take you a long way when you finally sit down to formalize your agreements with suppliers, customers and partners. If you are not a skilled negotiator, work with someone who is: an attorney, a financial backer, an accountant, someone to watch over you.

■ Proven Marketing and Sales Strategies

Your marketing strategy is the comprehensive approach your business will take to achieve your objectives. Steps to implement a marketing strategy that will work for your Web site objectives as an integrated component of total business are listed in Figure 7.2.

Figure 7.2 Marketing Strategies That Work

1. Get to know your customers.
2. Use your power to persuade.
3. Understand your competition.
4. Differentiate from others.
5. Price profitably.
6. Coordinate your campaigns.

Get to Know Your Customers

First define your customers: Who will most likely buy from you? Where is this market(s)? What are you trying to sell to them? Then consider the more complex questions: How can you reach them physically? How can you reach them psychologically? Your clients' behavior can give you clues that help you understand them better. As you learn about your customers' behavior, you can eventually gain a better understanding of their collective "personality" and what they want. Using the data-gathering tools of your Web site, you can track the behaviors of your customers for transactions during every site visit.

In Stephen Covey's best-selling book *The Seven Habits of Highly Effective People* (Simon & Schuster, 1989) he defines the fifth habit as "Seek first to understand, then to be understood." He wrote that when everything else is equal, ". . . the human dynamic is more important than the technical dimensions of the deal." The human dynamic of e-tailing is the buyer-seller relationship, and how you relate to your customers.

When you start e-tailing, what track record do you have to work with? If you started with a brick-and-mortar store, a printed catalog base of customers, or both, you have a profile to analyze. If this is your first venture, focus groups can help you to acquire firsthand information about customer preferences, opinions, buying patterns, price sensitivity, and more. Interview potential customers directly and get their input. (The case study later in this chapter is an example of how focus groups can help you gather data for your business.)

Learn as much about your customers as you possibly can. What are their hobbies? What are their leisure activities? What memberships do they hold? Where and how often do they take vacations? What are their families like? The more you understand about their lifestyles, the better your choices will be about other Web sites to link to, key words to attract their attention, how to select your advertising and promotions, and other related decisions.

What do customers and clients respond to? Why is it that a request presented in one way will be rejected, but one in a slightly different manner will be successful? Psychologist Dr. Robert Cialdini cites six fundamental patterns underlying the thousands of individual tactics that successful persuaders use every day to get us to say yes. (See Figure 7.3.). If you can use techniques of influence in your Web site, you can tap in powerful psychological principles that can be irresistible to some individuals.

Reciprocation. We are trained from a very early age to live up to the rule of repaying favors. The rule possesses awesome strength, according to Dr. Cialdini. Whenever we offer free samples of merchandise, we are not only letting people try out a product to see if they like it; we also engage the rule of reciprocity.

Commitment. Consistency offers us a shortcut through life, so we have a nearly obsessive desire to be or to appear to be consistent with what we have already done (i.e., to behave consistently with a commitment). The marketing "foot in the door" technique is based on this principle. If you can start with a little commitment, you can usually build on it.

Social proof. When a lot of other people are doing something, we usually think it's the right thing to do. We see the principle of social proof in action

---

Figure 7.3   Six Principles of Influence

---

1. **Reciprocation.** We feel obligated to repay favors, gifts, invitations, and similar offerings.
2. **Commitment.** We have an intense desire to be consistent with what we have already done.
3. **Social proof.** We view behavior as correct to the extent that we see others performing it.
4. **Liking.** We most prefer to say yes to the request of someone we know and like.
5. **Authority.** We are trained that obedience to proper authority is right; disobedience is wrong.
6. **Scarcity.** Opportunities seem more valuable to us when their availability is limited.

Source: Influence: The Psychology of Persuasion, by Robert Cialdini (New York: William Morrow & Co., 1993).

whenever a product is described as the "fastest selling" or "largest growing." You don't have to convince us directly that the product is good if you let us know that many others think so. Sometimes that's proof enough.

Liking. If we know and like someone, we are more likely to say yes to their requests. So how do perfect strangers get people to comply? They work with components of liking: physical attractiveness, similarity, compliments, contact and cooperation, conditioning, and association.

Authority. Obedience to authority is right, we are taught when we are very young, and disobedience is wrong. Authority can be invoked both directly and indirectly to influence us to buy. If an authority figure recommends that you buy something, that's a great endorsement (More doctors use . . . Most accountants prefer . . . Technical experts agree . . .). But if you counterfeit authority, it is just as effective. Even the flimsiest referral to "authority" has been proven to work. Think of all the "authorities" promoting exercise videos and you'll agree the possibilities could be endless.

Scarcity. When our freedom to have something is limited, and the item becomes less available, most of us experience an increasing desire for it. The feeling of being in competition for scarce resources has powerful motivating properties. Opportunities seem more valuable when their availability is limited. Every Christmas season seems to bring a new dilemma of scarcity, from Tickle Me Elmos to Beanie Babies to Furbies.

Know Your Competition

For the most complete insight about your competitors, you need to check each one out from all perspectives: storefront, catalog, and Web site. Who exactly are you competing with and via what forums? Your ability to learn about your competitors is vastly enhanced by the Web. You can spend as much time as you'd like investigating your competition's Web site without having to answer to anyone. Use this research tool; you can be sure your competitors will.

Search every Web site that competes with yours. Go through the sites thoroughly for design, format, and content. In addition, investigate the prices of their products and services. Do they offer discounts? Special offers? Check out their complete catalog. Who advertises on their site? This gives you a lead for potential advertisers for your own site. What rates do they charge? Just as shoppers at your site will compare prices, so will prospective advertisers or sponsors. Have your data ready to incorporate into your pitch. Check out traffic patterns, too. If a well-designed competitor's site draws very few "eyeballs," you are in luck. Your position is stronger.

Differentiate from Others

Use what you learn from your explorations into your competition's territory to formulate a sales pitch that clearly differentiates you from others. What's your unique angle? Specify how your products and services benefit the consumer. How do you meet their needs? Is your site more interactive, your products most popular, your services most highly rated by experts? We are all inundated by information and deluged by data. If your products are the same old thing offered in the same old way, it won't matter if your Web site wins design awards.

Price Profitably

Know what your competition is charging all the time. Should you be greater than, less than, equal to? You will not be able to build the complete cost to create and maintain your Web site into the cost of your goods and services, but you do need to cover your basic expenses. Additional expenses include your telephone costs, printing, office equipment, travel, mailing expenses, rent, and payroll.

Coordinate Campaigns

When you put together all the pieces of your marketing campaign, strive for a consistent look. This includes all components for your complete business and your Web site: marketing, sales, public relations, advertising, promotions, and networking. Have a logo that defines you and appears on all your materials in addition to your Web site: sales brochures, business cards, press releases, articles, reprints of news features, advertising (print, radio, television, and banners on other Web sites), promotional items, and networking tools (directories, dinner programs, etc.).

■ Sales and Service Solutions That Deliver

Your sales approach, whether you are personally responsible for selling or you have hired a sales staff, is the most personal aspect of your marketing strategy. How well you sell will ultimately make or break your company. Web site sales offer new opportunities to expand your reach and make a greater impact—and higher profits.

Sales Techniques

Techniques that work in person may not translate directly into effective Web tactics, but it is important to remember that the decision-maker is still a person, not a computer. Consider the behavior you would use in a face-to-face or telephone contact. You would generally follow a series of steps (probably four) before you could actually complete a sale. Following is a way in which this technique would take place on a Web site:

1. *Introduce yourself and grab their attention.* All of this activity takes place within a matter of seconds. Quickly and succinctly, your home page is the Web equivalent of a firm handshake, a smile, and an interesting opening comment.

2. *Highlight the benefits.* Effective sales presentations are more than a rundown of all your products and prices. Probing to find out what the customer needs first works more effectively. On your Web site, forcing your shoppers to click through a long list or catalog of all your products and services is the equivalent of an unfocused sales pitch.

3. *Handle objections.* Face-to-face, you can judge by an individual's expression when they are hesitating and you can jump in. You can also answer their questions right away. By designing interactivity on your Web site, you can accomplish a similar effect. Your objective is to pre-empt objections by providing information and answers to questions. What are your customers' possible concerns? Provide an opportunity to ask questions and receive answers quickly. Frequently asked questions (FAQs) can be addressed through lists on your Web site. The more obtuse questions can be handled one-to-one offline: Will you deliver on time? Is this transaction secure or will the customer's credit card number be broadcast to the universe? Is your product really guaranteed to be of the highest quality? These potential objections can be addressed through your FAQ list.

4. *Close.* When the buyer is ready, you would make a move to close the sale. You wouldn't continue your sales pitch just because you didn't cover everything you had planned to say. Your Web site should enable your customers to "close" their transaction with a "buy" at any point. No extra paging and clicking, please.

Sales Opportunities

Opportunities abound for the creative and entrepreneurial-minded marketer to make money on more than just the sale of products or services on a Web site. The site itself has value, and if the site is popular the value increases. Banner exchanges were the first trend; now links are hot. Projections? Continued growth through innovative ideas.

Banner exchanges let small businesses barter ad space on their sites with complementary partners, an ideal cost-cutting strategy for entrepreneurs. Instead of paying for a banner, small companies trade ad space. LinkExchange (www.linkexchange.com; now owned by Microsoft) claims steady increases in banner customers. SmartClicks (www.smartclicks.com) reports the same. How do the exchanges make money? They offer major corporations the opportunity to advertise on multiple sites. They also offer services to round out the transaction: They register companies with search engines, create banners, and handle direct sales. Banner exchanges offer a way to reach your target market at a national level quickly and inexpensively. To reduce your costs, you can create your own banner with graphics software, such as Adobe PageMill, which includes HTML.

Exclusives

Considering the importance of differentiation—from your competitors and from other forums within your own business—you will need to concentrate on techniques beyond design and appearance that make your Web site stand out. A successful strategy, while difficult to maneuver, is to increase the number of exclusives your business receives from popular manufacturers. If you are one of a very limited number of Web sites that handle Coach's new spring purse, you can draw attention away from other sites to yours. How many deals like this can you negotiate? This effort is worth placing as a high priority.

■ The Art of Cybershopping

Perhaps the first people to become hooked on cybershopping were the early Internet addicts who could totally lose track of time hopping from Web site to Web site. It was only a short leap from hopping to shopping, easily mastered by the Web-savvy. These pioneers had already discovered the Internet advantages of speed, convenience, 24-hour availability, the excitement of new surprises daily, and the lack of a dress code (in fact, no need to dress at all). Their attitude of indulgence was quickly transferable to Web shopping sprees. How easy it is to click now, pay later.

Shopping for the Web-wise is the fastest way to spend thousands of dollars in minutes. No trudging from store to store in a crowded mall; just click to another site. No need to stop to buy food; the refrigerator is only steps away. No lugging heavy bags and boxes; everything will be conveniently delivered. No hassles. You can probably exceed your wildest expectations of compulsive behavior at breakneck speed.

For an extra adrenaline rush, there are online auctions, with all the addictive power of real live auctions. Ebay has thrived through many peak shopping seasons. So have thousands of individuals who checked in at Ebay daily for the hottest new items to come up for bids. It's truly a great experience—until the credit card bills begin to roll in. Ebay has evolved into the first sporting event that you can participate in while sitting down, in pajamas. Winning in the bidding is described by self-proclaimed auction addicts as a "high." Now *that's* entertainment.

Those of us who purchase inconceivable gifts at irrational prices every holiday season are familiar with the pain of facing horrendous credit card bills before Groundhog Day. The ease of initiating an online shopping spree serves as an incentive to avoid the judicious step of thinking before buying. The anonymity of bargain hunting lets you examine an item, go to another site to check out the same or similar item, go back to reexamine, and so on until you're satisfied. Most of us would be too embarrassed to do this in person. While shopping online there's no sense of guilt for having wasted a salesperson's time when you ditch their product for a cheaper deal.

Seven Habits of Highly Successful Cyber-Shopaholics

To understand the phenomenon of cybershopping, you have to grasp the seven habits of highly successful cyber-shopaholics: immersion intensity, abbreviated attention span, compulsion to comparison shop, obsession with uniqueness, passion for credit card payments, delight with deliveries, and an indelible memory for incredible sites.

1. *Immersion intensity.* A paradigm shift of enormous significance transpired over past holiday seasons when vast numbers of U.S. shoppers simultaneously developed the ability to endure extended hours of sitting and snacking in pajamas while they shopped online. Intervals as long as nine hours were reported to have passed as minutes. This intense immersion in e-tailing serves as the foundation for future holiday seasons that may exceed our wildest expectations.

2. *Abbreviated attention span.* In an apparent paradox, although cyber-shopping sprees may last for long periods, each site must grab attention immediately or the visit will be brief, the equivalent of window shopping at a brick-and-mortar store. Cybershoppers have a low threshold of tolerance for the same old screen. Images must be interesting and appear quickly.

3. *Compulsion to comparison shop.* Because it is so easy to check for competitive prices, most shoppers will. They never need to move their car; they only move a mouse.

4. *Obsession with uniqueness.* The rare find, the unique antique, the hottest Beanie Baby are musts for many, explaining the enormous popularity of online auction sites.

5. *Passion for credit card payments.* Credit cards are still the preferred method of payment, making it possible to accumulate many large purchases in a single trip. Small price items are more difficult to handle by credit card, and may be slower to gain popularity.

6. *Delight with deliveries.* From slow-route UPS to overnight early morning Fed Ex response, the shopper can control the timing of arrival by paying more for shipping, and many people do exactly that. The volume of online shopping increases steadily in the final days before the holiday season, indicating that people are willing to pay more for convenience.

7. *Indelible memory for incredible sites.* They tell their friends and family about Web sites with great looks, great gimmicks, great prices, and great products. If they stay interested, and there is always something new to view, they'll be back again and again.

From Shopping to Buying

There are still significant differences between the number of people who seek product and pricing information online and the percentage who actually make a purchase. The number of individuals who actually buy something over the Internet instead of just browsing steadily increases. There has been a large leap into action in a short interval. Alternatively, Internet Travel Network (ITN) reports that only 25 percent of their customers book flights online, although 95 percent check flight schedules and prices on their Web site.

Are shoppers satisfied with their online purchases? A recent survey released by Jupiter Communications indicates 74 percent were satisfied, a level 14 percent below the previous July figure. Customer satisfaction with purchases is only one area of concern. We still have every indication that even dedicated

Internet users continue to complain about security and excessive download times. The CBS MarketWatch telephone poll found that 65 percent of the respondents were very concerned about Internet security issues, particularly theft of their personal identity or credit-card numbers.

■ Addressing the Top Three Customer Concerns

If three fundamental issues—product quality, security, and download time—remain a concern to dedicated Internet users, it clearly is the mission of any company that seeks success e-tailing to address each. Incentives for individuals to change from shoppers to buyers have to be stronger than well-crafted creative gimmicks. While great graphics, for example, might entertain the viewer, they will not drive a shopper to buy. "I get more requests to take graphics *off* the Web site rather than put them on," says Joan Leavey, president of Computer Insights, Inc., in Leonia, New Jersey. "People now realize that if a picture takes too long to load, shoppers won't wait."

Handling objections and consumer concerns, just as you would in a formal face-to-face sales presentation, will make the difference between a look and a buy (see Figure 7.4).

Concern 1: Product Quality

To start, work with what we already know. Because we know that consumer confidence in quality is important, let the online shopper know that quality is important to you, too. (Let's assume, of course, that you do offer a quality product or service . . .) How do you ensure quality? Let your recipe for success be known: For example, "We use only all-natural, totally purified, untouched-by-human-hands, direct from heaven, ingredients," and so on. If you were running print, radio, or television spots, you'd promote the quality of your goods, even if in a subtle way. There is no less a need for reassurance on the Web. There are a lot of con men (and women) out there, and you want to disassociate your business from theirs.

Concern 2: Security

We know that security is a major concern, too. Many people will not hesitate to hand their credit card over to a stoned-looking waiter in a no-star restaurant in a remote location, but will choke at the thought of putting that same card number online. Their cavalier attitude may not prevail when they

Figure 7.4 From Shopping to Buying (Guerrilla E-tail)

Consumer Concern	Approaches to Consider
Product quality	Promote quality as your highest priority. • Describe your quality control measures. • Explain your attention to detail and how you have earned the "seal of approval" from others.
Security	Describe your security precautions. • How do you ensure that credit card numbers will not be accessible to anyone else? • Will you promise that confidential information will not be passed along to other merchants, banks, etc.? • Are you displaying your little "key" at the bottom of your secure site to let users know that you have encryption and are secure?
Convenience	Don't waste their time. • Offer shortcuts through transactions for experienced shoppers, and for those who know your product line well. • Concentrate on presentation, not exasperation. • Limit the number of pages a user must click through.
Control	Provide interactivity. • Allow shoppers some control over the information they can receive. • Answer frequently asked questions right away.

shop online. How have you protected their interests (and your own)? Address their fears. Without getting into technobabble about your Web site design, there are some terms that can be presented to let the consumer know that the credit card or smart card information that they are confiding remains secure. No one else can access it, including your staff. No other entity will be able to use the data they have provided for you. No one else will pester them. And there will be no surprises when next month's bill rolls in.

Concern 3: Convenience

We know that convenience is a huge influence in the decision to shop online in the first place. You won't necessarily have to offer the cheapest prices around (although you had better be competitive with Web prices) because you've eliminated the time factor of physical shopping. Tack on your shipping and handling charge, and you'll still have one happy clicker. But make the same individual wait while you walk him or her through an endless repertoire of Web site embellishments, and your would-be customer will hit the road fast. It's just a click away to someone else's store. If photos or complicated graphics enhance the presentation of your product line beyond belief, then by all means seek the best. But beware if you cross that very fine line between presentation and exasperation. In a word, *don't*. Certainly add color and pictures to your text, but don't cause congestion. Reduce the number of pages a user must sift through. And always allow experienced shoppers (those who know your Web site, and those who already love your product or service line) a route to bypass your introductory material and cut straight through to "buy now."

Being in Control

What else makes consumers buy rather than just shop? Consumers like the feeling of being in control, just as if they were in a store or holding a printed catalog. How can you instill a feeling of being in control? Think about how a personal transaction might take place. There might be a question or two, a need to take a closer look, a desire for some background information. If you provide even casual browsers an opportunity to feel as though they can control their run through your Web site to get to what interests them, *and* allow for an opportunity to have their questions answered—live in an interactive arrangement or from a FAQ (frequently asked questions) list—you have a better chance of getting them to buy.

■ Niche Marketing

Niche marketing refers to the efforts a business makes to focus its marketing efforts on a specific segment of the total market. Niche markets are traditionally defined by characteristics of their members; however, niches can also be defined by specific customer needs. Niche marketing is widely believed to be small businesses' best strategy for achieving leadership positions. When a company targets marketing efforts to a particular niche, it can reap the dual benefits of increased sales and reduced costs. Business-to-business marketers came to this realization years ago. Now business-to-consumer specialists are moving in. Traditional mass marketing communications appealed to the lowest common denominator. Trying to be all things to all people was expensive and bland.

People with similar culture, background, education, training, or experience comprise a niche. They are experts in a particular area of special interest. Their depth of understanding in their field is greater than the mass market. To get their attention, you need to provide intelligent information and substantial content at their level of expertise. Examples of niche markets include:

- Baby boomers
- Generation X
- Children
- Internet users
- Hip-hop generation
- African Americans
- Hispanic Americans
- Asian Americans
- Caribbeans
- Health-conscious consumers
- Affluent/Millionaires
- Entrepreneurs
- SOHOs (Small Office/Home Office)

This list is just the beginning. Logical subcategories within each niche should also be explored. For example, children include infants and toddlers, but also the distinctly different 12-year-old market.

It isn't good enough to have a superficial sense of a niche market. It is more important to have an excruciatingly detailed knowledge of these prospective customers, where you can find them on the Web, and how you can approach them.

Visualize your ideal customer. In the past, which prospects turned into good customers? If you are coming from a shop or catalog experience, there is a track record to examine. What were your successes? If you are launching a business online, select an individual who embodies the characteristics of your perfect prospect and work with that profile.

Identify the source of leads. What has been (or what could be, if this is pro forma) bringing in your best customers? How did they hear about you? Can the same sources be used to lead these customers to your Web site? Consider trade shows, vendor leads, yellow pages, referrals, seminars, direct mail, flyers, radio, television, and other sources.

Determine where to find them. Where do your customers hang out? On the Web, which chat rooms (if any) do they frequent?

CASE STUDY: *Delia's* ■

Delia's, a New York clothing catalog company, has made its name among teenage girls ages 12 to 17. Teenage girls are finally being addressed as a unique niche, and their buying power is evident in the success of music groups Hanson, the Spice Girls, Backstreet Boys, and Britney Spears. Delia's Web site (www.delias.com, Figure 7.5) has a look distinctly different from Macy's and other retailers, because Delia's knows and appeals directly to its niche market.

Online shoppers at Delias.com are treated to virtual makeovers, New Dig or Dis (a chance to offer opinions on television programs), and monthly polls (such as "What could you give up for a month?") through a set of links to other sites.

Delia's has been immersed in the 12-to-17-year-old age bracket for over four years. They know their stuff. But behind the lighthearted approach of the Delias.com Web site design are truly serious business decisions. Online sales for all the Delia's companies are handled by a company called iTurf, which has been granted the exclusive rights to market Delia's brand online. ITurf marketing executive Renny Gleason says, "The goal of iTurf is to become the premier destination online for teens for content, commerce, and community." ITurf handles online marketing for eight entities that make up Delia's parent company, all serving the youth market:

1. Delias.com (clothing and accessories for girls 12 to 17 years old)

2. Droog.com (clothing and accessories for boys)

3. TSISoccer.com (complete line of soccer equipment and clothing)

4. DotDotDash.com (clothing for ages 6 to 12 years old)

5. StorybookHeirlooms.com (for the same younger market)

6. DiscountDomain.com (an online outlet store)

7. ContentsOnline.com (homewares and roomwares for college students and high school students)

8. Gurl.com

Figure 7.5 Delias.com Home Page

103

Cybermerchants

Wednesday 08.11.99

rEADY foR sChOOL?

165 new items oNLinE nOW!

SHOP ▼ GO

LInA PaNtS $36

discount domain $34.00 $7.99

oNLY aT dELiAs ✳ cOm

sHoP

rEQuEsT a cAtaLoG

Win Your Wishlist! Enter Here

Style in the Stars? Read your Fashion Horoscope.

FREE dELiAs✳cOm mousepad with ALL online orders.

FREE CD with ALL back to school orders over $75.

contents

The galaxy is growing. Fill it up with MORE NEW ROOMWARES!

sAVe

discount domain

discount domain is a sale shopper's dream. JOIN NOW for the best deals year round.

cONneCt

aFfiLiaTe NetWoRK

Make $$ create an online store and sell dELiAs✳cOm stuff.

gURL.cOm fReE e-MaiL aCcoUnTs & hOmEPaGeS!

contest --> the gURLmAIL get yourself together giveaway!

advice --> be an advice columnist for a day!

help me heather --> "my best friend hates herself...."

sPeAK

Play Twisted E-Mail. Let us twist your words.

tHe LiSt

Sign up for our E-Mail Newsletter. Receive News, Updates, Sales, Plus A Lot of Fun Stuff.

oR

eMaiL uS

General comments: espeak@delias.com specific problems: custserv@delias.com

iNFo

hELP

sToRes & eVeNTs

beYonD dELiA's

PriVacY PoLicY

tErmS oFuSE

Figure 7.6   Delias.com Web site provides a close-up look at special sale items for young online shoppers.

Figure 7.7   Delias.com encourages feedback from shoppers.

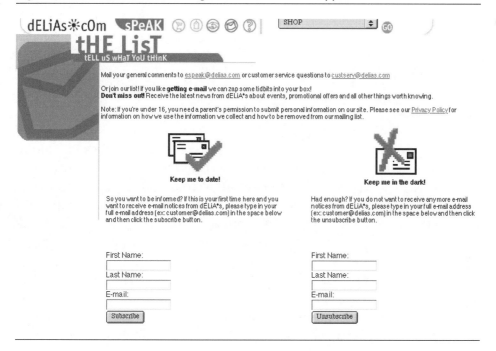

Delias.com today offers most of the Delia's catalog products, but they are moving quickly to put the entire line online. Delia's maintains tight control over production, distribution, and customer service processes to ensure the highest quality standards are met. All merchandising and sourcing is done in-house. They maintain their own customer service call centers. They have their own fulfillment centers. They have formed special relationships with vendors and suppliers who can be counted on. They also ensure that sizing is always consistent within and among vendors. Designers are also critical. "We find young designers who know this market, who will grow with us," says Gleason.

This astute combination of a structured approach to running the business and a spontaneous youthful look in their catalogs and on their Web site make Delia's and iTurf companies to keep your eye on.

■ Brand-Building and Image-Making

Creating a brand identity is the ultimate challenge to marketing and advertising specialists. Consumers are drawn to a brand that brings to mind a vivid image of something tangible. A powerful brand name can assume human qualities; it is also an implied promise of a high quality product. How can you make people see your company, product, or Web site differently? How can you add value?

In February 1999, Compaq Computer announced that it would increase its global advertising budget to $300 million, a 50 percent increase. During the CBS Grammy Awards, Compaq launched a new television advertising campaign to portray itself as a "dynamic youthful company in an Internet age," expanding from computer products to computer solutions. As part of its 1999 marketing strategy, Net.B@nk announced it would establish the Net.B@nk brand as the leading Internet bank, and rolled out a new print ad campaign with the signature line, "So, why aren't you NetBanking?"

Radio advertisements for Microsoft's Sidewalk.com Web site (www.sidewalk.com) spell out the tangible image they want you to conjure up. In their early 1999 commercials, an even-toned voice responds to a series of questions about the range of items Sidewalk.com will find for you ("from light bulbs to liposuction . . .") by simply saying, "Sidewalk can help." One of the ads closes with "Sidewalk.com is an information 18-wheeler." All the other ads have equally strong powerful images. As a result, a strong image emerged in a relatively short ad campaign cycle. See Figure 7.8 for Sidewalk.com home page.

Branding is no longer the exclusive technique of product lines. Personal branding, an exaggerated form of image making, is a phenomenon that gained rapid momentum in the 1990s. Martha Stewart and *Martha Stewart Living* expanded from a magazine, to television guest appearances, to weekly features, to a daily television show, with a line of linens and towels to top it off. Tommy Hilfiger and Michael Jordan became larger than life, with personal brand-name recognition that spanned the globe.

In 1997, the business magazine *Fast Company* published a special issue on "The Brand Called You." An article by best-selling business author Tom Peters, detailing the process of turning oneself into a brand name product, resulted in a deluge of requests for more information on the magazine's Web site. Have you developed your own personal brand, or are you a work in progress? If your company produces a product, packaging is essential to sales (What color? How durable? What shape?). If your company is you, and you provide a service, your image is like your package. It will sell you.

Figure 7.8   Sidewalk.com Home Page

107

Cybermerchants

Photo courtesy of Philips Magnavox Consumer Electronics

Your Web site is a vehicle to reinforce your existing brand or image and to build a new brand—or expand the range of your image if you're just a local personality. Product leaders know the value of launching new product offerings in a big way to ride on the power of a brand name. For large companies who spare no expense, the launch of a Web site can become an event in itself. By building the anticipation through other media, the launch can draw curious eyeballs that will return. For small companies, where expenses must be limited, launching a brand can be handled through smaller, but creative, events. Consistency with the image you want to evoke is key.

Online Stores: Dos and Don'ts

Some techniques just won't work online for the long haul, although you may reap short-term benefits. Beware of deep discounting as a gimmick, for example. Target and Wal-Mart, discount chain stores that offer year-round low prices, continue to show strong growth in profits although they offer few promotions. They are consistent, they offer an enormous variety, they keep overhead low. If you discount heavily to gain attention initially, you will not be able to hold interest if you later increase prices beyond what the cyber-market will bear.

Beware of the design considerations in Figure 7.9 when you create your online store.

Differentiating Your Web Site, Print Catalog, and Store

Should you present the same merchandise or services online as you offer in traditional stores and catalogs? Should prices be the same in each medium? Both approaches—consistency and differentiation—have been tried with varying degrees of success. Your decision may not be clear immediately; you may have to experiment with different techniques and monitor results carefully. As a general rule, consider where your customer base comes from. Will the same individuals visit your physical store as your Web site? Not if you're a very small business staging a nationwide Web marketing venture. What about print catalogs? How much crossover will you see from Web catalog to printed catalog? If in doubt, ask. Survey your customers through your site (more on this in Chapter 9). The following case study illustrates how customer consideration— What do they really need and want?—will go a long way to help you design a memorable Web site and attract buyers.

Figure 7.9 Dos and Don'ts of Online Stores

109

Cybermerchants

Do

1. Open with a strong introduction—great home page, that is.
2. Design creative visual images.
3. Create a company image that makes your Web site stand out.
4. Avoid a cluttered visual image (too many banners, too much information).
5. Reinforce your brand image. Build strength.
6. Use short, concise phrases in your narratives.
7. Vividly describe your products and services.
8. Offer a way to speed through your Web site to any specific known point.
9. Let shoppers get to the product they want in three clicks or less.
10. Build in customer interactivity—let them become involved in the site.
11. Serve as an information resource. Become an expert in your field.
12. Refresh your Web site regularly, just as you would change a storefront's window displays.
13. Offer competitive prices. Check your competition's prices regularly so you know what the market will bear.
14. Provide incentives to return to your site—giveaways, tips, coupons, advice, and jokes are popular choices today.
15. Include testimonials from satisfied customers to support product quality.
16. Offer a guarantee, prominently placed, near your order form.
17. See Chapter 9 for more ideas ("Checklist of Best Customer Practices").

Don't

1. Save your best page for last—many shoppers will leave you if the home page is dull.
2. Overwhelm the user with excessive photos and graphics that take too long to display.
3. Follow a template (one size fits all) if it doesn't suit your business goals.
4. Fill each page and allow for very little "white space."
5. Design without concern for your brand image.
6. Rely too much on narrative.
7. Use long-winded wording to get to your point.
8. Use a route to any specific product that requires too many clicks.
9. Design too many pages that must be clicked through sequentially.
10. Structure the site without allowing the customer to deviate from your pattern of responses.

(continued)

Figure 7.9   Continued

11. Offer superficial information that will be available on a thousand other sites.

12. Let information stagnate, get out of date, or look the same for too long.

13. Deep-discount if you can't afford to; and don't price gouge, or you'll lose shoppers.

14. Assume shoppers will return to your site without incentives.

15. Assume that your word about product quality is good enough.

16. Let your guarantee be lost in text.

CASE STUDY: *GoBabies®*   ■

Entrepreneurs who are armed with energy and optimism also need to support their endeavors with business savvy and a marketing strategy. Maura White, a former IBM manager who founded TigerRed Enterprises and created the brand GoBabies®, possesses a disarming combination of innate talent and professional expertise. TigerRed Enterprises is an example of a business that has used a strategic marketing approach since it was formed in 1993 to build brand recognition. White blends mail-order, telephone, onsite and Web site sales to sell her products, using a cohesive mix of marketing, sales, public relations, promotions, advertising, and networking to build momentum.

The marketing strategy. TigerRed Enterprises was founded to develop and market high-quality, competitive children's products and services. White discovered her market niche fortuitously during an airline flight delay when a fellow passenger ran out of diapers, an item ridiculously difficult to find in most airports. White created the brand GoBabies®, her own line of products for young children on the go, to make traveling with infants and toddlers easier and more fun. Her first products included the GoBabies® Diaper Changing Kit, Disposable Bibs, and the Grab 'n Go (an insulated travel bag filled with products for travel convenience). "The brand is anchored by a group of positive, energetic, and purposeful characters, the GoBabies," adds White. With the character as the brand logo, White is developing these characters through books and long-term plans for licensing the GoBabies® name and characters. The strategy for licensing extends to manufacturers who have travel-supportive products for families on the go.

White is a strong proponent of advertising and promotion and has traveled to trade shows and baby expos to promote her brand. Her goal is to become a Web-based business and be *the* Web site for families who travel with infants and toddlers. The GoBabies Web site (www.gobabies.com) serves as a vehicle to enhance the GoBabies® brand and build brand loyalty, not just as a place to take orders. This strategy became a key factor in the design of the site, which has a unique look and ambiance.

The Web site. The GoBabies® home page greets you with the character Simon traveling across your screen with an impish grin (Figure 7.10). The black-and-white standing version of this image does not do it justice, so check this out for yourself. The colors are vibrant.

Each character introduces a different theme: Simon has travel (Figure 7.11) and community (Figure 7.12), Lincoln offers activities (Figure 7.13), for example.

Click on the "Good Ideas" triangle and a set of questions is posted. *"What is your favorite toy to bring when traveling with your GoBaby?"* If your response is selected as a winning answer, you'll receive a free six-pack of GoBabies® Diaper Changing Kits. Responses are listed regularly and updated frequently. Free giveaways, and a bright and cheerful site, have helped to generate over 500 responses a month from 18 countries.

Maura White decided not to bring in a full-time programmer to support the GoBabies® Web site. "This is not my core business," she explained. Instead, she arranged to have the Web site designed for her (at a cost of about $1,600) and contracted with a Chicago company called I Works (www.i-works.com) for Web site hosting and maintenance. Her Web site hosting agreement includes twelve months of hosting services at $3 per page per month. Her cost for one year of hosting is $216. "Their cost was unbeatable," White said. On the other hand, her investment in graphics, which have multiple uses beyond the Web site, was a high priority. "I spent about $10,000 on graphics alone," she said.

Market research through focus groups. White used focus groups to obtain specific information regarding use of the GoBabies® name and logo, current and future product development, and identification of potential strategic alliances. Participants in her focus groups were a representative sample of upscale suburban mothers with children as young as newborn. Most families had two children and a household income of over $75,000.

These focus groups confirmed that "life is difficult" on the go with young children. Participants strongly agreed that products designed to simplify travel

Figure 7.10   GoBabies.com Home Page

First Stop for Parents
of Little Travelers

Vroom! Vroom! Vroom!

**Click Here to Hear
GoBabies Song**

Articles
How to Protect Your Home
While You Are Away

Featured Products
Earplanes
Inflatable Booster Seat

Ask the GoBabies
Custom Travel Tips

Message Board
Ask questions and get answers
from others like you around the
world

Stories
Simon Finds the Peanut Butter

Special of the Month
Buy One Get One Free

Win Free Products
Good Ideas

We'll guide you every step of the way.

Click here for your FREE Interactive Pregnancy Planning Guide

1-800-GoBabys (1-800-462-2297)
1-609-219-0239 (fax)
GoBabies@aol.com

Figure 7.11   GoBabies Simon has travel tips.

113

Cybermerchants

1-800-GoBabys
(1-800-462-2297)
GoBabies@aol.com
1-609-219-0239 (fax)

Special of the Month

FREE Medical Travel
Pack Checklist

ORDER
FORM

Travel Info

Message Board

 Visit Our Message Board

Articles

◆ **How to Protect Your Home While You're Away**

Travel to London

◆ **Accommodations**

◆ **Nutrition and Groceries**

◆ **Resources**

◆ **Safety and Medical**

◆ **Products**

Home   Product   Good   Ask The   GoBabies   About Us
        Ordering   Ideas   GoBabies   Songs &
                   Community   Stories

Figure 7.12 GoBabies characters guide the Web sites' community offerings.

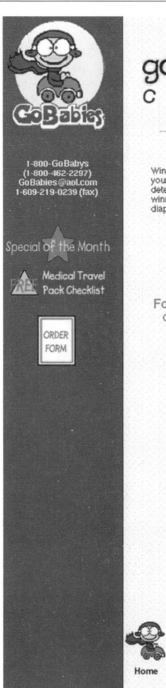

FREE
Win a ☀ 6 pack of GoBabies Diaper Changing Kits if your tips are used here at Good Ideas. Winners will be determined on a first come, first serve basis. Check out the winning responses for helpful hints on being mobile with your diaper-aged child!

QUESTION

For a child under 2 years old, what clothes do you pack for a weekend and a week vacation?

<u>Submit your answer</u>

Winning Answers

1. What medicine/first aid should you bring when you travel with your diaper-aged child?
<u>ANSWER</u>

2. What do you bring when you visit a friend's house that does not have children?
<u>ANSWER</u>

3. How do you plan a successful visit to the mall with your diaper-aged children?
<u>ANSWER</u>

4. What is your favorite toy to bring when traveling with your GoBaby?
<u>ANSWER</u>

Home   Product Ordering   Travel Info   Ask The GoBabies   GoBabies Songs & Stories   About Us

Figure 7.13 GoBabies character Lincoln provides tips on activities.

and emergency needs for baby supplies are a high priority. "If you can show me something that will make travel easier, I'm interested," reported one mother. In spite of their best efforts to be well organized and prepared for every trip, there was unanimous agreement by the participants that in every excursion at least one critical item is forgotten. Response to the GoBabies® product samples was extremely enthusiastic, indicating that the current product line meets these needs for travel-related items. The GoBabies® name and logo also drew highly positive responses from participants, with unanimous agreement that the name and logo connote travel and being on the move. Adjectives used to describe the GoBabies® name and logo included "very cute," fun, playful, happy, and adventurous. The groups outlined a wide variety of products that could fall under the GoBabies® name. One participant stated, "You could buy everything GoBabies® that you need for traveling."

White's focus groups were structured to meet specific objectives. The process involved three components: a structured questionnaire, unstructured group discussions, and a structured group interview. The structured questionnaire was used to document demographic and psychographic information, as well as compile ratings of travel-related service providers and restaurants. The unstructured group discussion was an open forum that served as a warm-up and an opportunity to gather input about life on the go. The structured group interview questions addressed the GoBabies® name/logo, current product line, and strategic alliances.

The evaluation process required the interpretation of both quantitative and qualitative data, as well as anecdotal information drawn from the round-table discussions.

- Quantitative data—concerning demographics, ratings

- Qualitative data—concerning opinions about present products, future product/service needs, personal preferences, characteristics of travel-related service providers

- Anecdotal information—about lifestyles and preferences

White found strong support for the GoBabies® fundamental focus on making travel easier when on-the-go with infants and toddlers. As one mother explained, "Traveling with children is horrific. Anything that will make this less painful will grab my attention!"

A comprehensive marketing approach. Maura White's GoBabies® Web site was recently selected by the Wharton School for analysis and review. Her input to their redesign is strong and confident. "I want extra space to surround the images to catch the eye," she said, noting that her present site has a unique look as it stands uncluttered with distracting details. "Design is such a personal thing. You have to know what you want." White's own insight into the needs and wants of her customers, confirmed by market research, drives her decisions as she works to build and grow GoBabies® into a national brand.

8

Selling Products and Services Online

■ Successful Business Models

Just before the online shopping craze started, *Fortune* magazine predicted the new business model of electronic commerce. The editors pronounced this new model the "e-corporation," a new kind of organization born by information technology. The e-corporation was, they avowed, "more than just Web-based . . . it's building a new industrial order." According to *Fortune,* a real e-corp would do more than use the Internet to change its approach to customers and target markets. It would combine "computers, the Web, and the massively complex programs known as enterprise software to change everything about how it operates."

According to this business model, working with the principle of consumer control is essential to building businesses that thrive. According to *Fortune,* mediocrity becomes intolerable as consumers assume a major role in defining which businesses succeed and which fail.

The business model for e-tailers needs to encompass all the steps it takes to complete the sales process with an intense customer focus. The steps in the sequence of events include following:

1. Understanding what customers need
2. Meeting these needs with state-of-the-art technology
3. Delivering the highest quality products and services
4. Ensuring total customer satisfaction
5. Adapting to high-volume holiday and peak shopping periods
6. Changing by the minute in a rapidly changing environment

No wonder a perfect business model has yet to evolve. We are, however, getting closer. Traditional business models seek a return on investment as quickly as possible. Too bad electronic commerce may take longer than a Main Street shop to show a direct ROI, as discussed in Chapter 4. But if the ROI is measured by increased sales to a company's physical stores *and* online sales transactions, a positive result can be detected sooner. If your Web site directs traffic into your store, you can *exceed* your business plan objectives. The best e-tailers devise ways to let customers shop online and offline at whim. If you need to touch, feel, and try on, go to Main Street. If you've tried it and like it, go directly to ".com" and save yourself some time and energy.

The objective of providing quality products and services is top of the list for e-commerce leaders. Flawless service, top performance, and timely information are additional e-tail objectives. Experts agree that customer demands will grow more intense with the proliferation of online shopping services. To achieve their objectives, successful e-tailers will need to ensure that they provide extrasensory perceptive customer service.

How will the successful e-corporation operate in e-tailing? Take returns, for example. Returns are a mundane reality that accompanies even the most successful sales season. How should the business handle returns? Will you accept Internet returns at your store, as JC Penney and Macy's do? Or will you separate Web sales from store sales, as Victoria's Secret does, and not allow returns at the mall shops?

Even with the best of intentions, mistakes can happen with both returns and purchases. Consumer reports of online fraud are increasing, according to consumer group Internet Fraud Watch. The Federal Trade Commission launched a 24-hour Internet fraud-detecting group to address this escalating problem. In order of complaints, the top ten company categories experiencing problems are: auctions, general merchandise sales, computer equipment and software, Internet services, work-at-home offers, business opportunities, marketing schemes, credit card offers, advance fee loans, and employment offers.

From a consumer's point of view, the rewards may outweigh the risks if a treasured object or highly valued service is acquired at a discounted price in a whirlwind time frame. From the merchant's point of view, the loss of credibility eventually will catch up and undermine future success. Businesses that sell products and services from other companies have to be extremely careful to insure that they are dealing with legitimate businesses with high-quality goods. Right now, there are no licensing requirements or government regulations specifically geared to people selling online. In the meantime, the Federal Trade Commission is increasing its surveillance of Internet fraud.

■ Creating Content

"Content draws people to the site, but then you need to make money," said Alyson Miller-Greenfield, associate director of the Rutgers University Small Business Development Center, the New Jersey state headquarters office. In the day-to-day job of dealing with prospective clients, entrepreneurs, corporate sponsors, government officials, policy and protocol, the Small Business Development Centers (SBDCs) come in contact with all shapes and sizes of start-ups and growing businesses. Miller-Greenfield and her counterparts across the nationwide network of SBDCs tend to be realistic and pragmatic.

Translate this into a game plan for online sales and the strategy you devise is straightforward. First, focus on content as *the* professional goal for your Web site. Second, ensure that your content is directed to a sales objective. Your sales may be all online if your business is only on the Web, or a combination of offline-with-online if you also own physical stores.

Even professional writers have begun to recognize the importance of content excellence and diversity. Newspaper and magazine Web sites, which once contained the same content as their print counterparts, are now featuring original material. Content that reinforces sales and firmly establishes the identity of the company works best. Customers shouldn't be forced to get lost in content, so structure and organization of material will also be important.

The depth of the content you provide should be geared to your purpose, but structured so that the shopper can control the flow and direction of information. The following should be considered when developing content:

- *Build in consumer control.* Let the viewer click or not, view or move on easily. Provide different routes through your site for new customers and for returning customers. If the customer is new to your site, but experienced in your product line, let them get to what they want without unnecessary words and slogans.

- *Don't oversell.* Do you want to see a belt with every pair of pants you order? Probably not. Maybe for the first pair of pants, to get you thinking. Offer each time, on the same shopping trip, and the Web site is acting like an overzealous sales clerk.
- *Show details on request.* Let the shopper choose to dig deeper and ask for more details.
- *When detail is desirable, go for it.* Not cluttered explanations, but catchy descriptions and well-placed photos or graphics. At the point when a shopper is ready to make a final decision about a cashmere sweater, for example, let him or her "feel" how luxurious it is before they buy.
- *Give niche markets clear signals that you know what they need.* Your approach will have to be at the level of sophistication that is appropriate for your target.

Sites that sell great volumes have a built-in capacity to adapt to change. If a merchandising strategy doesn't work, they change it, just like your favorite Main Street shop would change a window display. By gathering information about how well a site is doing, and keeping in contact with customer needs, e-tailers can learn from their customers where to modify their Web site to be more effective.

Content that drives the shopper's decision to stay, browse, and buy is the first consideration. In addition, Web sites contain revenue-generating features, like ads in a newspaper, which support the site and build relationships with other vendors. So some of the content on a Web site will be determined by contractual arrangements that are made with sponsors, advertisers, related Web sites, and additional content providers.

Banner Ads

These colorful rectangular advertising displays highlight the name, logo, and an occasional "grabber" of a company. Banners originally were placed on the top of a home page; now they can pop up almost anywhere. And some of these banners, in fact, *do* pop or run or flash or scroll with animated graphics.

You may choose to sell banner ads to any company from the largest corporation to the smallest start-up company. Prices of banner ads, however, are declining, so this will not be a huge source of revenue for any Web site. This is bad news when you are selling; great news when you're buying. Typically banner ads are prices per 1,000 online eyeballs or impressions. The average price per 1,000 today is $35.13 and dropping.

How many banner ads on your Web site are too many? The proliferation of banner ads is making them borderline offensive. They can make a site look cluttered. In addition, if the banner offers something unrelated to your site, your visitors may just totally ignore the ad. Consider overall visual impact when you add banner ads. Don't clash, don't smash.

There is an ongoing debate about how to measure the effectiveness of banner ads. Does an advertiser gain significant benefit from an ad that a browser has not clicked through or bought from? Analysts are finding that Web shoppers click on banner ads only about .5 percent of the time. Top sites can command high prices for their ads, just like prime time television shows. New sites may need to consider giving space away just to get attention. The range of prices runs from no cost to whatever the market will bear.

Editorial versus Advertising

The distinction between objective content and promotion of the products and services of companies that have paid to advertise on your site is one of the most complex issues concerning Web site content. Banner advertisements are clearly paid for; other business promotions may not be as clear to Web site visitors. Hardly any sites distinctly label paid versus unpaid advertising.

It was disheartening for many online shoppers to learn that Amazon.com is far from objective in its most prominent book reviews. The special treatment awarded to "destined for greatness" books that shoppers believed stood on their own merits was in fact earned by promotional dollars invested by the publishers. But as Web space has grown cluttered with banner ads, the hunt for other ways to advertise became more intense. Product mentions in site content seemed a natural outgrowth. Consumers, beware.

Search services Yahoo! and Lycos were among the first to contend with the content-and-advertising issue. Their searches were created to be objective, and their order of presentation was not intended to be influenced by corporate advertising dollars. What about links to other sites: Which are for content purposes, and which are paid for by sponsors? Yahoo! distinguishes "paid" by location on their home page. Those companies featured above their thin light blue line are partners who have paid a fee to display their products or services and also pay a commission on sales. Below the blue line is an index of Internet sites selected. Period. No dollars. (If you're wondering, *What thin light blue line?*, you're not alone. But once you go on www.yahoo.com, you will see what I mean.)

The Federal Trade Commission bureau of consumer protection has established a group to be on the lookout for deceptive Internet advertising practices. The simplest approach is to be up-front about the advertising that is paid for. Consumers and advertising can profitably coexist when both parties can stand behind the quality of the product or service.

Subscriptions for Information

Because so much information is available at no cost, it is difficult to pinpoint exactly what users are willing to pay for. Experts agree "not much" when it comes to information. As a revenue source, products and ads are a better way to bring in money. Subscription-based services work as long as the information provided is focused, in-depth, and not available elsewhere at no cost. Information—for free—serves another purpose on your site. Up-to-date bits of information can keep browsers coming back for more. GoBabies®, for example, keeps a list of helpful tips from traveling parents updated regularly, making it fresh and interesting.

■ Publicizing and Promoting Your Site

Extensive promotion of your Web site from as many different forms of media as you can afford will pay off. If you have a great site that nobody can find, you'll make no money. Should you be listed in a mall, take out ads on other Web sites, or hope that your listings with major search engines will be adequate?

Peter Levitan, president of New Jersey Online (NJO), is working to ensure that business owners who want to build a strong online and offline presence will have a forum. "Our mission," he said, "is to provide *the* marketing resource for advertising in New Jersey. Our goal is to develop a mass audience." NJO has a solid commitment to driving store traffic by attracting people to the Web, then enticing them to continue to shop. Besides offering assistance to retailers in building online stores, they also offer advice and practical solutions to build momentum and traffic. Using coupons and sales and deals, they create an air of excitement for New Jersey merchants. "Our goal is to make it as affordable as possible," said Levitan, so that all retailers can take advantage of this opportunity. The best news for e-tailers is that they don't have to do everything themselves. There are resources available, like NJO.com, to help you publicize and promote your Web site and your Main Street or megastores. And these resources get results—fast.

Net.B@nk is an example of how a well-crafted drive to publicize an e-commerce Web site should be executed. Net.B@nk was introduced in Chapter 2 as the first profitable Internet bank in the country. In their press release announcing bold new strategic marketing initiatives, the company outlined their 1999 efforts and described a sixfold increase over their 1998 marketing budget. Great plans aren't cheap, and the scope of Net.B@ank's efforts is well beyond the fiscal reality of smaller firms. However, their strategy reads like a textbook version of how to blast the competition. They promised to accomplish the following:

- Advertise on seven times more Web sites in the first quarter of 1999 than before.
- Add banner ads, poster ads, buttons, key words and more, on dozens of Web sites.
- Link to banking, investing, finance, shopping, real estate, technology, and business news sites.
- Invest in print advertising (including magazines like *Forbes* and *PC World*) and major newspapers (including the *Wall Street Journal, New York Times, Chicago Tribune, San Francisco Chronicle,* and *Los Angeles Times*).
- Invest in broadcast advertising later in the year.
- Use highly targeted direct mail campaigns.
- Redesign the current Web site.

This list can both intimidate and inspire. Major corporations will say, "We do that . . .", and start-up firms will sigh, "In your dreams . . ." But fitting all of the pieces together in a comprehensive strategy will enhance the already solid lead that Net.B@nk has achieved.

Search Engines

The role of search engines in directing people to your Web site cannot be overstated. As new and more powerful search engines are created, their potential to serve you—particularly if your product is high quality and competitively priced—will grow exponentially. Consider two new search engines by Junglee and C2B Technologies. Junglee allows consumers to look for bargains throughout the Internet, crossing over multiple sites and providing results in a single summary. C2B has formed a partnership with *Consumer Digest,* which helps them deliver recommendations for Best Buys and product reviews.

Banner Ads Part Deux

Internet advertising is a two-way street. Any Web site could potentially make money selling banner ads while spending money buying banner ad space on other Web sites. As the buyer rather than the seller of ad space, keep in mind the same considerations discussed earlier. How many eyeballs are attracted to this Web site? Is there a benefit to being seen on another site, even if the shopper does not click through to you? Also determine whether a given Web site attracts the same target market as your business. Portals offer access to large numbers and are also dropping their prices, but you could get lost in the clutter. Sites that offer products and services that are complementary to yours may provide a more focused first consideration.

Printed Materials

At the simplest level, your Web site address should be listed on all your printed materials. This includes your business cards and stationery, brochures, flyers, and all newsletters, articles, and handouts where you are quoted or featured. Make it part of your name.

Multimedia Ad Campaigns

Of course budget considerations govern the scope of your print, radio, and television advertising commitments. Whether your budget is in the multi-million-dollar range or has only one comma, the guideline remains the same. Every campaign you select should mention your Web site in the context of the pitch:

- "Be sure to visit our Web site at . . .", or
- "You can find out more from their Web site at . . .", and best of all,
- "Get a free coupon from our Web site at . . ."

If the idea of a "visit" bothers you, try "check out . . .", but always extend the invitation to browse. The tie-in from the audio or video ad to the Web site should be synchronistic; keep your image consistent, not schizophrenic. Remember Simon in GoBabies®? Simon reappears in all print ads, trade show displays, product packaging, flyers, coupons, and the Web site. The animated character of Simon is all about travelin', and so is the GoBabies® product line.

■ The Hottest Businesses Online: Sites That Sell

The best shopping sites are more than electronic versions of a company store or printed catalog. They offer a completely new shopping experience. Following are some examples of sites that sell, with suggestions about how any e-tail company can learn from their approach. Samples of home pages are included to help you become familiar with sites that people are talking about, if you have not already visited them. In addition, check these figures for details. The difference between success and failure for many companies is in *how* they accomplish their objectives, not only in the design itself.

Art and Music

Art and music sites were among the earliest to become and stay successful. Here are a few originals. They are classics.

Art.com (www.art.com). Art.com, "where you start for art," calls the site the world's "most inviting destination for discovering and buying art." They feature over 100,000 art prints, categorized by artist name, subject and title. The site's "frame studio" allows you to try out different picture mats and frames before you order your own custom frame. In addition to 20 to 50 percent discounts, Art.com adds new selections daily in their "what's new" section. The art experience is convenient and fun, and their home page lets you find your perfect art in three easy steps (see Figure 8.1).

What's good about this site? The site allows visitors to experiment with features before purchasing.

CDnow (www.cdnow.com). Owners of this site bought N2K, providers of Music Boulevard, as discussed earlier. This deal places CDnow in a strong position to challenge Amazon.com in the CD arena. CDnow has the pulse of the music lover, and calls the site "The Internet's Number One Music Store." It is easy and pleasant to navigate this site (Figure 8.2), which is constantly updated with the latest scoop. You could buy a Grammy winner and get free shopping minutes after the Grammys went off the air. For St. Patrick's Day, you can read about—and listen to—a selection of Celtic Music Picks.

What's good about this site? It's a very easy site to navigate and always has "hottest" new information.

Musicmaker (www.musicmaker.com). Consumers can create their own personalized CD's at Musicmaker, which has a terrific appeal to shoppers of

Figure 8.1 Art.com allows visitors to find and frame their art in three easy steps.

127

Selling
Products and
Services
Online

all ages. This site does not offer bargain-basement prices, although discount clubs such as the "Insider's Club" are available during limited time intervals. Shoppers can select a list of songs and artists from country through soul, and everything in between. The feature of customer configurations of CDs is right on the mark to meet the e-corporation target of consumer control.

What's good about this site? Customers can configure their own products.

Figure 8.2 CDnow

Auctions

Auction sites have gained such a popular following that they have become events to be reckoned with. Some people structure their social lives around the bid times of certain favorite items, or ask friends and families to submit bids for them if they were not going to be near a PC for an evening, even set an alarm to rise for one last bidding opportunity. These individuals know the addictive power of the auction sites, and they enjoy it.

eBay (www.ebay.com). Ebay, the world's largest online auction, does not have any inventory to sell. It allows people to post listings of items for sale worldwide, while potential buyers place bids over the Internet (Figure 8.3). After each auction, the winning bidder contacts the seller to close the deal. Ebay gets about a 5 percent commission on each listing and sale. Many sellers will post photographs so the buyer has a better view of the item auctioned. You just can't touch—or *totally* trust.

For every 1 million auctions, eBay receives an average of 27 fraud complaints. The worst occurred in January 1998 when the New York City Department of Consumer Affairs began an investigation into the authenticity of baseballs supposedly signed by Babe Ruth, Roberto Clemente, and Christy Mathewson. Whether eBay will be held accountable for unscrupulous sellers remains to be seen. As discussed earlier, the Federal Trade Commission is on record as saying, "I'll be watching you."

While eBay may not hear of consumer complaints, vigilant consumer groups are ensuring that fraudulent practices are halted. It would seem that self-monitoring would be a better idea than going head to head with the FTC. Ebay has systematically attempted to keep its site fraud-free, but there is little they can do when sellers completely misrepresent themselves. There are no lie detector tests on Web sites. What is the lesson to be learned for the nouveau auctioneer? Remember Pinocchio: The truth eventually wins. (See Figure 8.4.)

What's good about this site? If features constant action and the thrill of competition.

Onsale.com (www.onsale.com). With great public exposure comes tremendous public scrutiny. Onsale (Figure 8.5) has been spared the infamy of Ebay; they have also not achieved equal notoriety. Without covering nearly the daily volume of Ebay, and without the extra advantage of being the market leader, Onsale thrives. The tip? Consumers like choices, and there is room for one more.

What's good about this site? It allows easy navigation, and features clean-cut design.

Figure 8.3 eBay

Browse | Sell | Services | Search | Help | Community

your personal trading community™

search | tips

categorieS

Antiques (56926)
Books, Movies, Music (328927)
Coins & Stamps (89795)
Collectibles (748366)
Computers (79532)
Dolls, Figures (46601)
Jewelry, Gemstones (95247)
Photo & Electronics (42352)
Pottery & Glass (142504)
Sports Memorabilia (288181)
Toys, Bean Bag Plush (241627)
Miscellaneous (218069)
all categories...

Sell your item

Get news and chat

new users, **Click** here

Register It's free and fun

welcoMe

What is eBay?
How do I bid?
How do I sell?
Register, it's free!

statS

2,379,540 items for sale in 1,627 categories now!

Over 1.5 billion page views per month!

featurEd

Lexmark 3200/5700/7000 Series Blk Refill Kit
Epson Stylus Color 400/500/600 Blk Cartridges
New! 10,000 Graphics Pack Cd-Vol#1 * So Cool!
Joe Dimaggio 1938 Gowdey Rookie, Near Mint
Gorgeous Genuine Sapphire 1 Carat Nice Blue
Rockwell-Signed "First Airplane Ride" Litho.

more! see more featured....

fun sTuff

The special Charter Subscription offer to eBay magazine ends the 15th. Subscribe now!

cool feaTures

Looking for a surfboard, flashy red convertible, or filmmaking gear? Visit eBay LA, our first regional eBay.

Seeing is believing... try the gallery click here

cool happenings...

Announcements Register eBay Store SafeHarbor Feedback Forum About eBay Jobs
Get Local - eBay LA | Go Global! | Canada | UK | Germany | 日本語のヘルプ

Last updated: 08/10/99, 19:15:01 PDT

My eBay Site Map
Browse Sell Services Search Help Community

A Better Business Bureau Program
BBBOnLine CLICK TO CHECK

Copyright (C) 1995-1999 eBay Inc. All Rights Reserved.
Use of this Web site constitutes acceptance of the eBay User Agreement.

TRUSTe site privacy statement

Figure 8.4 Ebay provides the thrill of competition for the anxious auctions addict.

HOME   LISTINGS   BUYERS   SELLERS   SEARCH   HELP   NEWS/CHAT   SITE MAP

About ebay™

Jobs

Investor Relations

eBay in the News

eBay Foundation

eBay Community

Company Overview

Press Releases

Computers - Toys - Dolls - Bean Bag Plush - Antiques - Jewelry - Pottery
Trading Cards - Coins - Stamps - Photo Equipment - Glass - Advertising - Elvis

Books

Early success came to all vendors who narrowed their focus to goods that didn't require a dressing room or a road test. Although Amazon.com set the gold standard by which all online sales are measured, there are other players in the field.

Amazon.com (www.amazon.com). Amazon.com was discussed earlier, but just a few more comments about site organization are in order here. During holiday rushes, Amazon.com receives an overwhelming number of orders that truly could damage them. Great planning and foresight keep them out of trouble. They deliberately work to keep customers informed about the status of their orders, even if the news is not good. Despite heavy volume, for the most part Amazon.com meets customer needs. If they can't get the product on time, they let you know and offer alternatives.

Figure 8.5   Onsale

What's good about this site? Besides enjoying tremendous choice, customers always know the status of their order.

Barnes & Noble (www.barnesandnoble.com or www.bn.com). Even though they were slow to jump online, Barnes & Noble still attracts large numbers of visitors to its Web site (Figure 8.6). Online sales are still, however, less than half of Amazon.com's. Will they catch up to their main competitor? The site lacks the pizzazz of their main competitor, but they are catching up rapidly.

What's good about this site? They're fast learners.

Alibris (www.alibris.com). In spite of the hype about Amazon.com, Alibris (Figure 8.7) has found a niche and serves the needs of its market beautifully. Here's a place to find rare books from a collection of member dealers, including children's and science fiction books. Consumers can even request autographed copies or first editions, and set a price range. These special deals are not available from either of the two big book Web sites. There will always be room for specialty items on the Web, and companies like Alibris that learn to meet the needs of a market niche can thrive.

What's good about this site? It will hunt down special items for you.

Other Consumer Products

Online shoppers first gravitated to the Web sites of traditional retailers with a strong physical presence—like Eddie Bauer, Nordstrom, and Wal-Mart. Today, possibilities are endless for a wide range of consumer items. Well-designed e-commerce systems have stayed true to fundamental principles of great merchandising. They are not all things to all people. The best sites can be easily found, are simple to navigate, and provide what you would expect them to provide. More isn't always better when it comes to listing goods and services. Here are some examples.

Cars

- **AutoSite** (www.autosite.com). This is the place to check out almost all car models, purchase rebates, incentives, leases, and loans. You would have to pay *Consumer Reports* $12 for a review this detailed; this is free. The site also includes used vehicle book values. Although a car is definitely an item shoppers will test drive before buying, doing research in advance is the best way to approach a negotiation as an educated con-

Figure 8.6 Barnesandnoble.com

Figure 8.7 Alibris

ΛLIƷɹI5   subjects | community | resources | book search

advanced search >

Title

GO

The Ultimate Source for Used, Rare, and Hard-to-Find Books

how to shop | bookbag | checkout | your account | book hound | help

First-Time Visitor?

help
▶ searching
▶ shopping
▶ credit card safety
▶ shipping & delivery
▶ our guarantee

booksellers
▶ featured seller
▶ our network
▶ join us

contact us
▶ customer service
▶ webmaster

about us
▶ company profile
▶ in the news
▶ employment

Looking for Today's Bestsellers?

IN ASSOCIATION WITH

BOOKS, MUSIC & MORE
amazon.com

BARNES &NOBLE

BORDERS.com

For best results, download the latest browser from Netscape or Microsoft

Welcome to Alibris

New! -- Having trouble locating a book? Tried the Advanced Search and had no luck? Submit a request to Book Hound, and we'll keep sniffing around for your book during the next 30 days.

 Featured Book - _Trump: The Art of the Deal_ by Donald Trump - In this sizzling read, the maverick tycoon divulges his formulas for entrepreneural success.

 Special Offer - Own a signed first edition of Salman Rushdie's newest novel, _The Ground Beneath Her Feet_ .

Featured Author - John Kenneth Galbraith - This controversial economic theorist is notorious for his charateristic wit & insight.

Subject Spotlight - Business, Economics & Careers

 Summer Reading

 Award Winners

 Information for Libraries

 The Vault

The finest selection of rare signed books, manuscripts, autographs, maps, graphics, and more.

SALE **Uncommon Bargains**

Hard-to-find books at uncommon prices are here!

Skyscrapers: Form & Function

Was - $35.00
NOW - $11.00

CROSSWORDS

New Each Day!

THE NEW YORKER CARTOON OF THE WEEK

sumer. Shoppers are just three clicks away from full pricing information on the car of their choice (Figure 8.8). For customer convenience, this data can be printed on a worksheet that simplifies comparison shopping between dealers.

What's good about this site? It allows direct clicking to complete price information on your choice of product.

Children and Toys

- **BabyCenter, Inc.** (www.babycenter.com). This company first earned its reputation as an Internet information center for pregnancy and early child rearing. BabyCenter recently expanded into an online store. The company now sells everything from strollers to baby bottles, clothing, and toys. In the estimated $18 billion baby market, about 35 percent of the families are online. There are about 4 million babies born every year and research shows that most parents spend in excess of $7,000 on baby products in their child's first year of life. BabyCenter has an edge over larger and soon-to-be online ventures like Babies 'R' Us due to the quality and scope of information provided at the site. They gained credibility through professionalism before they started to sell products.

  What's good about this site? It features content with depth and vast product selection in one place.

- **eToys** (www.etoys.com). This site offers a huge inventory of today's best toys, easily classified by categories for shopper convenience (described in Chapter 1). Parents can check out award-winning toys, or follow "Picks of the Week" for the selection of a unique toy in every age group. Every holiday season, Etoys cultivates hordes of grateful consumers in the hectic preholiday weeks. Sometimes only Etoys can find hot items like Furbies in 1998.

  What's good about this site? It's easy to find what you want fast. If you don't know what you want, they'll offer suggestions at age-appropriate levels.

Clothing

- **Gap** (www.gaponline.com). For all the swing and other dance routines in the Gap's advertising campaigns, you once had to chug through a few steps before ordering the items shown on its home page. Breaking the minimum-click rule was one brief mistake; online sales are now excellent for the Gap. Their shoppers keep coming back. Apparently, if

Figure 8.8   AutoSite

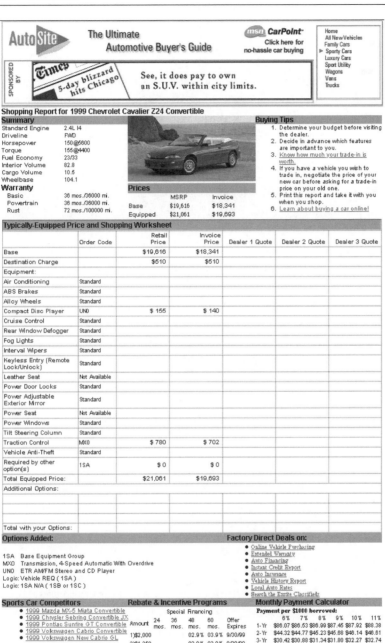

everything else about your site and product and marketing is excellent, shoppers will tolerate an additional click or two. This site lets you take a good look at products and descriptions before buying, but if you like any outfit on the home page you can click directly to "buy outfit" (Figure 8.9).

What's good about this site? Design provides great views of products.

- **Eddie Bauer, Inc.** (www.eddiebauer.com). International specialty retailer Eddie Bauer launched its Web site in 1996. Electronic commerce is used as a supplement to retail stores and printed catalogs, and all of their brand merchandise that is available through mail order is also available online. Eddie Bauer sells clothing, accessories, and home furnishings. The Web site lets you create a shopping cart, and one of their unique features is their "Wish List." Using the Wish List, you can register online for items you want, then offer the password to a limited number of friends. When you visit this site, you'll note that the box on the left side of the home page (Figure 8.10) hides a duck that escapes once in a while and flies off the page.

  What's good about this site? You've got to love the duck—and the shopping carts.

- **Lands' End** (www.landsend.com). Here is a warm and friendly-looking home page that lets you decide how much detail you would like to see on any given product. You don't need to see the inside seams of any product until you ask for a closer look. This site saves you time weeding through photos and descriptive text unless you request it. When you're ready to order, you'll be able to learn about every subtle nuance of that irresistible supple combed cotton cable crew sweater. Lands' End recently extended secure online payment to first-time shoppers who used to be required to buy by phone. See Figure 8.11.

  What's good about this site? You control the amount of detail you see, so if you're on a brief shopping trip, you can navigate quickly.

Flowers

- **1-800-Flowers** (www.1800flowers.com). This online site brought in 10 percent of the company's total sales of $300 million. While you won't be able to smell these flowers, the selection of photos is vivid and well chosen. In spite of the detail, the site is simple enough to load quickly. Even the home page is artistically designed, leaving the impression that this is a company that takes beauty seriously (Figure 8.12).

Figure 8.9 The Gap

139

Selling
Products and
Services
Online

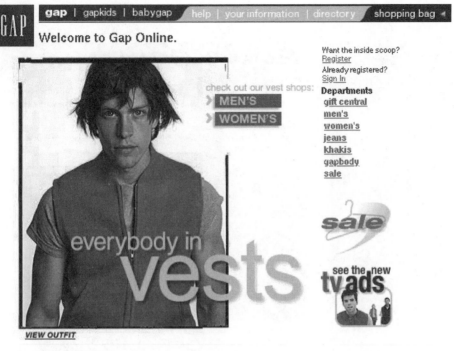

VIEW OUTFIT

gapstyle | store locator | company

Questions? Feedback? Email us or call 1-800-GAP-STYLE (1-800-427-7895).

Want it? Don't hesitate...product selection may vary slightly
between Gap Online and Gap stores.

Customer Information Policy
Use of this site constitutes your acceptance of these Terms of Use.

sites: [gap | gapkids | babygap]
departments: [gift central | men's | women's | jeans | khakis | gapbody]
services: [help | your info | directory | shopping bag]

Figure 8.10 Eddie Bauer

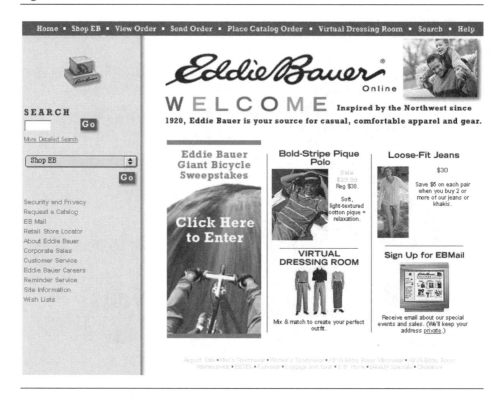

What's good about this site? It manages to make those gorgeous arrangements arrive on your screen quickly.

Outdoor Gear

- **L.L. Bean Online** (www.llbean.com). The site has outdoor and camping goods and services, as well as a full line of clothing for all seasons. One of the original mail-order catalog companies, L.L. Bean was cited by experts as a leading provider of excellence in customer responsiveness long before they began selling online. The company was known for its cheerful, helpful telephone salespeople. This positive customer interface prevails in the online store, too. You can e-mail or call directly if you have a question or problem.

Figure 8.11   Lands' End offers product details only if you want them.

Home | Our Store | Overstocks | Gift Finder | Catalog Requests | How To Order | Sizing | Site Map

LANDS' END

Your Privacy &
Security Guaranteed

Our Store / Women's Casual / Search Tips [　　　　　]   [Search]

Women's Cobble Cloth Crew
Tough as cobblestone, feels like "easy street."

Back | Store | Next

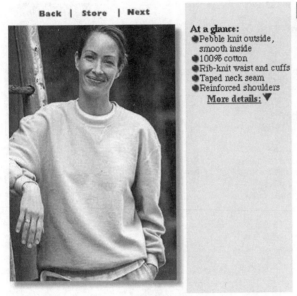

At a glance:
- Pebble knit outside, smooth inside
- 100% cotton
- Rib-knit waist and cuffs
- Taped neck seam
- Reinforced shoulders

More details: ▼

Shopping Basket   Checkout Now   Your Account

SELECT   **Women's Regular Solid Cobble Cloth Crew**
Available Colors
Size: XS, S, M, L, XL
$39.50
Item #: 6070-7A52

What's Cobble Cloth®? It's nubby, bumpy, pebbly-knit texture. Looks earthy, outdoorsy. Definitely not boring. Pure combed cotton makes it extra soft too, like a favorite sweater. It's substantial enough to handle roughhousing with Rover. Think of it as a dressier kind of sweatshirt. Where else can you find this nifty knit? Nowhere. Machine wash. Imported.

Return To Top

Home | Intelligent Order Blank | Our Store | Gift Certificates | Overstocks | Search | School Uniforms | Gift

Figure 8.12 1-800-Flowers

What's good about this site? If you need a human, you can still reach one.

- **REI** (www.rei.com). This Seattle-based company features camping and outdoor sports items. Best of all, besides helping you get your gear, they link consumers to an online community of like-minded outdoorspersons and expert advice. Their outlet site offers markdowns. Communities, expert advisers, and outstanding product information keep customers returning to this Web site for new information and new goods.

    What's good about this site? Community building is *hot*.

Wine and Food

- **Virtual Vineyards** (www.virtualvin.com). Featuring wines from all over the world, Virtual Vineyards emphasizes smaller vintners. The Cork Dork can advise consumers on the best food and wine combinations. This may not be the place to shop for a specific vintage; nor is it ideal for the strongly opinionated. However, this is a great place for those who are learning, or are open to suggestions from an online specialist. Note that shoppers can slip over to a chocolate treat, too, on this particular month (Figure 8.13).

    What's good about this site? It offers specialist suggestions for the ripening connoisseur.

- **Peapod** (www.peapod.com). One of the largest online grocers, Peapod provides home delivery of fresh produce, meats, and more than 25,000 other items. Shoppers choose products by price, fat or sodium content, and any other factors important to them. The process extends to personalized lists that allow reorders of items that are needed weekly. It is not available everywhere, although expansion is in the works. Online grocery shopping is predicted to grow to a $60 to $85 billion business by 2007.

    What's good about this site? Customization of shopping lists to avoid unnecessary steps for customers.

Distance Learning

Distance learning refers to curricula developed for presentation over the Internet. Many universities now offer online training courses for degree credit. At the simplest level, online courses provide a way to take advantage of educational opportunities without geographic constraints. The original online courses were a combination of instructional material presented by pages of a text-type guide, supported by contact with an instructor via e-mail, or with

Figure 8.13 Virtual Vineyards

WELCOME

Hello. I'm Peter Granoff, Proprietor and Master
Sommelier here at VirtualVineyard.com. Don't
let summer pass you by! Grab one (or more!!)
of our savory summer reds, whites or bubblies,
pack up your picnic basket and head to the park!

1997 Calera Estate Viognier, Mt. Harlan
What is it about fine Viognier that just makes you want to
loll about with your sweetie all afternoon...? $30.00

1996 Chinon, Domaine de Beausejour, Loire Valley
Although not widely known in the U.S., Cabernet Franc
from Chinon can represent excellent value in red wine. This
fine example is ready for your table now. $11.95

Romantic Duet
What could possibly be more romantic than a toe-tingling French bubbly and a
silky California Pinot Noir? $39.95

Find more tasty wines for your summer outings in our Wine Shop! Simply
click on the links to the right.

Happy Shopping!

PETER GRANOFF, *Proprietor*

SHOP FOR
WINE
Wine Shop
What's New
Monthly Wine Program
Bang For The Buck
Specials
Samplers

SHOP FOR
FOOD
Food Shop
What's New
Company's Coming
Specials
Samplers

SHOP FOR
GIFTS
Gift Shop
Gift Certificates
Monthly Wine Program
Corporate Gift Program
Samplers

SHOP
SERVICES
Sign In or Create an Account
Security and Privacy
Learn more about our site
See how to order
Site Help
Shipping Information
Press Room
日本語

Our Position on Recent Legislation

SIGN UP FOR
VV NEWS

e.g. youremail@provider.com

students and instructor via chat rooms. More advanced features are being incorporated in new courses offered by a few leading universities. Stanford University, for example, provides video lectures with synchronized slide demonstrations. Hardly the monopoly of academic institutions only, distance learning is an area full of potential for the private sector.

Small Business Administration (SBA) (www.sba.gov). The SBA made the expansion of distance learning programs one of its top priorities. Called the "Small Business Classroom," the SBA training programs are offered in both English and Spanish (Figure 8.14). Courses are short, self-paced learning modules. Available courses include: Y2K Issues, The Business Plan, and How to Raise Capital for a Small Business. At the end of each lesson, students are invited to participate in a scheduled chat room or call to make arrangements to talk to a SCORE counselor.

What's good about this site? Courses are short, self-paced, and available in English and Spanish.

Figure 8.14   Small Business Administration's "Small Business Classroom"

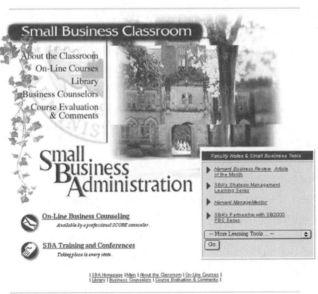

ZD University (www.zdu.com/catalog). ZD Net offers an extensive list of courses in three categories: instructor-led, workshops, and self-study tutorials. Some courses are available by subscription and some are free. In the catalog of programming courses, for example, instructor-led courses range from introductory to advanced levels. You can learn to program, compile, and download. Notice in Figure 8.15 that ZD University attempts to replicate the feel of a physical campus by directing you to the "Student Union" and "ZDU Handbook." The list of more than 100 online courses, priced at $7.95 per month, complete with easy registration and information searches, make this a popular site.

What's good about this site? A variety of courses are offered with easy registration and help finding information.

Information Brokers

By placing vast information resources at our fingertips, the Web can overwhelm, intimidate, and confuse us with details. With more than 350 million sites available, how can we ever expect to find what we want? If a search engine lists half a million responses to a keyword search, how in the world do we make any sense of the response?

Information brokers are subject experts who sift through data and form some logical order. On a huge scale, Lexis-Nexis organizes a database of 1.8 billion documents, including the *New York Times,* the *Wall Street Journal,* and the *Washington Post.* On a smaller scale, some ambitious entrepreneurs have carved out packages for niche markets.

Information brokers use different methods of charging a fee for service. One-time fees can be used to order a single substantial product, like a book. Subscriptions work for newletters and magazine products that are published weekly or monthly but billed annually.

CEO Express (www.ceoexpress.com). For the busy executive who doesn't have time to sort through all the potential junk on the Internet, CEO Express provides highlights of the best available material on a daily basis. Visitors can customize a home page to bring up categories of information in which they are most interested: Stock reports, news headlines, weather, etc. (See Figure 8.16)

What's good about this site? It features customized categories and daily updates.

Electronic Commerce Research Room (www.wilsonweb.com/research). Under the direction of "virtual librarian" Dr. Ralph Wilson, the Electronic

Figure 8.15 ZD University's "Course Catalog"

Figure 8.16 CEO Express

Sponsors | WADJET "Top 5 Games '98" Mensa Awards | Are you running your business or is your business running *you?* CNA UniSource | GET IT NOW NECX #1 PC Superstore | BE beta tester for the new CEO Express!

Customize CEO Express!
My Page: Sign-in
Register: Free and Easy!

Tell a friend! Spread the word about
CEO Express THANKS!

What's New

CEO Express!®

The $0/20 Rule applied to the Internet
Designed by a busy executive for busy executives
Make CEO Express your Opening Page| Help!

Solar Eclipse, Aug. 11
Editor's Note: NASA's webcast
tracks the last total solar eclipse
of the 20th century, with live
feeds from around the world.
Best U.S. Views
Great Sites Archive

| Become a Member! | Bookshop | Career Center | Feedback | Suggest a Link | Sign-in |
| Daily News & Info | Business Research | | All Things Internet | Tools, Travel & Fun | |

Fortune 500 | Global 500 NEW! | Private 500 | Inc. 500 | Web 100 | Forbes Toolbox

BACK TO TOP

DAILY NEWS & INFO

Daily News: Boston Globe | Chicago Tribune | Christian Science Monitor | Los Angeles Times | Nando Times | New York Times | San Jose Mercury News | USA Today | Washington Post | *Major Metros* | *Other Newspapers* | *Alternative Newspapers*

Business News: Barrons | CNN*fn* | Crain's: NY, Chicago, Detroit | Financial Times | Investor's Business Daily | Journal of Commerce | Kiplinger | Law News Network | Singapore Business Times | Wall Street Journal | WSJ: public site | *Daily Business Journals* | *Weekly Business Journals*

International News: Herald Tribune | Le Monde | London Times | *Africa* | *Asia* | *Australia* | *Canada* | *Caribbean* | *Central America* | *Europe* | *Mexico* | *South America*

Business Magazines: Business Week | Business 2.0 | CFO | Context | Economist | Far East Economic Review | Fast Company | Forbes | Fortune | Harvard B. School Publishing | Inc. | Industry Week | Institutional Investor | Money | Newsweek | Red Herring | Smart Money | The Industry Standard | Strategy & Business | Time | Upside Online | US News | Wired | Worth

Technology Magazines: CIO | CNET | Computerworld | Electronic Markets | First Monday | Intranet Journal | MIT TechReview | TechWeb | ZDNet

Online Magazines: American Demographics | Arts & Letters Daily | Atlantic Monthly | Golf Digest | Harper's | National Geographic | Salon | Scientific American | Slate | *Magazine Database*

Newsfeeds: AP Wire | AP Wire (Int'l) | Bloomberg | Bloomberg Radio | Broadcast.com | Business Wire | Canada Newswire | Drudge Report | NewsLinx | NewsPage | NewsReal | PR Newswire | Reuters

Internet Search: About.com | Alta Vista | Ask Jeeves | Deja | DirectHit NEW! | DogPile | Excite | Google! | HotBot | Infoseek | LibrarySpot | Magellan | Metacrawler | Northern Light | ProFusion | Wall Street Search | WebCrawler | Yahoo **Search Tips:** *How best to use a search engine*

Website Locator: Broad Search | Company Locator | Domain Registration | InterNIC 'WhoIs'

Health: Alternative Medicine | AMA | Ask Dr. Weil | Dietsite | Dr. Koop | Healthfinder Search | InteliHealth | Internet Drug Index | Mayo Clinic

Commerce Research Room tracks more than 1,500 articles about Internet commerce. The Research Room organizes the material into 43 categories of articles. Some articles are free, but the service is primarily subscription. For an annual fee of $49.95, subscribers can receive Web Commerce Today, which includes book reviews, original material, and other additional features.

Investing

More and more of us want to take control of our own financial future, or at least try to. Online investors tend to be more aggressive and self-assured than the average human being. They view themselves as savvy and experienced, as compared to the novice offline investor. These experienced investors feel that the information available on the Internet is as good as what they could get from any traditional broker.

There are major Web sites that offer investment advice, and sites that let you make your own trades. This is an area where experienced and qualified investment advisors can still fill a need by offering tips and investment strategies. Do this with the most careful attention to separating advice from sales. The Securities and Exchange Commission recently sued 13 people and firms in six states, claiming that they had conned investors by using the Internet to pitch companies that paid them for promotions. These individuals were supposedly providing unbiased opinions in their stock recommendations. Their sales techniques ranged from using unsolicited e-mails to recommend low-priced stocks, to online newsletter features and articles that glorified companies' prospects while neglecting to mention that they were paid by these companies.

CBS MarketWatch (www.cbs.marketwatch.com). This site covers investment strategies in detail. This site offers free information, helping consumers track their portfolio and the stock market, and is extremely easy to use (Figure 8.17). Investors can check stock prices during the day, as well as obtain prices on stock options. There is always an interesting insight into a company's decision-makers, or marketing strategy, or strategic partners. With the benefit of this additional information, consumers have an opportunity to ponder their decisions overnight, and jump into action the next day.

What's good about this site? It offers free information and easy portfolio tracking.

Charles Schwab & Co. Consumers can buy and sell securities at home or at work without using a broker. Schwab, a San Francisco-based brokerage,

e-tailing

Figure 8.17 CBS MarketWatch

is the dominant player in the exploding online trading industry. Schwab handles about 153,000 online trades per day, which is 28 percent of all online trading transactions. To their credit, they have hustled to keep up with Internet trading growth by adding a new mainframe computer. When a software problem caused the system to go down for about two hours one February morning, Schwab moved extra employees to their phone lines and offered discounted trading fees to calm angry investors.

What's good about this site? The company matched skyrocketing online trading volumes with upgraded computer technology to best serve customers.

E*Trade Group, Inc. (www.etrade.com). E*Trade has branch offices in 22 million PCs, which made $6.1 million in profits in first quarter 1998, double that of the previous year. E*Trade is one of the most high-traffic trade sites. E*Trade did not offer mutual funds trading when it first went online, but as this book went to press, E*Trade had more than 4,000 funds. E*Trade is tailored to individuals who want to assume more responsibility for their own finances, and also lets customers link to sites that offer mortgages, car loans, and insurance (Figure 8.18).

What's good about this site? You can link to sites offering mortgage, car loan, and insurance information.

***Wall Street Journal* Interactive Edition** (www.wsj.com). This site offers more than a daily online version of the *Wall Street Journal* newspaper. It also offers a "briefing books" database with information on all sorts of stocks. Dow Jones news-wire stories are highlighted for significant companies in "Personal Journals." This is a subscription service, available for $59 per year, or $29 for current newspaper subscribers.

What's good about this site? It features extensive databases of background information for all sorts of stocks.

Professional Services

Web site design and maintenance companies are among the limited number of professional services that have thrived online. Companies that help businesses set up e-commerce Web sites are in huge demand. E-commerce support services include marketing, graphics design, data security, and order processing, to name a few. Not every potential e-tail business has sufficient staff or adequate training to take this task on themselves. There is a big demand for companies that can help with e-commerce. These firms can set up Web sites and operate them for other businesses, or offer their products and

Figure 8.18   E*Trade

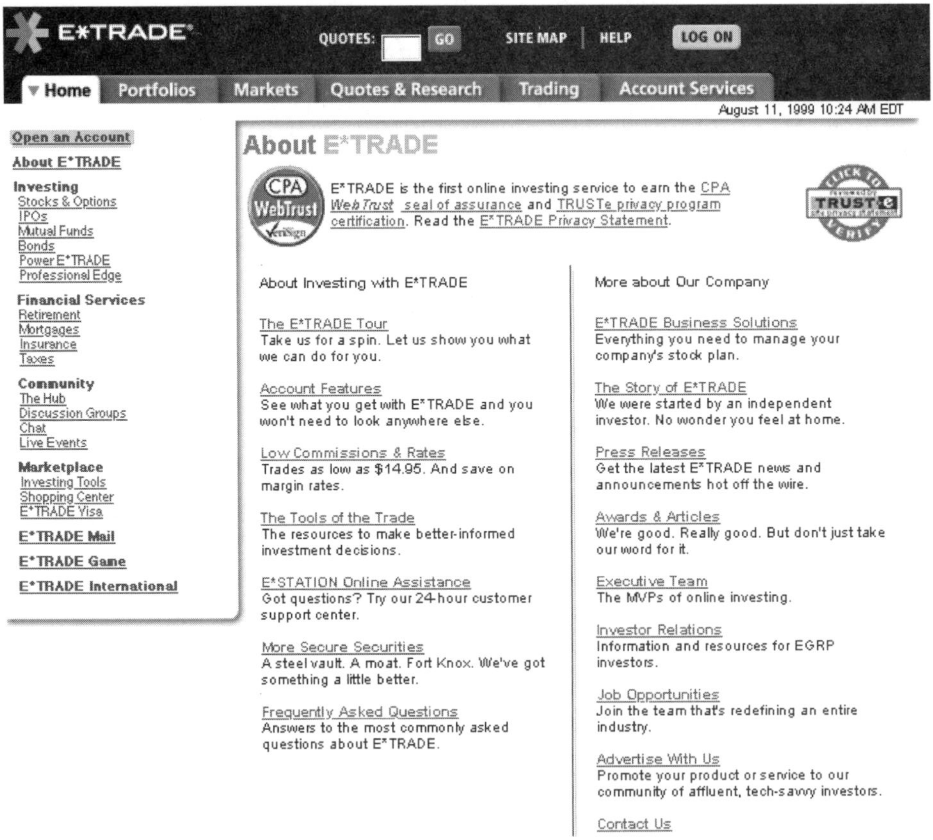

About E*TRADE

 E*TRADE is the first online investing service to earn the CPA _WebTrust_ seal of assurance and TRUSTe privacy program certification. Read the E*TRADE Privacy Statement.

About Investing with E*TRADE

The E*TRADE Tour
Take us for a spin. Let us show you what we can do for you.

Account Features
See what you get with E*TRADE and you won't need to look anywhere else.

Low Commissions & Rates
Trades as low as $14.95. And save on margin rates.

The Tools of the Trade
The resources to make better-informed investment decisions.

E*STATION Online Assistance
Got questions? Try our 24-hour customer support center.

More Secure Securities
A steel vault. A moat. Fort Knox. We've got something a little better.

Frequently Asked Questions
Answers to the most commonly asked questions about E*TRADE.

More about Our Company

E*TRADE Business Solutions
Everything you need to manage your company's stock plan.

The Story of E*TRADE
We were started by an independent investor. No wonder you feel at home.

Press Releases
Get the latest E*TRADE news and announcements hot off the wire.

Awards & Articles
We're good. Really good. But don't just take our word for it.

Executive Team
The MVPs of online investing.

Investor Relations
Information and resources for EGRP investors.

Job Opportunities
Join the team that's redefining an entire industry.

Advertise With Us
Promote your product or service to our community of affluent, tech-savvy investors.

Contact Us

Sidebar navigation:

Open an Account
About E*TRADE

Investing
Stocks & Options
IPOs
Mutual Funds
Bonds
Power E*TRADE
Professional Edge

Financial Services
Retirement
Mortgages
Insurance
Taxes

Community
The Hub
Discussion Groups
Chat
Live Events

Marketplace
Investing Tools
Shopping Center
E*TRADE Visa

E*TRADE Mail

E*TRADE Game

E*TRADE International

Top navigation: QUOTES: [ ] GO | SITE MAP | HELP | LOG ON
▼ Home | Portfolios | Markets | Quotes & Research | Trading | Account Services
August 11, 1999 10:24 AM EDT

services as an adjunct to the full-time staff of the company going online. These functions are discussed further in Chapters 11 and 12.

Professional services, including lawyers, accountants, financial service advisers, and medical professionals tend to use their Web site as a marketing, rather than a sales, tool. Not all professionals are Web-ready. Some may never be. Consider lawyers: Can you seek legal advice online? Or would it be better to simply use a law firm's Web site to learn more about its capabilities and track record before deciding if it meets your needs? Maybelle Cowan of M.L. Burke, Inc., has helped many professionals establish a presence on the Web, and said, "Many professionals hope to get referrals from their Web site. They don't sell their services online." But even without online sales transactions, Cowan's clients have experienced increases in business. She found that this has been particularly true with lawyers. "They have had a better response than anticipated. The Web has turned out to be a great vehicle for professionals to connect with their peers in other parts of the country when they need referrals." Medical professionals? Cowan's clients have had great success using their Web sites to advertise jobs and recruit personnel, in addition to spreading the word about their business.

Nonprofit agencies and associations have also used the Web to their advantage. Association newsletters and membership benefits can be promoted and updated easily. Can you apply for membership online? Cowan's experience is that many nonprofits ask that membership forms be filled out online, then ask a member of their organization to make personal contact by e-mail or phone to obtain billing information.

Accountants? Can you do your taxes via the Internet instead of in person? Advice and how-to columns in local newspapers and national publications regularly dispense counsel on the full gamut of legal and accounting issues with mixed results. All include qualifying statements to protect themselves from potential lawsuits down the road. Cowan predicts that some professional services will continue to market rather than sell online. It may be a while before we see Lawyers R Us and Accountants R Us billing clients online.

Let's stick with a safer, more conformist topic that is less likely to send the founder into litigation. In these litigious times, the following is a safer venture:

HotJobs.com Ltd. HotJobs.com is an online recruiting company that made a name for itself as the smallest company to advertise on the Super Bowl. The company operates a subscription-based membership, charging $600 per month for up to 20 postings on an account. The company began catering to Fortune 500 corporations, but has expanded to include 870 members and is still growing. HotJobs.com differentiates their services from their competition by allowing a user to prevent a member company from seeing a réumé that could jeopardize current employment status. They offer access to a résumé database, and let users track the jobs they have applied to.

What's good about this site? Users can block a current employer from seeing their résumé online.

Technology

Cyberian Outpost (www.outpost.com) As discussed in Chapter 1, this Web site delivers what it promises: "A phenomenal selection of computer products and a whole lot more" (Figure 8.19). To help answer customer questions quickly, Outpost.com has a comprehensive frequently-asked-questions (FAQ) list.

What's good about this site? It has a comprehensive FAQ list.

Dell (www.dell.com). Discussed earlier as a leader in electronic commerce, a few more points need to be included about why Dell works so effectively as an online shopping site (Figure 8.20). When customers specify their computer configuration, they use an easy-to-read pull-down menu. Customers can specify their selection of video monitor, speakers, sound card, videocard, and memory capacity. If a particular component is not available immediately, Dell lets the customer know how this could delay shipment. If a customer selects incompatible parts, Dell advises about potential problems (Figure 8.20).

What's good about this site? The pull-down menu is easy to read, and customers are advised about component availability and compatibility.

ZDNet's Software Library (www.zdnet.com//swlib/). Here's a place to download utilities—the ultimate in shareware. They offer tips and free advice, articles, as well as product information that seems endless (Figure 8.21).

What's good about this site? It offers tips, free advice, articles, and endless product information.

Beyond.com (www.beyond.com). This online software store is truly geared to consumers over business. It offers a wide range of software packages, and helps the consumer search to find a match for what they are looking for (Figure 8.22).

What's good about this site? It matches customers to software products that meet their needs.

Figure 8.19 Outpost.com Home Page

Figure 8.20 Dell

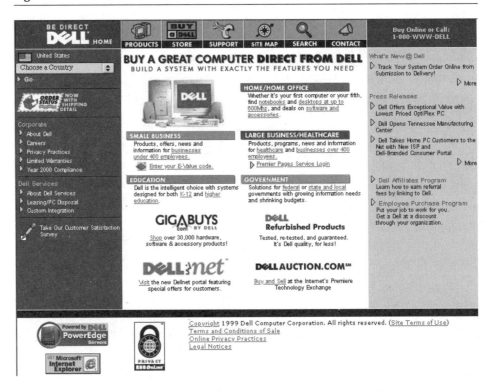

Travel

Priceline.com (www.priceline.com). Priceline.com began with the revolutionary idea of letting consumers define the price they are willing to pay for airline tickets. The customer receives a response within one hour (for domestic flights) to 24 hours (for international flights). Priceline.com has expanded to include hotel rooms, new cars, home mortgages, refinancing, and home equity loans. (See Figure 8.23)

Travelocity.com (www.travelocity.com). This is one of the original online travel agencies which offered airline reservations, hotel rooms, car reservations, and all the vacation package frills (Figure 8.24). It was recently cited by *Business Week* as a site worth visiting.

Figure 8.21 ZDNet's Software Library

Figure 8.22 Beyond.com

A **Better** Place to Buy Software

SOFTWARE | HARDWARE

Advanced Search | Browse Categories | Bestsellers | Recommendation Guide | Gifts

SEARCH [   ] GO   Mac
Advanced Search   Go to Windows

Welcome to Beyond.com
Home of the Safe Shopping Guarantee

SHOPPING CART
Empty

CATEGORIES
Games
Video Games
Kid Zone
Business
Graphics
Utilities
Internet
Communications
Reference
Hobbies
Programming
Operating Systems
Handheld

BUYERS' GUIDES
Customer Reviews
Antivirus Center
Computer Essentials
Free Products

Corporate Customers
Government Customers

SUPPORT
Customer Service
Download Help
Customer Forums
Expired Rebate Archive

SHOWCASES
Adobe
Macromedia
MetaCreations
All Showcases

COMPANY
About Beyond.com
Affiliates Program
Free Newsletter
Investor Relations
Publisher Sign-Up

Dr. Seuss Deals
Find great titles like Dr. Seuss Learning Buddies Kindergarten, Preschool, Reading, and Toddler in our Dr. Seuss Center. Bring your children's favorite characters to life on your computer. Enter to win a trip to Florida in Beyond.com's Florida Adventure Sweepstakes.

Locate Any File
Download ACTION Files 1.2 today and manage your files, documents, and folders like never before. Easily find files by name, size, kind, label, creation date, modification date, file type, creator, and more. $27.95

Strike a Pose
Poser 4.0 makes designing 3D figures easy, even for first-time users. Shaded, textured, and fully interactive real-time previews of your 3D figures enables fast posing and animating. $226.99 after $20.00 rebate

Hardware Head-Turner

Now available in our Hardware Store, keep your schedule, contacts, and other information safe in the Palm V, this elegant device -- and get it at our exclusive price. $359.99 after $30.00 rebate
Find software for your new Palm in our Platinum Software Center.

StarCraft for the Mac
Lead any one three futuristic races through an epic real-time strategy adventure in StarCraft. Play 30 single-player missions, and then test your skills against thousands of players online. $34.95 after $15.00 rebate

Full-featured Font Manager
Make font management quick and easy with Adobe Type Manager 4.5. The latest version of ATM boasts font smoothing, font sample previews, and automatic font activation. $65.45

Put PC Options on Your Mac
Get the flexibility to run any PC operating system on your Macintosh with Virtual PC Windows 98 2.1. Buy now and upgrade to version 3.0 for free (minus shipping and handling) as soon as Connectix releases it. $174.99

Top 10 Downloadable Software
MACINTOSH
As of Aug 11, 1999
1. AudioCatalyst
2. MacTicker
3. BBEdit
4. Norton AntiVirus 5.0
5. eMerge
6. Dr. Solomon's Virex
7. MacLinkPlus Deluxe
8. DreamWeaver 2.0 Introduction
9. Conflict Catcher
10. Action Files

GSA Store Now Open

Summer Fun For Kids!

Visit Our Hardware Store

Join Affiliates - Earn Money!

win a complete memory-making package!

Free Newsletter

SEARCH [   ] GO   Advanced Search | Browse Categories | Bestsellers | Recommendation Guide | Gifts

Home | Shopping Cart | Customer Service | Order Status | About Beyond.com | Contact Us | Jobs
Safe Shopping Guarantee | Privacy Policy

Copyright © 1998, 1999 Beyond.com Corporation. All Rights Reserved

Figure 8.23   Priceline.com

159

Selling
Products and
Services
Online

Hotel Reservations Network (www.180096hotel.com). This company prebooks hotel rooms in bulk in 27 U. S. cities so that it can offer rooms in places that generally would be unavailable. They offer instant confirmation, great discounts, but little information about what you've just reserved. No problem—neither would any 1-800 call to the hotel itself.

Virtual Communities

GeoCities (www.geocities.com). If you want to build connections, here's a place to meet and greet. So much for business networking social hours— just make your anonymous online contacts and hide behind a cheap suit. GeoCities has more corporate sponsor tag lines on its home page than infor-

Figure 8.24   Travelocity.com

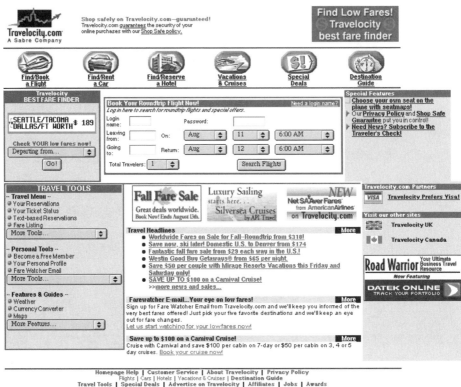

mation (Figure 8.25). It's a challenge to find substance here, but the site serves a different purpose. People . . . people who need people. It's the luckiest Web site in the world.

Xoom.com (xoom.com/communities). Just when you thought you'd communed enough, here are even *more* communities, sorted by "areas of interest," no less (Figure 8.26). Best of all, this site asks the question, "Are you a people person?" If you are, they have a job for you as a "community leader." Community leaders are always needed to head up scheduled chats, manage the message boards, and more.

■ Moving On

This is just a sampling of what's out there already. Hopefully these sites' successes will inspire and encourage you. These are some examples of the great and quasi-good sites that have lasted longer than since the beginning of this manuscript. Here are the good; you'll surely find the bad and the ugly soon enough on your own.

Figure 8.25 GeoCities

Yahoo! - Help

Yahoo! Calendar - get your free web-based calendar

Welcome, Guest - [Sign in]   Get a free home page

BUILD A PAGE
Create a
new webpage.

EDIT PAGES
Use File Manager to
work on your site.

UPLOAD FILES
Import or FTP
sounds, pictures
or HTML files.

Returning GeoCities members, learn how to sign in for the first time.

Search Home Pages

[Search]

Explore Neighborhoods

Area51	Hollywood	TimesSquare
Colosseum	SouthBeach	Tokyo
Heartland	SunsetStrip	WestHollywood

Take a vacation in TheTropics, one of our 41 Neighborhoods.

Cool Home Page Add-Ons

Interactive
Forms, Guestbook

Fun Stuff
Java applets,
Tic-tac-toe

Multimedia
Streaming audio/video

Make Money
Cash-earning links

Art
Free clip art

Up-to-the-Minute
Counter, Headlines

Five Great Reasons to Get a Free Home Page

1. Yahoo! PageBuilder - Use your mouse to build a professional-looking page in minutes.
2. Home Page Add-Ons - Free clip art, headlines, guestbooks and more to enhance your page.
3. Neighborhoods - Meet people just like you in one of our 41 themed communities.
4. Pages That Pay - Add sales links to your pages and earn cash! Plus, you're automatically eligible for cool contests.
5. GeoMedia - Publish streaming audio and video on your pages for your visitors to enjoy.

New and Notable

Have you tried the new Yahoo! PageBuilder?
The preview version is here! If you can point and click with a mouse, you can build great pages in no time.

Make money with your home page! Now you can earn money by adding merchant links to your pages. When visitors click, you get commissions.

Spice up your home page with some toys.
Your visitors will have a blast playing with "Gadgets." Add a countdown, video poker, sports trivia or stock charter Gadget to your pages.

Getting Help

If you need help getting started or have other questions, visit our Help section for frequently asked questions and tutorials.

Figure 8.26 Xoom.com

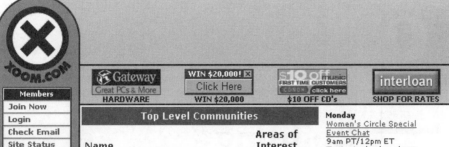

Members		
Join Now		
Login		
Check Email		
Site Status		
Help		
XOOM.com Hubs		
Communities		
Auctions		
Online Chat		
Connections		
Communications		
Search		
Hot Spots		
Find a hot date at Match.com		
travelscape.com Low Hotel Rates		
Buy, Sell, Trade at eBay		
Resources		
Pay Bills Free		
FREE STUFF!!!		
Job Options		
Classifieds		
Yellow Pages		
White Pages		
ActiveShopper		
Research Center		
Shopping Guide		

Top Level Communities

Name	Areas of Interest
Arts Graphic Arts, Photography, more...	10
Business & Money NEW! Personal Finance, Business Center, more...	3
Computers & Technology WWW, Programming, Video Games, more...	8
Education & Career Scholarships, College, Career, more...	10
Entertainment NEW! Movies, Music, DVD, more...	10
Health & Recreation NEW! Healthy Living, Illness & Diseases, Medical Reference, more...	21
Hobbies & Crafts Antiques, Jewelry, Metalworking, more...	12
Home & Family Families, Genealogy, Parenting, more...	7
International	30
Lifestyles New Age, Romance, Singles, Gay	4
Organizations Charity, Government, Volunteer, more...	6

Monday
Women's Circle Special
Event Chat
9am PT/12pm ET
Topic: Let's chat about
Internet relationships!
HelpCenter
6pm PT/9pm ET
Topic: Creating Frames in
HTML - Beginner Class

Tuesday
Religion Chat
3pm PT/6pm ET
Topic: General Religion and
Spirituality Chat
HelpCenter
7pm PT/10pm ET
Topic: Beginning HTML
Arts Special Event Chat
7pm PT/10pm ET
Topic: Computer 3D
Graphics...The fun never
ends!

Wednesday
HelpCenter
9am PT/NOON ET
Topic: HTML Chat
Computers and Technology
Special Events Chat
11am PT/2pm ET
Topic: Open Forum: Bring
ideas and topics that you'd
like us to highlight in our
Community!
Entertainment
7pm PT/10pm ET
Topic: Come chat with us
about new movie releases!

Thursday
Arts - Anime
12pm PT/3pm ET

9

Building Effective Customer Relations

■ Analyzing the Online Customer

An old truism of sales is that it is far less expensive to retain existing customers than to recruit new ones. Customer retention could also be one of the keys to increasing profits for e-tailers.

Online customers run the gamut from new visitors who will browse a few times before buying, to militant shoppers who arrive at a Web site as if they're on a mission. The majority of customers, however, are somewhere in the middle. Studies of online buying behavior indicate two phases of customer purchases. First, a small initial purchase lets the shopper test the trustworthiness of the merchant. If they are satisfied, they'll return for larger purchases later. Remember the "foot in the door" technique discussed under "Influencing" in Chapter 7? There you go.

Besides a range of shopping expertise, you'll also detect the full magnitude of surfing proficiency. Novice Web users will find some of the simplest technological issues to be baffling. Proficient Internet users will be able to speak geek right along with you or your programmers. Web sites that learn to identify the new visitor versus the returning customer, and distinguish between the Web-elite vs. the Web-impaired, can provide the best "welcome" for the user. There is a big difference between new prospects and returning customers, just as there is in any Main Street shop. Recognize returning customers and don't force them to re-enter billing and shipping information. Also consider that the degree of hand-holding needed to navigate your site or your product catalog will differ.

What degree of service will online customers expect? In general, people appreciate the value of good service. Stores like Nordstrom that provide excellent customer service have gained a following of loyal customers who behave like fans. Nordstrom is widely recognized as the model for exceeding customer expectations, not merely meeting customer needs. Once the bar has been raised this high, anyone who can't reach that level looks like a wimp.

■ Communicating with Your Customers

Experts agree that content is and will remain the major differentiating factor among Web sites. This trend is already apparent as more people grow accustomed to shopping online and the novelty of online bells and whistles wears off.

BabyCenter Inc., a privately held Internet company, realized this from the start. BabyCenter launched its Web site in October 1998 to tap the $18 billion baby-supply market. Today they deliver baby products, toys, clothes, diapers and more to your door, but they originally made their name delivering *information* to expectant and new parents. BabyCenter (www.babycenter.com) provides articles on pregnancy and parenting activities, chat rooms, and bulletin boards. It has become a trusted resource to gather information.

BabyCenter raised $10 million from Intel and four venture capital firms to make the transition to electronic commerce. Advertisers include Johnson & Johnson, Procter & Gamble, and Clorox. These advertisers are much more than banners. Each advertiser sponsors a different area of the site, providing up-to-date expert content. Johnson & Johnson sponsors an area on touch and massage for infants; Charles Schwab sponsors an interactive college savings calculator, for example.

Stay focused on the fact that if your site offers new (fresh), innovative, and relevant content on a regular basis, and is simple and easy to navigate, visitors are most likely to hang around. The best techniques to keep customers coming back to your site, and loitering when they get there, are inexpensive and easy to produce. "Stickiness" is the term for getting people to spend more time on your Web site. For a sampling of techniques for keeping customer interest, see Figure 9.1.

■ Personalization and One-to-One Marketing

Strengthening ties with customers is a high priority. For many customers, strengthening ties means focusing on *me*, with dedicated one-to-one attention. For most customers, as for the population in general, the favorite topic is themselves. *What's in it for me?* Smart salespeople learn early that unless you address the personal benefits of your products, nobody listens. They'll go off into their own private Idaho with eyes glazed over. The Internet equivalent of that glazed expression is a click.

Personalization is a way to get to everyone's favorite topic immediately. Tell people something about themselves and you've captured their attention. Personalization can include letting shoppers

- Check the status of an order.
- Check out "frequent shopper points" to see what they've accumulated.

Figure 9.1 Techniques to Encourage Customers to Linger and Return to Your Site

---

Web sites that are "sticky" thrive. What is sticky? Stickiness refers to the process of getting people to spend more time on your site. Stickiness should never cost you a customer, but should support customer retention.

Current articles on subjects related to the company, product line, and image. Articles should not be a direct copy of printed text. They should be written or adapted for the Web, using short sentences, bullet points, and lists.

History articles or information that you keep on the site that will intrigue a new visitor.

Expert articles like those used by BabyCenter, on topics relevant for your niche.

Chat rooms where like-minded spirits can share advice, experiences, and ideas.

Bulletin boards to post notes, tips, hot flashes, and news items.

Instant messages to let your customers know something important and unique to them.

Free e-mail newsletters on a regular basis, to stay in touch.

Jokes and allowing visitors to add their jokes to the list.

Entertainment of some type that creates an "experience" for the visitor unlike other sites. Some sites have their clothing "modeled" for interested buyers, for example.

Free prizes, and requests for the visitor to register for your contest.

- Receive personal responses to their purchases with a follow-up e-mail.
- Receive news flashes on topics that are of interest to them.
- Benefit from other creative connections you can dream up.

Mattel toy company (www.mattel.com) has a site that lets shoppers choose their doll's skin tone, hair color, and name. Musicmaker.com allows shoppers to browse through decades of recorded music treasures and produce personalized CDs with their own favorite songs and artists. Amazon.com uses a technique called "collaborative filtering" to recommend a new book to you by comparing your past choices with those of other book buyers who reported similar taste in reading material.

With a technique referred to as "mass customization," e-tailers can use technology to make all their customer contact unique and personal. Mass customization refers to the process of giving individual customers exactly what they want, when they want it, and in the way they want it. Technology for mass customization enables any business to provide this type of personalization for thousands of customers. In *Unleashing the Killer App* (Harvard Business School, 1998), Larry Downes and Chunka Mui refer to this as treating each customer as a market segment of one: "The power of these applications comes from the fact that customers like the appearance of a personalized product, especially when they have done the personalizing themselves." Using technology to customize has become the rule.

Individualized customer pricing is another appealing technique. Taking into account earlier discounts and the quantity of purchases, the Web site can automatically offer a lower price to frequent shoppers.

NBC Television sells NBC merchandise online using "My Snap," a free service that helps you customize your own Snap page to display only information you want: weather, sports, lottery, and more (Figure 9.2). In order to use My Snap you must, of course, *register*. After you register, you can even customize the color scheme.

■ Simplifying Your Site for Ease of Use

The online shopping experience should emulate as closely as possible a perfect offline shopping trip: The shopper should get to the destination quickly, with no waiting for a parking space, find the department he or she needs, locate the wanted item(s), track down a cheerful sales representative as soon as you need him or her for advice, decide what to purchase, pay, and leave. The more similar the online experience is to the offline experience, experts agree,

Figure 9.2   My Snap allows users to customize their page down to the color.

Home: Help: Topics: Using My Snap

My snap.

- Personalize Content and Color

- Edit Your Portfolio

- Edit Your Weather

- Edit Your Scoreboard

- Edit Your Lottery

- Edit Your Headlines

- Edit Your Bookmarks

- Edit Your Topics

Help Topics ○

My Snap is a free service that allows you to customize your own Snap page to display the information you want.

You can personalize your portfolio, weather, sports scores, horoscope listings, lottery, news, Internet bookmarks and topics of interest to you.

Using My Snap
To use My Snap, enter your Snap member name and password. If you forgot your Snap member name or password, visit Snap's Registration Help.

If you don't have a Snap member name and password, you need to register for Snap. To do this, complete the Snap registration form.

Getting Started
Once you sign in, you can customize your settings. The first thing you'll want to do is choose your content and color settings. Click Personalize Content and Color to learn how.

 Click a personalization topic from the list on the left to learn how to customize My Snap features.

Haven't found the answer to your question? Send a message to our support group.

snap.com   Home Search Membership Info Feedback Help Free E-mail Newsletter

About Snap Ad Info Snap Jobs Privacy Policy List Your Site Add Snap to Your Site the more likely a shopper will make positive decisions to buy. Structure the online catalog around the way shoppers really think. Do they think department or outfit? For online sales, probably outfit. *Would you like to see a sweater with those pants?* Peapod.com reminds coffee buyers to purchase cream.

Shopping carts are a favorite way for shoppers to pick up a number of items from the same online store while "paying" only once at the end. Shopping cart technology allows shoppers to gather items from all over a site for one-stop checkout. Unfortunately, of all the purchases that begin on the Internet, about one-half to two-thirds are not completed. Shoppers ditch the cart and move on.

How could a tool like shopping carts that looked like a sure thing to simplify online shopping have such a low success rate? Apparently the billing process shakes shoppers up. Some browsers are strictly "window shopping" and leave because they never intended to buy. "Just looking, thank you." But what about the others? The first shock could be the cost to ship their product selection; often it's much higher than expected. The next surprise is the registration process that many Web sites have introduced to gather customer profile data. While this is great data for the merchant to have, most shoppers will balk at giving their date of birth and other private information just because they want to buy a shirt. Finally, some individuals are still hesitant about divulging credit card information. In that case, offer an alternative method of payment. Let the customer complete the ordering information online, and give their credit card information offline by telephone.

Simplify your site for your customers by eliminating issues that interfere with shopping. Tips are summarized in the checklist in Figure 9.3. First of all, be patient with window shoppers. When they've had a chance to become comfortable, they'll eventually buy. Keep shipping and handling costs to a minimum. Offer shipping alternatives, and let the customer choose which one they want to meet their needs. Not every purchase absolutely positively has to be there overnight.

Remember that "cost" to your customer is his or her bottom line, not yours. All extras, like tax (for those states that have it) and shipping are lumped together in the buyer's mind.

Addressing Security Concerns

In the past, some customers balked at giving credit card information on the Web. In fact, some merchants were equally hesitant about online payment processing. Why? Not everyone is convinced that online transactions are safe. Adding the final step of online payment processing is not the most expensive

Figure 9.3   Checklist of Best Customer Practices

☑ Be patient with window shoppers. Give them time and money and they'll be back.

☑ Recognize returning shoppers and simplify their visit. Don't make them repeat information about themselves.

☑ Emulate a successful offline shopping trip as closely as possible with each on-line expedition.

☑ Offer suggestions to returning customers based on their previous preferences (but don't overdo it).

☑ Use smart technology. Learn what mistakes in spelling or typing are typical of your customers and teach your system to interpret.

☑ Maximize the effective use of shopping carts. They are a great way to save the customer time at check-out and billing.

☑ Don't ask for too much personal information. Protection of privacy may cause the customer to leave—fast.

☑ Avoid asking lengthy registration questions at check-in or check-out.

☑ If you ask for data, stay with questions that would be typical for a warranty, then don't expect answers at the "cash register."

☑ Answer customer e-mails *as soon as possible.*

☑ Offer simple and fast ways to get through your site, at levels appropriate for new and experienced Web shoppers.

☑ Give information that enables a customer to reach a human voice in a reasonable amount of time.

☑ Create communities, and encourage customers to bond.

☑ Remember that cost to your customer is his or her bottom line, not yours. All extras, like tax (for those states that have it) and shipping, are lumped together in the buyer's mind.

☑ Beware of posting exorbitant shipping rates. You'll frighten off potential buyers.

☑ If your shipping rates are necessarily high, offset the cost to the customer with an enhanced discount. (If your products cost too much more than any other source, you'll be ditched.)

☑ Offer shipping alternatives, and let the customer choose which one they want to meet their needs.

For more information, see the list in Chapter 7 of "Online Stores Dos and Don'ts."

component of e-commerce. "Their resistance is not a financial decision," says Maybelle Cowan of M.L. Burke, Inc., a Web site design and service firm. "They were concerned about security." Cowan says this fear is unwarranted. "When you give your credit card over a cell phone, you run the risk of interception. The same is true with cordless phones. These are easily intercepted by walkie-talkies, short-wave radios, and other headsets," she warned. "You could be broadcasting those credit card numbers all over creation." A secure Web site and encryption technology are safer than cordless or cellular phone transactions.

■ Building Brand Loyalty

The look and feel of a site should be consistent with your brand image. If your image is sleek and trendy, your Web site should be the same. Some experts feel that companies may need to adapt their image when they begin to sell online. Not so. Images that transfer from print to store to Web site reinforce brand image and let the shopper know they are clearly in the right place.

Peter Levitan, president of New Jersey Online (www.nj.com), believes that it is important for e-tailers to understand the power of promotion to increase brand loyalty. "Recognize the unique ability of the Internet to drive people to the store," he said. NJO provides a marketing resource for advertising and recognizes the importance of branding. It designs tools to encourage online shoppers to visit Main Street, too, further reinforcing the strength of a brand. The goal is to have customers return, to the site or to the shop. Examples of techniques designed to bring customers back include coupons and loyalty (or frequency) programs.

Coupons

"If a Web site includes coupons, the shopper can take a printed copy of the coupon to the store and incur a bigger discount," said Levitan. Other specials and promotions, sales, and deals can be announced on the Web site and used in person or online.

Loyalty/Frequency Programs

Rewarding loyal customers with special treatment is another inexpensive but high payoff strategy. A number of sites use club memberships as a technique. Macy's, for example, has E-Club, a personalized express check-out service that offers additional benefits if you—that's right—*register*. E-Club benefits include reminders of important gift dates so you "never forget a loved one." Automatic replenishment establishes delivery dates for life's necessities like facial wash so that you never run out of your survival items.

■ Assessing Competitors

While tracking your current customer activities will help you refine your site and keep it current, tracking your competitors' sites will also help you. Two routes are helpful: (1) obtain current information about your specific competitors on a regular basis, and (2) eavesdrop in online discussion groups.

Check Out Your Competitors' Web Sites

In the past, if you sent away for a rival's marketing materials, you probably used someone else's name and address when you snooped. If the company was privately held, you had no information about their financial stability. If you wanted advertising rates, you had to request a different packet of information. The comprehensiveness and timeliness of their responses were a shot in the dark.

Today, you only have to call up your competition's Web site to get the complete scoop on everything they are doing. And you don't even have to give your name. Use any search engine (see the Appendix for lists) to locate a competitor's Web site and browse for details such as the following:

- *What do their catalogs look like?*
- *How do they position their products and services?*
- *What claims do they make about their products? (Can you counter them?)*
- *What are their pricing structures?*
- *What can you learn from their press releases?*
- *Do new product announcements have an impact on you?*
- *Do they provide any financial information?*
- *Where applicable, what do their advertising rate cards look like?*
- *Who advertises on their sites now? What links do they have to other sites?*

Check Online Discussion Groups

The online discussion group can be an invaluable—and free—market research tool. Discussion groups often engage in lively arguments over the pros and cons of products and services and companies. An open mind in these free-flowing dialogues can soak in a wealth of information. The drawback is that the data is totally unscientific, based on a biased sampling of online conversations. But the additional benefit is that you can jump into the scene if you choose (as long as you are not blatantly self-promotional). "Netiquette" prohibits selling in discussion groups. You'll be thrown right out.

■ Tracking Customer Interactions

The goal is to give a customer what he or she wants with little effort. Customers want personalization, so collaborative filtering (the personalization technology discussed earlier regarding Amazon.com book recommendations) is important. There are additional information filters that can help users retrieve responses to their inquiries. *Rules-based filtering* is a technique that asks the customer to select features desired in a product, then searches its database to find the closest match.

According to Jupiter Communications, ten of the top 25 online vendors now personalize their Web sites in some manner. Sites are now expected to remember what the customer bought previously and to offer helpful recommendations. *Learning interfaces,* a technology modeled on video games, are "interfaces that adapt automatically to a user's level of skill, advancing them through the system's functions as they are ready, and calling on a human being when the situation requires," according to Downes and Mui (*Unleashing the Killer App,* Harvard Business School, 1998). And all these interactions are tracked and recorded.

To make things even easier, a Web site can interpret typos. Using smart technology, any Web site can accept common mistakes in spelling or typing that are typical of many customers. The system can be taught to interpret. "Cookie technology" is another tool to obtain general (not too personal) information from online visitors. Cookies track aggregate information to a site, which allows a merchant to update and improve the site.

Creating Customer Profiles

Customer profiles create a wealth of information that enables e-tailers to target their marketing efforts and reduce advertising costs. With a customer profile, e-tailers have a good idea of where they should advertise on other Web sites, print, television, and radio. The information obtained from their Web site can help in the decision about what Web sites are important to link to.

Many Web site designers recommend that companies use the first encounter with a customer as a way to gather information (as well as to sell). Others warn that customers are put off by questions that seem intrusive or inappropriate in relation to their purchase. "The Web is designed to speed the process, not to slow it down," warns Jim Stoddard, president of Hook Mountain Marketing, Inc., in Ridgewood, New Jersey. He recommends "cloning" your best customer to increase sales revenues, and helps businesses of all sizes create their own databases.

E-tailers walk a fine line between asking too many questions and not asking enough. Ask too much and the customer may drop off. Ask too few questions, and you are missing a golden opportunity to create customer profiles and create a database that potential advertisers on your site are willing to pay for.

Registration questions have been used surreptitiously since the first site went online. Customers have been asked to register for access to the site, to download utilities, and to participate in special programs (e.g., loyalty programs, special sales, promotions). At this point in time, the registration process has been overused to the extent that it has become a sensitive issue for many buyers. On the other hand, e-tailers need to know something about their customer base in order to grow.

The difference between accomplishment and alienation through registration may be a matter of how you request data. "Look at this from the customer's perspective," says Stoddard. "If you go too far beyond shipping information, customers won't want to fill it out. Purchasers don't like to give out a lot of personal information. There are different levels of acceptability in questioning customers. Questions that are typical of a warranty are not perceived as threatening by most individuals because they are familiar with the process. However, customers are used to filling out warranty cards after a purchase—not when they visit a store. Consequently, they will not expect to provide warranty-level information in order to open the door to your online store. Don't expect answers to detailed questions when visitors arrive at your site. Customers prefer to offer information at their convenience, or ignore the request completely.

Web site managers have far more leeway with business customers. "You can get a lot more information about someone's business. They will tell you what kind of business they're in, how they intend to use the product, their title, and additional contact names," says Stoddard. Not so with the average consumer. However, there are circumstances in which consumers will bend a little. Customers are more willing to divulge personal information if they perceive an immediate personal benefit. If the product is complicated or they believe they might need help later on, customers are willing to give away more private data.

Many e-tailers elect to differentiate between mandatory (for shipping purposes) and optional ("to help us improve our products and our site") information. As long as a customer completes the mandatory information, he or she can continue through the site. Optional items must be clearly identified as such, so as not to hinder the purchase process.

As a final point of differentiation, if the perceived quality or complexity of a product does not warrant the Spanish Inquisition, consider requesting data or feedback using a brief follow-up questionnaire on e-mail or phone call. If you choose this approach, offer a "thank you" in some form of giveaway that in some way is related to the business. Beware: Most of us have enough refrigerator magnets. And for home-based businesses, the refrigerator magnet only serves as an annoying reminder that the business owner frequents the refrigerator too often during official business hours.

Figure 9.4 is a hierarchy of derivable data from Jim Stoddard's guidelines for information gathering.

■ Providing Customer Support Services

How much help, and what type, should be provided? Should the help be online, offline, or both? Existing companies can answer these questions by examining what they can learn from their offline sales and customer service. Their transition to online sales can incorporate some of what is learned from the offline process. For example, careful monitoring of questions that are raised

---

Figure 9.4   Building Customer Profiles—What Can You Ask?

Keep in mind that you can advance a level or more in depth if a customer regards the proportion of data requested vs. perceived personal product benefit to be high.

Level 1: Information Needed to Ship the Product(s)

- Name, address, phone
- E-mail address

Level 2: Information Related to Product "Warranty" (in a category, checklist format)

- Family income
- Education level
- Number of people in household
- Date of last major purchase
- Other similar products owned

Level 3: Going for Broke

- What type of Web sites do they visit now?
- What organizations do they belong to?
- What sites do they find the most useful?
- Do they have a Web site and can you link to theirs? (Look for links. Some can be arranged through reciprocity; some will be fee-based deals.)

---

to customer service reps and sales personnel will help to anticipate product/ service related Web site questions. Customer concerns that are strictly related to the Web site can be predicted by observing some of the sites that have been online longest. Their help buttons often send the shopper over to a technical explanation of the best software to use to view the site, which can then be downloaded right away if the shopper doesn't have it.

Helping Customers

Online companies have tried several different approaches to provide help. At the simplest level is a listing of frequently asked questions (FAQs) to handle the most basic concerns. FAQs are acceptable for easy questions that have uncomplicated and straightforward answers.

> Q: "Does your company accept clothing designs from outside sources?"
> A: "Get real," or more effectively, "No thank you. We have our own internal design staff."

Heavy reliance on self-help will not work. Most online shoppers are there for speed and convenience, so if you make it inconvenient to get an answer, they'll be more likely to click off your site. 1-800-Flowers lets shoppers click on an icon to begin an interactive conversation with a sales representative. Remember, this company started out by taking telephone orders, so they know the value of human-to-human contact. Provide a phone contact that can be accessed quickly and you're back in business.

E-mail contact can work, but not when instant answers are necessary for sales or site maneuvering to progress. E-mail customer contact can serve other purposes, which will be discussed later, and is more equivalent to dealing with a letter of complaint or compliment. Answer customer e-mails *as soon as possible*. These contacts may allow customers to vent, praise, or make their own recommendations for a Web site. Instead of guessing what customers want, ask for their input. Encourage e-mail correspondence as a feedback mechanism for your marketing efforts. An analysis of customer communication with any business will reveal a lot. Look for patterns that tell something about where enhancements are needed.

Creating Communities

Online communities facilitate exchanges of information among customers. Like spirits in the night, lovers of Furbies can seek kindred souls and e-mail one another, engaging in loving correspondence. In the safety and security of the online community, no one will tease or remark, "I just don't understand what's so great about those things."

The appeal of online communities is enormous. Given the information presented in Chapter 5 on the psychology of Internet usage, this is borderline disturbing. But it works. Communities are the online equivalent of networking meetings, which overall are losing the battle for attention and drawing much lower attendance than in the past. Online communities allow members the opportunities for personal publishing, experience sharing, and creating geography-free friendships. Groups can be moderated by a host or open. E*Trade offers the opportunity to engage in live chats about stocks at any hour of the day. And you can even customize your community experience (see Figure 9.5). E-Trade lets you block out "noisy" members with special member filters (try *that* in a Chamber of Commerce meeting), and allows participants to vote on news events with hypothetical "What would *you* do . . ."

CASE STUDY:　　　　　　　　　　　　■
Dynamic Customer Interaction—CDnow

CDnow has a charming way of making you feel like the people who work there are your friends. They're not really selling you anything; they're simply recommending things to enhance the quality of your life. The first customer contact from CDnow is a personal thank-you note for creating an account with the company. There normally wouldn't be anything unusual about a thank-you note, except that in this case it comes from CDnow president and co-founder Jason Olim, who shares a few of his ideas with you about his vision of the company's mission. See Figure 9.6 for details.

As a repeat customer, your continued support is always appreciated. CDnow lets customers know that they value your loyalty, and they reward you with additional discounts. Because they are tracking your purchasing history, they can respond to you with the appropriate type of promotion. See Figure 9.7.

Although the company president does not personally respond to all subsequent orders, customers are treated with a letter from Customer Relations that describes this and other special discounts and services. There is always a sense of a relationship building and growing between the shopper and the merchant.

Figure 9.5   E*Trade's Online Community

Community @ E*TRADE

Investors Are Talking

- Stock Talk: Over 1,000 of your favorite tickers in Stocks A - Z. Also here: the most active Community @ E*TRADE discussions!
- Join the most active stock discussions: EGRP, BIGG, AOL, SNMM, and MSFT.

Community Buzz

191,534 Community Members!

Mutual Fund Live Event
Wednesday 8/11 at 6:00pm PT

Here's your chance to get access to the movers and shakers in the mutual fund industry.

This week: ask Kevin Landis from the Technology Value Fund about his investment strategies.

Visit Live Events for more info!

- Join the fifth edition of the red-hot Intenet High Flyers discussion, IHF V.
- Tacos? Tin? Transistors? Tell us your pick in The Next Hot Industry.
- Interested in ways to invest for the benefit of children? Tell us your strategies in Investing for Your Kids.
- Fixed Income Investing. Connect with other fixed-income investors to trade ideas and make the most of what you've got.
- Looking for stocks that might net you rapid rewards? Discuss them in Quick Gains.
- Check out the Women's Stock Club Or create your own club!

Get The News

Get the news about all the exciting talk in the Community @ E*TRADE.

Your first name:

Your last name:

Your e-mail address:

SUBMIT

Top 10 Nasdaq
E*TRADE's Most Active
August 10, 1999 MARKET CLOSE

EGRP	E*TRADE Group, Inc
CSCO	Cisco Systems Inc
EBAY	eBay Inc
YHOO	Yahoo! Inc
MSFT	Microsoft Inc
CMGI	CMGi Inc
AMZN	Amazon.com Inc
ATHM	At Home Corp
DELL	Dell Computer Corp
STMP	Stamps.com Inc

This information does not constitute by E*TRADE a recommendation or endorsement to engage in any securities transaction.

Daily Poll

A study conducted by the Milken Institute claims that regional growth is tied to high tech industry activity. How about your region? Do you think the area where you live is growing its high tech activity adequately so that it stays economically vibrant?

○ Yes, the wildfire economic growth I see around me is tied to high tech.

○ Well, there's some high-tech powered growth, but the region I am from balances itself among a number of industries.

○ No. Even in these boom times, the area I where I live isn't driven by high tech in any significant way.

SUBMIT

jobs of the week
hotjobs.com

Hot Jobs of the Week
1. Andersen Consulting - Alliance Mktg Mgr
2. Forbes - Chief Financial Officer
3. Levi Strauss — Dir, Global Portfolio
4. Goldman Sachs - Sr Web Strategy Analyst
5. CitySearch, Inc. — EVP, Marketing

The Experienced Professional's Job Board

It's time for ✳ E*TRADE®

Figure 9.6   CDnow establishes a rapport with their customers from the moment
                  they open an account.

Subj: Thank You for Visiting CDnow
Date: 99-03-06 00:50:49 EST
From: presmail@cdnow.com
To:

Dear Bill,

Thanks for creating an account with CDnow. As the company's president, I am
writing to introduce myself and to tell you about some of the unique benefits that
come with shopping online at CDnow. I hope you will think of us as a resource
when you are shopping for music or seeking music information.

If you want to listen to music before you decide to purchase it, we have hundreds
of thousands of sound samples in all musical genres. If you are interested in
personalized recommendations based on the kinds of music that you like, visit
My CDnow on our home page. We understand that security and privacy are
important to you, and we pledge the following:

- an unconditional 30 day money back guarantee on your purchases
- safe shopping through the use of powerful encryption software
- we do not sell personal information about our customers
- we will not send you unsolicited email

I started CDnow with my twin brother Matt because I couldn't find what I was
looking for at a conventional record store, and I realized that there must be other
unsatisfied music lovers out there. Since then, our goal has been to build a better
music store. When you visit CDnow, we want you to have the best possible
experience shopping for music. So if there is anything that we can do for you,
please let me know.

Again, thanks for visiting us. We look forward to serving you and helping you
discover great music for a long time to come.

Yours truly,

Jason Olim
CDnow
President and Co-founder
http://cdnow.com

P.S. If, for any reason, you'd prefer not to receive future emails about CDnow,
please reply to this message with "PRIVATE" in the subject line.

Figure 9.7   CDnow offers discount coupons to repeat customers, applied automatically to their shopping carts.

Subj: 15% off Music from CDnow
Date: 99-04-09 19:28:41 EDT
From: managerFT@cdnow.com
To:

Dear Bill,

Thanks for visiting CDnow recently. I'm writing to you for a very simple reason: we want to be your favorite music store, and we're even willing to put our money behind it!

I'd like to offer you a 15% discount towards your next CDnow purchase*. To redeem your discount — for an additional 15% off — you must use this link: http://cdnow.com/from=rek:x:cdn:fq526 You'll see your "coupon" at the top of your screen to indicate that your discount is waiting for you. Start shopping, and when you make your first selection, your discount will automatically appear in your shopping cart! But you'll have to hurry, because this offer expires on April 29th.

CDnow is the ultimate music store, with plenty of reviews in all musical genres and feature articles by top music journalists, all at one great Web site. Plus, at CDnow we have more than 300,000 sound samples, so you can listen to music BEFORE you buy!

Enjoy your CDnow discount. Use it to purchase anything in our store.

Sincerely,

Geoffrey Carr
Manager, Customer Relations

P.S. If, for any reason, you'd prefer not to receive future emails about CDnow, please reply to this message with "PRIVATE" in the subject line.

*Limit one 15% discount per person. Limit one discount per order. This discount is good only on CDnow products. This offer expires on April 29, 1999. Offer does not apply to orders that have already been placed.

10

Secure Commerce on the Internet

■ Issues of Security

Experts agree (and consumers confirm) that security remains a dominant concern in the growth of e-commerce. Defined as freedom from danger, risk, anxiety, doubt, or care, *security* assumes a new meaning in e-commerce. The dangers we face relate to potential financial loss, data damage, consumer havoc, or publication of trade secrets. As e-commerce grows exponentially, so does the potential for major security failures. On the positive side, there is also a more aggressive pursuit of the development of security software, systems, and hardware today. Our biggest challenge is to guarantee security at all levels of e-commerce, from complex corporate configurations to individual consumer transactions. Our future challenge is to ensure that technological security system developers stay at least one step ahead of those who seek their demise.

Failures in e-commerce security make news headlines weekly. Perhaps the most disturbing aspect of these headlines is this prevalent theme: The smallest flaw in the design of a security system can cause tremendous repercussions. Every e-commerce business is only as secure as its weakest link. The best security is provided when a business considers all possible targets for trouble, starting with software used by the business. Smart e-commerce businesses are prepared rather than paranoid about security.

Major corporations face security issues on all fronts, from the fear of invasion of privacy to the risk of invasion of service providers. Small businesses are equally vulnerable to corruption of company and consumer data, inappropriate access to proprietary information or financial records, copyright infringements, and invasion of private database records. Destroying, changing, or disclosing information to unauthorized users is a real security threat. Even solitary Web page owners need to concentrate on prevention of tampering with their sites. Covert activity that causes the alteration of information on a Web site, the disruption of service, or theft of information is costly and hazardous to the health of any business.

Finally, there is the issue of consumer confidence that security is being handled properly. The ultimate determinant of the success of e-commerce rests in the hands of shoppers, not net moguls. Consumers demand guarantees that their credit card numbers and personal purchasing patterns won't be broadcast or used illegally. Consumers must feel they can trust the security of a Web site. As consumers, we are most likely to think of security in terms of the impact on us.

■ Requirements of E-Commerce Security

Electronic commerce security is based on five requirements: authentication, authorization, confidentiality, integrity, and nonrepudiation of origin (Figure 10.1).

- *Authentication* involves proving your identity using a password, personal identification numbers (PINs), key, fingerprint, or some combination of methods.
- *Authorization* is the control of access to specific information, using an access control list (ACL). Some users will be authorized to read and browse only; other users will be authorized to modify content.
- *Confidentiality* protects secret information from unauthorized access. Encryption techniques (discussed below) help to ensure confidentiality.
- *Integrity* is the protection of information from changes during transmittal or storage.
- *Nonrepudiation of origin* protects against cheats and liars who attempt to deny involvement in specific transactions or nefarious actions.

Figure 10.1   Five Requirements for E-commerce Security

1. **Authentication:** proves identity (password, PINs, keys, biometrics, etc.)
2. **Authorization:** controls access to specific information with an access control list (ACL)
3. **Confidentiality:** protects secret information from unauthorized access (encryption techniques)
4. **Integrity:** protects information from changes during transmittal or storage
5. **Nonrepudiation:** protects against cheats and liars; prevents anyone from denying they sent or received data

What are the most serious threats to your business? Can you afford to be incapacitated for hours or days while problems are fixed? What are the consequences if someone messes with your data, or infiltrates your site and wipes out critical information? Can you purchase a software package that will provide the protection you need, or is your best solution a more expensive hardware configuration?

Security is not the appropriate place for any business to cut costs; on the other hand, not every business requires incorporation of the most complex security systems. The best policy for any company, regardless of size, is to work to identify the best solutions to accomplish its goals. At the consumer level, you know that you will lose business if there is even a remote possibility that shoppers will not develop an immediate sense of trust in you and your business. *You will not get a second chance to make a first impression.* Not only will you need to arrange for the tightest possible security in all payment transactions, but you will also need to promote this security intensely on your Web site.

Can you afford a software package that will provide the protection you need, or is your best solution a more expensive hardware configuration? To determine the level and type of security technology to be instituted for your e-commerce business, consider these questions:

- What are the most serious threats to your business?
- What network resources need to be protected (intranets, extranets, internets, telecommunications connections)? How should each be protected?
- Within a network, who should be able to communicate with whom?
- What information should be permitted to travel through each of these communication paths?
- Who should be allowed to access specific information within each communication path? Specify your access control list (ACL).

- Who should be allowed to change information (specifically delineate which information): add, modify, delete?
- When are changes allowed: before, during, or after what time intervals?
- If you are transmitting tons of data on a regular basis, how can you ensure that it arrives at your destination in the same format that it left you (with all dollar signs and commas intact)?
- For your purposes, what is the best method to verify identity to determine authorization for access to information—passwords, personal identification numbers (PINs), keys, cards, fingerprints, other, a combination?
- How should you insure confidentiality? Which encryption technique(s) should be employed—symmetric or asymmetric key encryption?
- How quickly must you track down troublemakers? (What about those users who insist they sent money, products, information, or deny receiving the same items from you when you know they did . . .)
- How much of a system delay is tolerable? Some encryption technology, like asymmetric encryption, adds to processing time. What is the trade-off between security and transaction processing time? Are there ways to get around this problem?
- What issues of customer privacy are of concern to your business? Will children be potential consumers? How will you guard the privacy of children and stop online ordering by minors?
- What type of notice should be displayed on your Web site to indicate your level of security? How should you describe your protection of consumer privacy and confidentiality?

■ Protecting Yourself and Your Customers

The amount of trust that consumers will place in e-commerce is tightly connected to security and privacy issues. To achieve maximum security and ensure consumer privacy, consider the following:

- Start with all software on the user side of the total e-commerce system. Have you protected your business from threats of viruses, active software, flaws in browsers, weaknesses in mini-applications? Your security will only be as strong as your weakest link.
- Identify the layers in the network that represent your greatest security threats. Address these immediately.
- Know precisely what type of security guarantees your Internet service provider (ISP) can offer.

- Decide how you should guard against attacks on your Web site.
- Write privacy guidelines. Address not only the concerns of adult users, but also include special provisions for protection of the privacy of children.
- Write a security policy. Use this policy to initiate specific security actions. Be sure your employees understand this policy.

These strategies are addressed in further detail throughout this chapter.

■ New Technologies and New Risks

The increase in threats to networks and systems has caused IT managers to closely examine their systems' susceptibility to hacker attacks. This has led to a growing demand for assessment and detection systems, which are projected to increase in sales from $50 million in 1997 to more than $100 million in subsequent years, according to a study by the Aberdeen Group in *InternetWeek* magazine. Assessment systems include vulnerability scanners that probe networks and systems for holes in security. Detection systems include intrusion detection systems (IDS), which are like high-tech burglar alarms that detect suspicious activities and alert system administrators. Intrusion detection tools are among the hottest new technologies.

The definition of risk differs from the perspective of the Internet user, the merchant, or the Web site administrator. In general, risks have an impact on both clients and servers (the end users and Web sites), on the end user alone, or on the Web site alone. Risks that affect everyone require overlapping solutions. Critical areas of concern follow, and are shown in Figure 10.2

- *Eavesdropping.* With the increasing complexity of the design of computer transactions, with long and winding paths from computer to computer, eavesdropping is a problem that has an impact on users and Web servers. There are any number of steps along a message route that can invite eavesdropping: a machine at an ISP, a computer connected to a LAN, the Web site host, to name a few. Interlopers use devices like packet sniffers to intercept network communications and read text, including passwords being transmitted over the Internet by protocols such as Telnet. Packet sniffers are small software programs that can be installed anywhere on a network path to listen for interesting information (like passwords and credit card numbers) and report back to the cyber thief. Encryption, which will be discussed further on in this chapter, can prevent such tampering.

Figure 10.2   Examples of E-Commerce Security Risks

Risk	Description	Technology
Eavesdropping	Intercepting data as it passes through several computers to reach its destination.	Encryption prevents tampering.
Fraud	Impersonating legitimate businesses or setting up phony businesses to steal from shoppers.	Digital signatures provide authentication using encryption.
Forgery	A person pretends to be someone else.	Personal certificates authenticate users.
Break-Ins	Hackers steal passwords and take over Web sites and corporate computers.	Firewalls only allow specific Internet addresses to access the site.
Vandalism	Hackers attempt to crash computers by a deluge of messages or log-in attempts.	Firewalls and other security software check for unusual activity.
Theft	Unauthorized user gains access to a network and intercepts data.	Firewalls prevent entry to the network or server. VPNs limit traffic.

- *Fraud.* Fraud on the Internet can take the form of impersonating a legitimate business or setting up a phony business to steal from consumers (e.g., taking orders and payments for products that don't exist, from companies that don't really exist). Digital signatures help to verify the identity of sender and receiver and reduce the potential for fraud. Personal certificates authenticate individual users; site certificates authenticate businesses.

- *Forgery.* Forgery, or impersonating a person, can also be prevented by the use of personal certificates.

- *Break-ins.* The amateur and professional hacker alike, who can be anyone from a teenager testing his technical expertise to a disgruntled and malicious employee, love to break into Web sites and corporte computers. Most break-ins are never publicized, perhaps due to the fact that many major corporations would prefer not to spread the news that their sites are penetrable by twelve-year-olds. Highly secure firewalls help to prevent break-ins by allowing only specific Internet addresses to access the Web site. The firewall is also the checkpoint for dangerous software.

- *Vandalism.* This occurs as a result of attempts to crash computers by a deluge of messages or log-in attempts. Firewalls and other security software can check for unusual activity that could lead to vandalism, and switch off connections to sources of potential trouble.
- *Theft.* Corporate records or confidential data can be stolen when an unauthorized user gains access to a network. Firewalls prevent entry to the network or server by unauthorized attempts.

■ Attacks on Web Sites

If you think for one minute that it can't happen to you, guess again. Ebay, the Internet auction site, was penetrated by a hacker who managed to attack the company's home page and delve into the content. The attack included changes to auction prices, the addition of fake ads, and diversion of traffic to other sites. The 22-year-old college student hacker who invaded Ebay had the potential to take the entire network down. The company claimed that all credit card information was safe, however.

One of the worst things about Web site attacks is that most of the time the break-in is covered up. Hackers are notorious for altering system logs to remove evidence, even altering dates on file modifications to insure they match originals and never reveal the date of the break-in. Another "worst thing" about Web site attacks is the follow-up process of plugging holes in a system. When hackers gain access to a system, they often design "back doors" to let them in again . . . and again. The only way to truly secure a system that has been altered in this way is to settle down to the tedious task of perusing every critical file for even the slightest change. Passwords could also have been stolen, so to be on the safe side all passwords should be changed too.

■ Break-ins at Internet Service Providers

When a business makes a decision to use an Internet Service Provider (ISP), the business decides that the ISP will become their network. This is an important strategic decision, as discussed in Chapter 6. Selection of an ISP involves an assessment of the service provider's track record and ability to deliver the best service. Consequently, when customers sign on with an ISP they expect immediate trouble-free quality service. And they expect the ISP to provide a secure network management solution. Companies that rely on an ISP to run their e-commerce business will lose money quickly if the ISP experiences trouble.

ISPs are expected to deliver and manage security services for their customers. The security services they provide should be customized to each customer's stipulations, not one-size-fits-all. Company security policies provide the guidelines to help an ISP decide how to design each customer's solution. ISPs also need to be sensitive to changes in customer requirements. Firewalls, for example, provide protective barricades to ensure private data remains inaccessible to unauthorized users. As customer networks grow and change, there may be a need to use more than one firewall. With multiple firewalls, a business can create multiple security zones, allowing different individuals or businesses to access different data.

ISPs have additional pressure to seek the best security solutions to make their own networks safe so that ISP customer networks will be assured of safety. If something happens to the ISP, all customers are affected. If an ISP goes down, their customers go down, too. For an e-commerce business, this means the company is shut down until the ISP problem is fixed.

Perhaps the most vicious Internet attacks are those that bring down ISPs, referred to as "denial-of-service" attacks. One method of denial-of-service attack is to overwhelm the site with hundreds of incomplete Internet connections. This prevents authentic network connections from being made to the ISP. An example of this type of attack is the SYN flood attack. The SYN flood attack works against systems that use the Internet TCP/IP protocol, affecting both Windows NT and Unix platforms. (SYN refers to a "SYN request," which is part of the TCP/IP connection protocol.) Another type of denial-of-service attack attempts to exhaust system resources or crash the main computer. A highly publicized example of this type of attack is the "ping o'death." The ping o'death attack can hang up, crash, or reboot a system. The extent of the malicious attack depends on the platform used.

Other types of attacks threaten confidentiality. Unauthorized access to proprietary information (such as credit card numbers) is possible through cracks in the firewall. An attacker could also steal or delete files, deface Web sites, open cracks for others to enter, or place bogus programs on the server. But how can there be a crack or a backdoor in a firewall? Cracks can exist through even the most minute flaw in a software program installed and executed on the system. These flaws are publicized and exploited by hackers. And there is another infuriating and unintentional route inside. Even when a firewall is secure, there can be a break-in through a modem. For example, sometimes modems are attached to company computers so that employees can have dial-up access from home. If a modem attached to a corporate computer is also attached to a LAN, that modem is able to listen to any other corporate computer on the LAN. The firewall can be bypassed by a malicious user who has access to the network of company computers through the modem.

Security systems at this level are provided by the pioneers and major players. Lucent Technologies, for example, offers Bell Labs technology for network security solutions. Hewlett Packard provides Network Node Manager as one of several options.

■ Invasion of Privacy

Most ISPs now identify their detailed privacy policies to quiet the fears of customers concerning how their personal data may be used. E-commerce Web sites would do well to follow suit. In its "Terms and Conditions," Prodigy promises it will not sell or release any information to third parties. America Online offers terms and conditions of service that include "Eight Principles of Privacy." AOL promises never to give out information that would link screen names with actual names. However, as the public learned with the Melissa virus scandal, there are two exceptions to this AOL promise. AOL will release private information (1) to comply with a search warrant, subpoena, or court order, and (2) if there is a physical threat to anyone. In fact, regardless of the stated privacy policy, all ISPs must release the identity of their subscriber if presented with a valid subpoena.

The Electronic Communications Privacy Act

Consider two aspects of protection of privacy: the federal law and your own privacy policy. Federal law takes shape in the Electronic Communications Privacy Act (ECPA). The ECPA was initiated as an antiwiretapping act in response to the Watergate scandal and government eavesdropping on telephone conversations. As technology advanced, so did provisions of the ECPA so that it now covers all forms of digital communication, all people and businesses, and all unauthorized access to messages stored on computer systems. Is this a perfect document? Hardly. The biggest loopholes, according to experts, are in the nonvoice (e.g., e-mail) message transmissions, where guaranteed rights to privacy are somewhat loose. The ECPA is a major federal law covering electronic privacy. Other provisions for privacy for online systems and their users exist at the state level; these rights, however, differ greatly from state to state.

In addition to federal and state law, consider the formation of your own company privacy policy. General principles can be drawn from the Organization for Economic Cooperation and Development (OECD) in 1980 which presented the following privacy guidelines:

- *Openness.* Obtain data lawfully and fairly with knowledge and consent of subject.
- *Data quality.* Data should be relevant to purpose of use, up-to-date, and accurate.
- *Specificity of purpose.* Purpose of data collection should be stated when data are collected.
- *Use limitation.* Disclose data only with subject's consent or by legal authority.
- *Security.* Use reasonable safeguards to protect personal data from access, use, or disclosure.
- *Disclosure.* Disclose policy changes, nature of data held, and who controls it.
- *Individual participation.* Individuals should be able to determine whether relevant data about them is held, and review, change, correct or challenge it in a reasonable manner.
- *Accountability.* There should be some requirement to comply with these measures.

Company Privacy Policies

E-commerce company privacy policies should incorporate general considerations for all users, and special provisions related to children. A privacy policy should include the following general information for all users:

- A description of how data is collected and used.
- A standard way to choose *not* to provide data or permit data to be shared.
- A description of the procedure for users to request and update data.

Special provisions related to children should include the following:

- A notice that children should check with parents before participating in certain activities.
- Instructions and disclosure written at the vocabulary level of the targeted children's age.
- Clear notice to children that this is a *sale*.
- Instructions that children must get parental permission before they "click here" to order.
- Provisions for a parent or child to cancel any online order.

- Notice to children and parents about what information is being collected from children online and how it will be used.
- Notice that children must have parental permission before answering any questions, with encouragement to only use screen names, not real names.
- Reasonable efforts to obtain parental permission whenever e-mail is solicited from a child, with the opportunity for a parent to choose to discontinue e-mails at any time.

■ Security Policies

Your business decisions about who should be allowed to access specific company information are fundamental to forming your e-commerce system security policy (see Figure 10.3). Without a written security policy, you cannot be confident your site will be secure. What's allowed on your network? The security policy is not a technical document, but it is the basis from which technical security guidelines can be written.

Your high level analysis of security policy considerations will then be translated into a detailed process of identifying specific names, codes, and addresses—all of which are needed to implement your security policy.

Figure 10.3 Examples of Security Policy Considerations

Access Levels	Permission	Privilege	Item/Information
Who?	Is allowed	access	Internet Web sites
Executives	Is not allowed	no access	company e-mail
Managers		exchange	Internet e-mail
Human resources department		change	personnel files
Accounting department		delete	budgets
All employees		read only	company Web site
System administrators		modify	
Consumers			
Field reps			

■ Security Problems and Solutions

The following security problems and solutions will be addressed in this chapter:

- *Client software*—Java, Java applets, JavaScript, ActiveX, and push technology, which may create new opportunities for hackers
- *Virus protection and control*—considerations for everyday personal computer use and corporations
- *Cryptography*—plaintext, ciphertext, cryptographic algorithm, and key
- *Encryption technology*—including symmetric and asymmetric key encryption
- *Digital certificates and certification authorities*—to verify digital signatures
- *Firewalls*—restricting access to intranets and extranets
- *Text encryption algorithms*—secure socket layer (SSL), pretty good privacy (PGP), secure MIME (SMIME), and secure HTTP (SHTTP)
- *Security protocols*—serving different but complementary purposes, including SSL, secure electronic transaction (SET), and IP security protocol and Internet key exchange (IPSec-IKE)
- *VPNs*—virtual private networks to protect your data

Which security options should be implemented and when? Remember the seven layers of communications protocol—application, presentation, session, transport, network, data link, and physical? Security protocols are used at different layers in this hierarchy. Some technologies are designed to provide security at the network level, while other technologies work at the transaction level, or even at your own personal computer. A combination of procedures will provide the most comprehensive protection for your business.

The following paragraphs cover security options in further detail. Figure 10.4 outlines some of the fundamental components of security.

Client Software

We don't tend to think of simple Web pages and e-mail as threatening, but the truth is that the first break-ins to any system can occur at the very simplest level. Small problem programs can be embedded as attachments to e-mail messages or embedded in applets, the mini-applications that add interactivity to Web sites. It doesn't matter if most of your system is a fortress if you leave the front entrance wide open. The following items affect everyone who uses the Internet. The significance increases for companies engaged in e-commerce.

Figure 10.4 Internet Security Protocols

Security issues cover the gamut from concern about virus protection for personal computers to prevention of corruption of data at the network level.

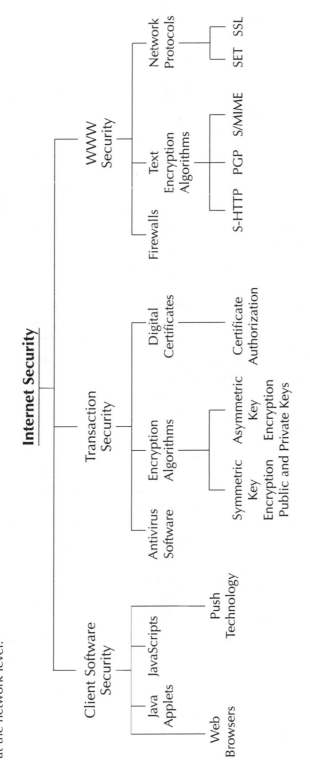

Web browsers. The most well-known browsers are Microsoft's Internet Explorer and Netscape Navigator. Web browsers make it simple to download and run software from anywhere. The problem is that software we download, which we assume is safe, can contain "active content" that could trigger a virus on our system. Active content is a collection of technologies that are used to add spark, interest, and interactivity to Web site designs. Java Applets, Java-Script, ActiveX, and push technology are among the most well-known active content technologies. But active content alone won't cause a Web browser to decrease a user's security. Plug-ins installed on a Web browser or downloaded from a vendor may also contain flaws that can affect security. Plug-ins, which are usually needed to view complex graphics files or listen to audio files, are like interpreters that enhance the viewing of multimedia presentations. Finally, there may be weaknesses in the browser software itself, although when these holes are discovered the response to correct the problem occurs swiftly.

Java applets. The Sun Microsystems, Inc., programming language Java is a multiplatform language, which means it can be run anywhere, regardless of where it was programmed. Java programs written in Unix can run on Windows, for example. Java programs, called Java applets, are small portable programs with a strictly defined set of functions. Java applets, JavaScript, and ActiveX go well beyond the limitations of HTML (the original Web programming language) to create features that appeal to most users and e-commerce businesses. Customized buttons and pull-down menus, rich graphics interfaces, and other user-friendly features to enhance Web site designs can be created easily with these programs.

The creators of Java quickly realized the potential security risks of these mobile programs and devised the "Java sandbox" as a security model. The sandbox restricts Java applets from gaining access to any surrounding system resources. It prevents Java applets from reading or writing on any file systems, permitting applets to work only within a restricted area. Unfortunately, hackers have found ways to manipulate Java by moving quickly, evading security checks, and invading corporate computers.

JavaScript. JavaScript, developed by the Netscape Corporation, is a scripting language. Scripting languages are more powerful than HTML, but are not quite as complex as Java applets. They can be used to improve the look of a Web page or browser interface, write short programs, or send messages to Java applets and ActiveX controls. News flashes and stock quotes that appear on running electronic tickers are examples of JavaScript displays.

Security holes were detected in JavaScript, and attempts have been made to patch them. Not all problems have been addressed. Experts have stated that the problem with JavaScript from the start was that security was never built into the original design, unlike Java applets' sandbox and ActiveX protection.

ActiveX. Microsoft's ActiveX is not a new technology, but a repackaging of existing technologies. ActiveX programs are called "controls," and accomplish many of the same things as Java applets. Controls can be written in any number of standard programming languages, such as Visual C or Visual Basic, which makes ActiveX a popular choice for programmers. ActiveX enables programmers to work in the language with which they are most familiar.

The danger of ActiveX lies in its power. Controls can ruin files, spread viruses, break through firewalls, and more. Microsoft was aware of the potential misuse of ActiveX controls and worked to prevent security holes from the onset. In partnership with VeriSign, Microsoft set up Authenticode. With Authenticode, all software developers "sign" their software. A certification authority checks out software developers who want to release ActiveX programs to make sure that they are legitimate. If they are, they will be given a software publisher's certificate. Authenticode cannot prevent problems created by malicious software developers with impeccable credentials.

Push technology. Web users have traditionally "pulled" data to their computer using a Web search engine, unless they know which site to go to directly. Searches often end up accumulating more useless than useful information; separating excellent content from the junk can be tedious. Push technology changes all this. Instead of searching for information, users can subscribe to a service that will do the search for them, filter information, and offer only relevant and high quality information. PointCast Network (www.pointcast.com) "pushes" stock market reports, news updates, entertainment highlights, and sports scores to its Web subscribers at regularly scheduled intervals. Both Microsoft Internet Explorer and Netscape Communicator have added push technology in their browsers.

The security risk with push technology is that the technology writes directly to a user's disk, in effect opening the door for security violations and privacy exploitations. While no news headlines have highlighted push technology as a major security threat, it creates the same type of potential risk as active content applications if it is abused.

Virus Protection and Control

Most computer viruses are spread through some direct action on the part of a user. For example, if you insert an infected disk or file into your computer you will contract the same virus. If you download an infected Internet file, you'll also be a target. You will find a warning appears before you download, designed to remind you that you should always know the source of your information before you accept files over the Internet. Finally, an infected file could be transmitted via e-mail. In this case, by opening an infected e-mail transmittal, you unknowingly become an accomplice in your own infection.

When the Melissa computer virus struck the global community of Internet users, it created shock waves reaching from the smallest home office personal computer to the largest corporate headquarters. Within only three days, Melissa infected almost 100,000 computers, according to the *New York Times*. At its worst, the virus clogged corporate e-mail servers and forced a shutdown of e-mail systems at DuPont, Lockheed Martin, Honeywell Inc., Compaq Computer Corp. and the North Dakota state government. Although Melissa did not prove to be fatal, the virus sent chills through professionals who instantly realized the implications of this insidious problem. An FBI investigation was launched immediately.

What was so threatening about Melissa? Three aspects of this virus were particularly disturbing: the sneaky manner of introduction, the high speed of transmittal, the exponential rate of replication, and the invasion of supposedly "safe" institutions. Melissa was introduced by e-mail messages labeled "Important message from" with the sender's name in the "subject" line. The message itself was harmless; the virus was stashed in the attached document. When the attachment was opened, Melissa took over and sent e-mails to the first 50 addresses in the recipient's address book.

Here come the Men in Black. While the FBI refused to comment, the rumor network passed along stories of suspects and situations that were being investigated. Posting of the virus was tracked to Scott Steinmetz, a civil engineer with a clean slate who claimed his AOL e-mail account had been ripped off. And in fact it was. We thought at least AOL was safe. Then the plot thickened. The transactions attributed to Steinmetz were initiated with his own password from his own AOL account that had been broken into to start the spread of the virus. This bordered on sacrilegious.

Virus cures can generally be circulated very rapidly, so for a virus to reach as many computers as Melissa it had to travel at an extraordinary pace with the unwitting assistance of a huge number of individuals. That's the second truly creepy aspect of this virus. Each time it moved, it spread simultaneously to 50 more Internet addresses. The "subject" of the e-mail transmission led recipients to believe that the e-mail correspondence was generated by someone they knew. Imagine how devastating the results could be if the same set of steps were used to transmit a fatal virus to corporate networks, individual computer systems, or personal computer users.

Is it *ever* possible to embrace technological advances and simultaneously hold the virus-generators aside? Absolutely yes. The technology available to protect you is simple, inexpensive, and accessible. *Don't miss it.*

Antivirus systems. An antivirus system for a personal computer costs an average of $50. Corporate system rates generally run at about $15 per machine. Updates cost about $3. When a high-profile virus like Melissa strikes, updates to existing anti-virus software and brand new software packages are available almost instantaneously. Often these updates and new software can be down-loaded from the Internet. So if you are out of touch with current events (with your nose too deep in your business to read the daily newspapers and follow television news broadcasts), you may miss the instant announcements of Internet trouble and miss the fast, economical solutions that are offered at no cost to Internet users in the aftermath of any classic infection scenario. *Pay attention.*

Precautions. To withstand computer viruses, take the following precautions consistently:

- Use antivirus software.
- Update your virus software at least once a month, and whenever a major virus becomes widespread.
- If you don't use the macros in Microsoft Word and Excel, disable macros in the programs.
- *Don't take this instruction lightly.* It will save you infinite problems, with no loss to the efficiency of your system.

Dozens of antivirus software systems are available, including Guard Dog, VirusScan, ViruSafe, Sweep, and eSafe Protect. Antivirus vendors like California companies Symantec and Network Associates, Inc., respond quickly to large-scale viruses with teams of analysts and specialists.

Cryptography

Cryptography is the study of techniques of secret writing, such as codes and ciphers. In terms of Web security, cryptography makes it possible to keep data private, to check if an individual is really who he claims to be, to ensure the authenticity of transaction requests, and to determine if someone really received (or failed to receive) certain data.

Cryptography has four parts: plaintext (the original text of the message or document); ciphertext (the original message after it has been encoded); cryptographic algorithm (the mathematical formula to translate plaintext into ciphertext and back again); and a key (to decipher messages). Video, sound, and software can be changed with cryptography just as easily as plain text. A good cryptographic algorithm is difficult to "crack" or break the secret code because it contains no visible patterns or connections to the original message.

Encryption technology. Encryption is a method of scrambling data before it is transmitted so that it is only readable by authorized individuals who know the secret to unscramble. Encryption, or secret coding, techniques were once the sole domain of the military, intelligence services, and law enforcement agencies. Today encryption technology is essential for all e-commerce transactions, serving as a critical factor to achieve confidentiality, but also supporting authentication, authorization, integrity, and nonrepudiation services (those five requirements listed in Figure 10.1).

If you have ever downloaded an e-mail attachment that looked like alphabet soup, a series of seemingly unrelated letters and symbols, then you've seen an encrypted message that was not decrypted. Encryption is used at several levels:

- At the network level, encryption algorithms delineate the rules. Encryption algorithms are mathematical formulas that explain how to encode (encrypt, or scramble) and how to decode (decrypt, or unscramble).
- At the transaction level, encryption technology operates with secret "keys." There can be private keys and public keys.
- Symmetric (one pair of keys) and asymmetric (a public and a private set of keys) key encryption ensure confidentiality.
- Digital certificates (or digital signatures, which then must be authorized) also use this key approach.

The way in which various security technologies are interwoven and used interdependently can be confusing. It's important to remember that no technology stands alone; these techniques support each other.

Symmetric key encryption. With this technology, the same secret key is used to encode and decode ("encrypt" and "decrypt") information. Data encryption standard (DES) is the most popular symmetric key encryption algorithm. (Translation: DES is the most popular set of mathematical formulas and rules for coding a single pair of secret keys that can be used to scramble and unscramble data so that nobody but your friend can read it.) A user encrypts data with a key, which in turn is used by someone else for decryption, i.e., to read the information. In theory, no one else could read this information because no one else would have the private key to unlock the message. The tricky part here is to get a copy of the key to both parties without some unauthorized party jumping on the key. The transmission of the key needs as much security as the transmission of the message.

Asymmetric key encryption. This technology uses a private key and a public key, two keys for double security. It's almost like double-locking your front door. The public key is used to encrypt; the private key (known only to the key owner) is used to decrypt. A popular asymmetric key encryption algorithm is RSA, named for its inventors, Ronald Rivest, Adi Shamir, and Leonard Adelman. Anyone can transmit a message with the public key, but only the private key can turn the message back into its original form. The RSA algorithm is also used for digital signatures. Private key and public key algorithms use different key lengths. Key length refers to the number of characters (bits) in a code. Private key lengths can be as short as 56 bits and as long as 128 bits. Public key lengths range from 384 bits to 2304 bits. Longer keys take more time to process; however, longer keys are also more difficult for hackers to break the code. The time and cost to break a code of 80 bits, for example, is exponentially far greater than to break a code of 56 bits. For highly sensitive data, it is important to use an encryption algorithm and key length that are extremely difficult to crack.

Digital Certificates (Digital Signatures)

Digital certificates are electronic signatures that verify that the individual sending a secure message is really the sender, not an imposter. Using the RSA encryption algorithm, an individual can sign a digital document by decrypting it with a private key. Someone else who knows the individual's public key and the message content can verify that the signature is from the right person by encrypting the signed message. For example, I can send a private message to you by this sequence of encryptions: (1) I scramble the message with my private key; (2) then I scramble the message again with my public key; (3) you then unscramble the message with your private key; and (4) then you unscramble it again with my public key.

If the individual signing the digital document is *not* who he or she claims to be, that person will be caught (in theory) because he or she does not know the private key. Digital certificates are issued in four different levels of classification: Class 1 verifies name and e-mail address; Class 2 adds checks on driver's license, Social Security number, and date of birth; Class 3 includes credit checks (using a company like Equifax); and Class 4 verifies an individual's position in an organization (details for this are not final yet). The fees for digital certificates vary with the degree of verification involved. Higher class verifications incur higher fees and also provide strong confirmation of identify. To ensure that imposters cannot slip through the system, certification authorities are used.

Certification authority. Certification authorities vouch for individuals and businesses. Certification authorities perform the same function as a notary would for a paper document. They verify that you are who you say you are and that your signature is valid. Vendors like CyberTrust, VeriSign Inc., Nortel, and Entrust Technologies, Ltd., act as certification authorities and issue digital certificates. Digital certificates are given built-in expiration dates. Certificates can be revoked by a certification authority if they are lost, stolen, or a person's position in a company changes. A certificate revocation list (CRL) identifies certificates that are not valid.

Firewalls

Firewalls are like digital gatekeepers, providing security at the network level. Firewalls protect private networks from unsupervised access (although they cannot protect against viruses). They allow you to control access to your data. Firewalls are programs that are located in servers' computers, at the networks' edge. Typically firewalls separate a business' local area network (LAN) from the Internet. They can also protect data between the company's intranets by separating and controlling access between internal corporate networks. Firewalls analyze data packets and determine who has the right to enter the private network. Security policies are enforced at the firewall, where packets of data flowing in and out of a corporation are analyzed and the question "To see or not to see" is answered.

Firewalls separate intranets from extranets, a private network from a public network. Servers can be split, allowing some (but not all) information to be accessible to some (but not all) individuals. Everything is done electronically. This separation enables corporate employees to share information over the intranet, while not making this information available over the extranet to field representatives, suppliers and distributors. For an illustration of how a server can be split, see Figure 10.5.

Firewalls use a "screening router" to block packets of information from being transmitted unless the owner gives the okay. Firewalls also include a "proxy server" which handles the flow of communication between the private and

Figure 10.5 Where's the Firewall?

201

Secure
Commerce on
the Internet

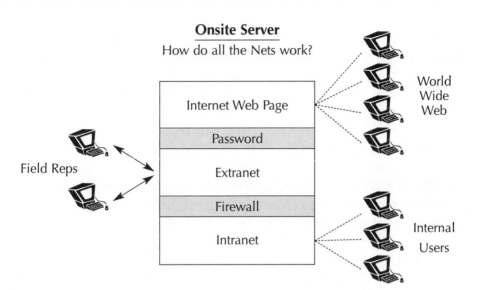

Onsite Server

How do all the Nets work?

Internet Web Page

Password

Extranet

Firewall

Intranet

Field Reps

World Wide Web

Internal Users

Source: Reprinted with permission from the University of Scranton Electronic Commerce Center.

public networks. Passwords also can be used to isolate specific sections of a server, but firewalls are the most difficult for hackers to break through. In general, the security offered by a firewall is only compromised when a company configuration is not set up correctly and there is some kind of "back door" entrance to the corporate network.

Smaller companies who choose to have their Web pages hosted offsite will not specifically select the procedure to be used for passwords and firewalls; however, they should select a host based on a careful analysis of the security procedures the host implements.

The biggest objection to firewalls is that they do not prevent attacks from people within a company. They also require an extensive amount of time to manage, since all information packets and the flow of who-can-access-what-data must be manually defined before it can be automatically implemented. Firewalls usually have to be built on-site.

Text Encryption Algorithms

Security standards for the Internet cover connections and applications. In general, secure socket layer (SSL) is designed to provide secure communication on the Internet, primarily for Web applications. Secure HTTP (S-HTTP), Secure MIME (S/MIME), and Pretty Good Privacy (PGP) are designed for applications: S-HTTP for Web applications; S/MIME and PGP for e-mail applications. Secure Electronic Transactions (SET) is the most advanced, providing security only for electronic commerce transactions.

PGP. Pretty Good Privacy (PGP) protects e-mails and files using RSA public key encryption. PGP is used as a plug-in to standard e-mail programs or on its own. The problem with PGP is that keys don't expire, so if there is a problem with a key everyone has to be notified.

S/MIME. The secure MIME is used to encrypt e-mail messages in order to send files with attachments over the Internet. S/MIME uses RSA encryption and digital signatures.

S–HTTP. Secure HTTP was designed to work with Web protocols only, and is less favored—to the point of being almost obscure—than SSL, a more flexible encryption tool.

Security Protocol

The most popular security protocols are SSL, secure electronic transaction (SET), and IP security protocol and Internet key exchange (IPSec-IKE). Although each of these protocols are different, they can work together since they each accomplish a different purpose. Security protocols are transparent to the user, but they can make a system run less efficiently, primarily because of the processes involved in encryption. Asymmetric encryption, in particular, takes time and can create system bottlenecks. On the other hand, with proper use of security protocols, business owners and consumers can engage in e-commerce, transfer sensitive data, and send personal communication over the Internet without breach of security.

Secure socket layer (SSL). This is a client/server protocol that can be used in any network application, in addition to the Web. With SSL, the server must prove its identity (authentication). Proving the client's identity, however, is optional. After the client checks the server's identity (and vice versa, if the option is chosen), a symmetric key is established. Next, the client and server can begin the exchange of data. Messages will be checked to be sure that the message was not messed with (integrity). For a summary of how SSL works, see Figure 10.6.

Figure 10.6 Secure Socket Layer (Transport Layer Protocol)

- Client initiates session.
- Server responds to client—establishes capabilities.
- Server and client exchange certificates.
- Client generates key = Secure data

For example, as a consumer I can type in my credit card number to make a purchase on a Web site. The browser uses SSL to do a background check on the merchant's digital signature. Is this who I think it is? (Is this truly the merchant I think I'm buying from?) My credit card number will then be scrambled and sent to the merchant securely, without interception.

Here's the catch: If I were making this purchase in person, the salesperson would have the additional verification that this was valid by checking the signature on my credit card to be sure it matched the signature on my sales slip. There can be physical verification that I am really the cardholder, authorized to use this credit card. SSL, however, does not require a digital certificate from me to make sure that I am an authorized credit card user. As a result, this security method can leave the merchant open to the possibility of fraud.

In secure transactions, the lock symbol will be displayed to let the users know that a connection has been secured with SSL to ensure security of payment information. For an illustration of the "lock" in an SSL secured transaction, see Figure 10.7.

Secure Electronic Transaction (SET). Secure electronic transaction is a step above secure socket layer. MasterCard and VISA led a consortium of

Figure 10.7 The lock symbol indicates that a connection has been secured using SSL.

companies to push for the widespread adoption of SET for more secure transactions. They had zero tolerance for credit card fraud and believed that SET was a better solution. The protocols for SET involve four participants: the customer (the credit card holder), the e-retailer (the merchant), the bank that issued the credit card, and the merchant's bank. Credit card information remains confidential throughout each purchase (and refund) because the data is encrypted as it is passed from the customer to the bank. SET performs extensive signature verification, a big advantage over SSL. In addition, with SET, merchants only receive encoded versions of credit card information. Hackers are less interested in files of encrypted card numbers that would have to be cracked than with an easy list of plaintext.

Some objections to SET arise because the time to complete the encryption process is long, and during busy periods this can be a problem. However, with SET e-tailers can decide to hold their transactions until night and run them in a batch. The disadvantage of this approach is that the consumer does not get immediate feedback about whether or not their purchase has been approved by the bank.

American Express, Visa, and MasterCard prefer SET, but have agreed to accept SSL for secure credit card transactions for e-commerce.

Figure 10.8   Secure Electronic Transmission

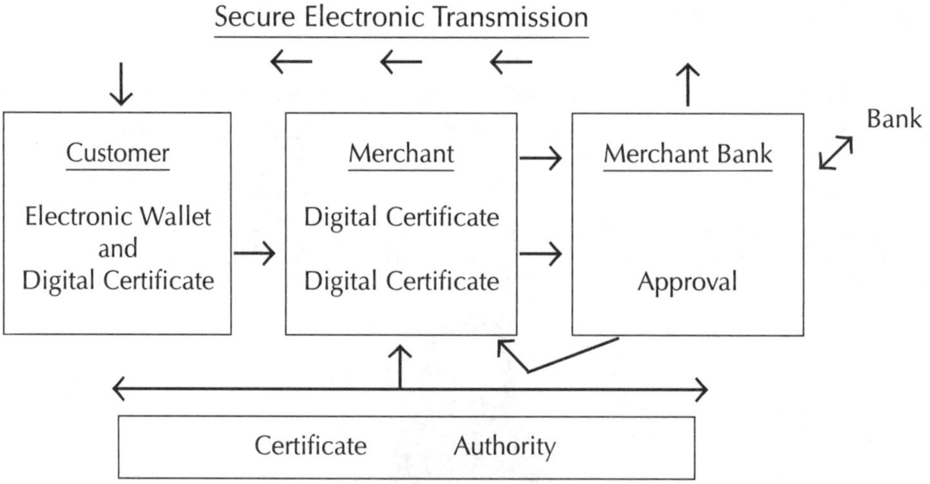

Source: Reprinted with permission from the University of Scranton Electronic Commerce Resource Center.

Virtual Private Networks (VPNs)

Over 90 percent of businesses are using VPNs. Virtual private network technology is a way of running a private data network on service provider networks. In other words, the technology uses public data networks to deliver service that equates to private leased-line networks. At first glance, VPNs have an advantage over private leased lines because they cost less. On the other hand, businesses need to carefully assess the actual total cost to use a VPN. The total cost to any company includes the ability to connect all their users and a guarantee of tight security. Users can include telecommuters, offsite workers, customers, corporate headquarters personnel, suppliers, branch offices, and more.

In addition, VPNs raise many of the same security issues that concern private leased lines. Every business that invests time and money in a VPN also wants complete assurance of security, and confidence that unauthorized intruders cannot access confidential information and resources. The goals of data security and integrity remain the same. A VPN therefore requires the same additional security provisions of network monitoring, a secure socket layer (SSL) interface, and IPSec (Internet protocol security) encryption of transported information.

■ Web Site Disclaimers

Legal notices, use or access restrictions, and disclaimers should be clearly identified on every Web site. These notices should be displayed on the home page or readily accessible from the home page. Notices include the following:

- *Disclaimers associated with site content.* It should be clear that information on this site does not imply warranties as to accuracy, appropriateness for a specific purpose, or timeliness. Disclaimer of liability for damages associated with reader reliance on information from this site or other linked sites.
- *User privacy.* This notice lets visitors know what type of information is being collected about them, the use and distribution of this information, and specific information regarding children and parental releases (see discussion in the "Company Privacy Policies" section earlier in this chapter for further details).
- *Copyright and trademark notices.* Copyright designations should be identified for content provided on the site. Trademarks should also be identified (including licensing arrangements).

- *Restrictions on use of content.* The most common restriction is on commercial use of content. Most sites permit noncommercial use of content as long as the copyright notice is displayed and the proper credit is given to the Web site owner, designer, or both.
- *Release associated with user input.* E-mail and other messages sent by site visitors can be used by the owner of the site for any purpose without compensation or written permission of the provider.
- *Restrictions on links and framing.* Site owners can prohibit the creation of links to their site without their approval. In this case, instructions about obtaining approval should be provided.
- *Revocation of access authorization.* The site owner can revoke access and use authorizations given to visitors at any time.

11

The Cast of Characters and Their Roles

■ How to Select Your Support Team

For a business to stay on the bleeding edge of Internet technology, it will have to eliminate the do-it-yourself mentality. The Internet industry changes so quickly that unless you are totally immersed in new technology developments on a day-to-day basis, you're falling behind. Rent a geek. If you want to look professional and operate efficiently, introduce a site that incorporates the most up-to-date technological gimmicks, and maintain a support team.

It is difficult to stay on top of your Web site and on top of your company at the same time, unless the Web site *is* your company. Even if you decide to use your service provider and their template approach to setting up your e-commerce activities, you should consider having some in-house system support. This applies to small business owners, too. Small business owners, who usually empty the trash one minute and negotiate contracts with senior executives the next, often balk at hiring for any task they think they can handle themselves. That's when they get in over their heads. Unless you are truly technically trained and have more time than you know what to do with, consider getting help. A staff member who also assumes other job duties and responsibilities can serve as a Web site coordinator.

When you are hiring an individual to work for you, look for someone who has kept current with new technology. High-tech business owner Joan Leavey of Computer Insights, Inc., recommends, "My ideal candidate would be someone with up-to-the-minute training who isn't afraid of the computer." People who have complete ease and comfort with the Internet, use it frequently for research and shopping, and have the most up-to-date training will be your best bet.

When you hire a company to develop and maintain your site for you, go for the same level of reference checks that you would use if you were bringing in a new hire. "You are really outsourcing part of your sales," said Leavey, "so you want to know as much as possible." Obtain at least three or four company references from anyone you are considering hiring. A nontechnical business owner can easily be overwhelmed by jargon and buzzwords.

Look for a company that often engages in strategic partnerships with other businesses. Companies that form strategic partnerships (also referred to as strategic alliances or joint ventures) on a regular basis are more likely to understand precisely how successful teams work together. Sharing information and maintaining open channels of communication are critical to the management of larger projects, and a company that has experience partnering with others will recognize this.

Computer Insights, Inc., for example, frequently partners with other firms to take on larger jobs than they might be able to handle alone. CII specializes in coding and back-end processing. Their clients include major corporations such as AT&T and Lucent Technologies, as well as start-up companies. They work the full gamut of technology projects. CII also handles behind the scenes functions for Web sites. But they are not artists, photographers, illustrators, graphic artists, or authors. As a result, they seek partnering arrangements with graphics design companies whenever client projects involve complex photography or illustrations. Web catalogs, for example, demand as much attention to details about the "look" of the pages as they do on the programming.

Companies that often form strategic alliances to take on larger projects know the importance of sharing information among partnering companies and enforcing the highest standards of quality. They are also well connected and well networked—from the human perspective, that is. These team-oriented companies may be a safer bet than companies that primarily work solo.

Figure 11.1   Critical Criteria for Selecting a Vendor

Find individuals who are on top of the latest technology.

Check for e-commerce expertise, not general programming experience.

Look for flexible contract terms, quality, and reasonable pricing.

Look for companies who frequently partner with other companies.

Get references from at least three or four companies with whom they have done business.

Check out their reputations.

View a live demonstration of other sites they have worked on.

Don't let anyone snow you—technology should make sense.

Never make a decision about hiring an individual or a company without seeing real demonstrations of how their ideas work. Do *not* rely only on a written proposal report for this information. Get a live demonstration. Examine the work they have done for others. Can they make you look better than your competitors? If not, hire one of their competitors.

Outsourcing will be a dangerous proposition for any company that does not have its own act together. A clear strategic plan, with specific goals and objectives, will help to keep your business and your vendor on track. These objectives should govern the contents of the contract established with a vendor or vendors, and guide decisions made throughout implementation of the site. Open communication with the staff directly involved in your project will be critical. And the boss, whether the owner of a small consulting firm or a senior executive at a larger company, should be accessible and informed about your venture.

Following are more details about the individual members of a comprehensive e-tail project.

Figure 11.2   Managing the Outsourced Project

Review goals and objectives with the vendor.

Define responsibilities and finalize an action plan.

Structure a contract that covers contingencies.

Specify terms of personnel assignments and changes.

Ensure the owner/senior executive is accessible and aware.

■ Web Professionals

No Web site can remain static. As your business changes, so will your site. But that's not all. With the data you gather from visitors and consumers at your site, you'll be obliged to use what you've learned to continuously improve its functionality, efficiency, and simplicity. And to keep consumers coming back, you'll need to keep your content fresh, your product descriptions current, and your interactive components lively.

Outsourcing, using the template approach offered by portals or servers, and opening up shop in a cybermall are fast and relatively inexpensive start-up alternatives. When a business is ready to expand, growth options may include outsourcing more customized design and maintaining a private server. At the most complex level, doing the work in-house is feasible for high-tech companies and major corporations.

Whatever your choice, you will be dependent on a diverse cast of characters who will help you achieve your objectives. The quality and frequency of your interactions with this motley crew will buoy or sink your site.

Most outsourcing falls into the information technologies (IT) category, including network consulting and support, hosting, e-commerce services, application development, and security. Additional opportunities for outsourcing are in the marketing and sales category. Marketing support services include market research, product packaging, branding research, and advertising consulting.

Network Consulting and Support

Network consulting activities (which include determining how to set up e-commerce systems, handling high traffic volumes, and meeting your strategic goals) are handled by both major corporate consulting firms and small business consultants alike. Included in this repertoire are all the usual suspects of consulting: Andersen Consulting, Ernst and Young, Unisys.

Network support activities include technology functions like help desks, desktop management, client-server management, and maintenance. Systems engineers with expertise in information management and networking in distributed systems handle these activities. They combine voice, video, and data communications into a seamless package. AT&T Solutions, Compaq Services, and Hewlett-Packard are examples of companies that provide network support.

Web Server Hosting

Web hosting services should provide high-performance, high-bandwidth, highly reliable, secure, and scalable Web sites. This is the company you will depend on the most to keep your Web site up and running, even during peak loads. *Internet Business* magazine evaluates vendors and contractors and lists both the large and the up-and-coming companies who provide the full gamut of Internet-related products and services. Web server hosting companies that made this list include Concentric, DIGEX, GTE Internetworking, and UUNET.

E-Commerce Services

E-commerce services provide the nuts and bolts of assembling a catalog and putting it online, streamlining interactions with customers to achieve the ever-popular "one click" handling online orders, and every activity connected with paying, shipping, and taxing the order. Key players in this arena include Open Market, BroadVision, IBM Global Services, Pandesic, and NexGen SI. These companies often subcontract portions of the work to other vendors (such as CyberCash for payment processing) but take the leading role in project management.

Application Development

Web application development companies usually combine features from strategy through design and technology. These firms help integrate software packages as well as develop customized applications, looking at business use of all communications and commerce tools. Examples include USWeb, Sapient, and Proxicom, all recommended by *Internet Business* magazine.

Security

Complete network security solutions are a combination of processes, as discussed in Chapter 10. Security can be part of a contract delivered by an e-commerce support company or handled separately, depending on the scope of your project. Security assessment, virtual private networks, Web security, firewalls—these components and more work quietly behind the scenes to keep you in business. Secure Computing, Denver Technological Laboratories, and Security Risk Management are a few providers.

Marketing Support

Cost-effective, tangible results are a goal of your marketing strategy as much as any other component of your Web site. Marketing support can be handled by a single firm that assumes responsibility for all parts of the whole, or subcontracted to different specialists. In-house marketing efforts may be simpler to manage and maintain a consistent look and feel than outsourced, but still demand communication and coordination among all the staff. Components of marketing support include market research, product marketing, branding research, and advertising.

Market research. More and more small businesses opt to handle market research in-house using resources available on the Internet to gather data. No doubt this is a great way to start and build a foundation. Larger firms make market research an ongoing activity, knowing that if a company is not moving forward, it's really falling behind. When the process becomes too time-consuming, or begins to take the business owner too far away from managing the company, it's better to hire a specialist.

Focus groups can be a time-saving method of gathering new information when basic research yields conflicting or inclusive results, when a company needs to measure reactions, or when very detailed information is required. Market research firms and independent consultants can run focus groups as part of a larger contract or as a one-time-only service.

Product marketing. Material that communicates information about your business and your products should look professional and refer back to your Web site. Graphic artists handle artwork and design, and if you find artwork you love it can be used on your printed materials as well as on your Web site. Check for how extensive the services of any firm are: Will they produce print-ready copy for you? Do they include printing services? Can they adapt your designs to multiple forms?

When you produce a product, packaging sells you. When you provide a service, image sells. Your image is your "package," and it's worth the money to create a positive one. The graphics that represent your business, online and offline, make a strong statement about your business.

Branding research. Many marketing consulting firms will offer assistance in creating a brand or measuring the effectiveness of an existing brand. Some firms specialize in this niche. Branding research may even influence the selection of your domain name, if you don't already have one.

When you select a domain name, which is the primary vehicle for people to find your Web site, it should be memorable. It should connect with what you are selling on the Web. For existing companies with a strong brand appeal, the transition is common sense. But existing companies that have not reached brand recognition should consider using their transition to e-tail as a new opportunity to build a stronger brand. Through branding research firms, businesses can test new names and determine the best image to meet their online and offline sales goals.

Advertising consulting. How do you determine the most appropriate media vehicles for your company? At the basic level, online advertising includes at least four different types of ads: banner ads, classified ads, paid listings, and sponsorships. Advertising consulting companies specialize in media planning (where to advertise), media buying (paying for the ads at the right time, in the right place, at the right rates), execution (creating the ads, graphic arts, multimedia), and campaign management and optimization ("How'm I doin'?"). Most ad firms offer the option of selecting full-service or select programs when you work with them.

Advertising agencies that specialize in Internet companies offer extra appeal. These firms have more experience in this relatively new field, have the best research, and can usually recommend more diverse solutions. They also have contacts at the major ad networks, search engines, and major Web sites that can result in lower rates and more flexibility. Online advertising companies offer advice for campaign design, search engine optimization, targeted e-mail, banner buys, content sponsorships, and press release distribution services, to name a few functions.

Traditional offline advertising should support the online campaign to the extent feasible within budget limitations. Can your budget afford advertising on network television or cable, radio, print at the national or local level? Media planning, buying, and execution require special handling on a limited budget. Additional functions, which can be handled by an ad agency or promotions specialist, include: special events, trade show appearances, speaking engagements, sponsor procurement, sales promotion items, incentive program design, and cross-promotion.

■ Bootstrapping

How can a start-up business enter the world of e-commerce on a tight budget? It would seem that the use of all these consultants could cost a fortune. Do most small businesses hire all of these types of services? No. Savvy small business owners are selective about what functions are outsourced based on their individual experience, knowledge, training, and time.

The most common start-up approach for businesses with limited financial resources is to have the Web site hosted by an Internet service provider (ISP). As discussed earlier, a business can elect to have the ISP handle Web site design (using standardized prototypes), maintenance, security, and credit card payments, among other services. Fees are arranged on a monthly basis, with contractual terms subject to annual renewal. For a more detailed description of options, see Chapter 12.

12

Products and Technologies

■ The Phenomenal Rate of Change

The first online sellers were responsible for developing most of their own technology in-house. Businesses moving into electronic commerce today have a huge advantage over the pioneering companies. Now we have a proliferation of companies that offer Internet-related services, software, and other products. And the pressure is on to accelerate new product creation as growth in online selling breaks all previous speed records.

Technology advances met the challenge of keeping pace with advances in online sales in 1998. Among the winners were the following events:

- Java 2 platform and Enterprise JavaBeans specification were released by Sun Microsystems.
- Virtual private networks (VPN) became the new favorite of information technology managers as a way to cut costs on WAN and remote access.

- XML (eXtensible Markup Language) gained respectability and was incorporated into databases and application servers.

Early in 1999, announcements of technological paradigm shifts seemed to occur daily. For example:

- AT&T Corporation announced that it would begin a transition to packet switching, retooling its entire network.
- Microsoft announced the upcoming release of Biztalk, a new language that is designed to integrate business practices and e-commerce technologies. Many experts marveled that Microsoft finally woke up to e-commerce.

This chapter deals with the core components of electronic commerce systems and recommendations from technical pros. Note that whenever specific products and technologies are referenced, we run the risk of quickly becoming outdated. It is our hope that generic guidelines offered here will help you assemble the system architecture that will work best for you. Specific products and companies are mentioned as examples, not endorsements (lest better models supersede these after this book is published). Products and technologies discussed in this chapter include:

- *Network and communications solutions.* Technical advances enable faster transmission of data from all media, including video, voice and data. With less expensive and more widely available DSL (digital subscriber lines), ISDN (integrated services digital network) lines, the growth of cable, and the creation of new technology, high speed and high quality telecommunication solutions empower small businesses and major corporations.
- *Host companies and Internet service providers (ISPs).* The pressure is on to expand the features, capabilities, and range of services they offer, so watch out for more cybermalls and more corporate consolidations as little companies are absorbed by the big guys.
- *Internet software.* Electronic commerce software is more complicated than posting documents in HTML (hypertext markup language) format. The transactional systems used for e-tailing require specialized programs that are unique to Web sites that sell. Software to power Web sites has dramatically improved in a relatively short period.
- *Commerce suites.* Packaged commerce software offers any firm a way to get to market quickly. Dozens of vendors offer commerce software, and new releases are announced daily.

Workflow refers to the coordinated set of business activities that are carried out to meet business objectives. A total business workflow is a combination of human and computer processes, application programs, and database management systems.

Technology should enhance business processes, not restrict them. After careful definition of business functions to be performed, technology and products that support each function can be investigated. See Figure 12.1 for a list of some of the basic functions involved in processing customer orders.

What technology will support this series of functions? *Are you starting from scratch or building e-commerce into an existing workflow?* Your list of business functions and required characteristics will guide your selection of tools and vendors. See Figure 12.2. Also consider usage volume and traffic periods. Will you experience seasonal peaks or slow periods? To what degree? Will you be using intranets and extranets?

Figure 12.1   Your Business: Functions Required to Process Customer Orders

---

1. The customer accesses YourBusiness.com.
2. Check the customer out.
   - Determine if they have visited YourBusiness.com before.
   - Recognize return visitors and handle appropriately.
3. The customer accesses catalog, reviews products, and decides to buy.
   - Direct experienced customers to "Buy."
   - Present levels of catalog detail as requested by customer.
4. The customer completes order information and payment information.
5. Record data about this customer transaction in a separate database for analysis and interpretation, market analysis, etc.
6. Check inventory to see if the order can be filled.
7. Confirm status of order for the customer.
8. Complete payment authorization and send confirmation to the customer.
9. Pack order for shipping.
10. Process payment.
11. Ship order.
12. Send confirmation of shipping date to customer.
13. Handle customer inquiries, complaints, and communication.
14. Handle returns.

Figure 12.2   Some Functions and Characteristics Needed to Build Your E-tail Web Site

Functions Needed:

Simple Services
Customer authentication
Site design (templates, other)
Custom graphics
Custom order forms
"Wizard"-like help screens
Order processing
Payment processing
Order tracking
Feedback forms
Shipping capabilities
Links to other Web sites

Advanced E-Commerce
Full-featured catalog
Custom payment options
Shopping cart
Product level searching

Back-Office Functions
Customer service
Sales reports
Database integration
Database analysis
Site traffic statistics
Market analysis and research

Specific Technical Features
Secure site management
SSL encryption

Characteristics Required:

Scalability
Backup
Redundant Internet access
Great design and graphics capability
Availability
Interoperability
Security
Reliability
Support for multimedia information
Order maintenance for the Web merchant
Speed

The size and scope of your business impacts the extent to which you can take advantage of pre-packaged combinations of software. Does your company handle all aspects of your product (e.g., manufacturing, warehouse, distribution)? Do you use multiple suppliers and vendors, and if so, where are they located? See Figure 12.3 for a basic illustration of the components of your e-tail business.

Figure 12.3   Your E-tail Business Components

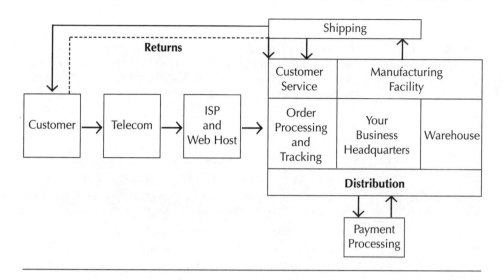

■ Setting Up an E-Commerce System

The first and most significant question is, What is your budget? Your financial capability constrains your design and implementation choices. What are your limits? Today there are alternatives for every size of business, for any range of products and services, and for every budget. Even if you are a start-up company with 50 products to sell, you can find a low-cost e-commerce system solution. As your financial reserves increase, you can make the transition step by step to more sophisticated technology as your budget permits.

The degree of customization and comprehensiveness varies in accordance with the cost of any e-commerce system. Generally, there are three categories, according to Joan Leavey of Computer Insights, Inc. Figure 12.4 features a brief summary of what your company can achieve with e-commerce systems, from the sublime to the simple.

Building a Comprehensive System: $300,000 Plus

These Web sites involve more than selling online. The largest and most expensive systems cover your business from start to finish from front-end order-entry processes, and automatically connect to shipping and receiving functions. Intranets and extranets keep all trading partners and corporate employ-

Figure 12.4   Examples of Choices for E-Commerce Systems

Your Budget	Possible Choices
Over $300,000	The site design involves more than online selling, and covers front-end order-entry processes that automatically connect to shipping and receiving. Intranets and extranets keep all trading partners and corporate employees up to the minute with customer information and product status.
$10,000–$300,000	Build your own customized e-commerce site. Your approach could be: • Have your in-house technical staff create your site. • Contract the work out to another company (i.e., outsource).
Less than $10,000	An Internet service provider (ISP) can handle everything for you. Some ISPs offer three levels of service to choose from: • Template (no flexibility, lowest cost). • Template with some ability to manipulate. • Modify HTML (you can customize, but you pay more).

ees up to the minute with customer information and product status. Costs are cut as just-in-time manufacturing becomes de rigueur. Database management systems analyze customer buying patterns and feed information about market trends to sales and marketing departments.

This is no-nonsense system design. These projects encompass Workflow Management tools, Project Management software systems, and PERT (Program Evaluation and Review Technique) charts galore. They control and analyze systems and programs to determine time and money, and dollar and labor status at regular intervals. These are not for the faint-hearted. This is the stuff of major corporations, big budgets and thick skins, and these projects can range into the millions—easily.

But bigger is not always better. Peter Levitan, president of New Jersey Online (NJO), cites a great example of this. NJO worked with Citibank to reconfigure its complex million-dollar Web site. "NJO was able to do more for them on a small site than they were able to accomplish with the multipage site design," says Levitan. Beware the risk of spending over $1 million to develop a Web site that will be doing nothing for the business. It is easy to be lured into building a site that is complex, huge, and loaded with information. Today experts agree that a reconfigured Web site, cut down to a few simple focused pages, can increase hits dramatically. In Web sites, size isn't everything.

Building a Customized Site: $10,000 to $300,000

Well-funded small businesses, medium-size companies with high-volume products, and large corporations seek this solution. Two approaches are possible: (1) assign the project to an in-house technical staff or (2) outsource the work.

To build your Web site in-house takes a dedicated team of experts. This approach generally works only with major corporations that already have software support teams in place. However, the support teams in corporations that undertake in-house development should be skilled in developing *e-commerce* systems, not one-size-fits-all programmers. Their training must be up-to-the-minute. An all-purpose programming staff could be in over their heads when it comes to programming online sales transactions.

If programming and database maintenance are *not* core components of your business, doing the work in-house will be more of a distraction than you could ever imagine. *If there is a chance that the logistics of operating your Web site will detract from your ability to run your core business, find another company to handle the work for you.* There will be no point in having an elegant Web site if your business collapses under the weight of maintaining it.

When you outsource work, the company you hire can handle just about everything for you, including the daily maintenance of your system. It becomes the responsibility of the company you hire to make sure the system is up, and that the system is backed up, that all lines are up and running, that security is thorough and complete, and that transactions flow smoothly all the time, even during peak traffic periods. This is not to say that you can sit back and relax. As a business owner, you need to understand exactly how your system is being designed. Know *everything* that is being done. Specifically, ask representatives about the company's service provider, method of credit card payments, programming packages, programming language used. Then read the following sections below to gain a conversational knowledge of what company representatives are talking about.

To some extent, you will act as a project manager when you outsource, even though you are not doing the work yourself. It helps to know more than Microsoft Word and Excel in order to do this. Work with familiar products, and you'll be able to assume more control over the outcome. Or at least you'll be able to ask the right questions. If you aren't up to speed, do your homework. Get to know more about design options, about what possibilities exist.

If you've ever taken on a construction project in your home, you know what project coordination means. The first time you renovate a house or build an addition, you might hire a general contractor (GC) to run the whole project for you. The GC brings in a team of electricians, plumbers, masons, and tile specialists to supplement his or her own crew. Very often the GC only handles the hammer-and-nails stuff. But after a few years living in the home, you eventually select your own plumber, electrician, mason, and others as the need arises. This new team of loyal tradespeople now know your home, for better or worse. When it comes time for the next "this old house" project, you're more capable of handling the job of GC yourself (time permitting), bringing in your favorite "staff," and hiring a construction-only building crew. You'll save a few thousand bucks, too.

While you may never pick up a hammer in true Bob Vila–style, you will definitely know what questions to ask the second time around. Get to the same level of intelligence with computer systems. Speak geek. If you don't, you'll be taken for the financial ride of your business life. Welcome to the new money pit.

Using an Internet Service Provider: Less Than $10,000

The best choice for start-up businesses and businesses that are just beginning to sell online, and medium-size companies with a small volume of product sales, is often to use the services of an Internet service provider. This is probably the easiest and least expensive route to follow, and you don't have to be technically astute. You can be online quickly, look professional, and have a support team working for you.

To start off, your company will need to define your workflow and your product information. Then the service provider can take over, working on an established fee schedule. In many cases, service providers will also offer different levels of service to work within your budget. Packages usually include the following:

- Domain name registration
- Acceptable graphics
- Guaranteed security
- Transaction processing
- Payment processing
- Report generation

As the least-cost approach, service providers offer basic templates. You simply fill in the blanks. For higher fees, there are templates that allow for some customization, granting a little more flexibility, and creating an image that will look less canned. The highest cost approach offers the ability to modify HTML and be the most creative. See Figure 12.5 for a summary of questions to ask

Figure 12.5   Checklist of Questions for Service Providers

Ask Any Internet Service Provider . . .

What is your track record for downtime? If your ISP is down, your business is down, as discussed in Chapter 6.

Do you have back-up systems? Describe. Be sure that the recovery method is swift, if not immediate, so that your business can be back online quickly in case of trouble.

Are you filled to capacity? How much growth can you handle? If the ISP is stretched to the limits and your business (or any other business they provide for) grows at Internet speed, they may not be able to deal with the sudden increase in demand. This will also be a problem if your business is subject to sudden seasonal volume increases.

What type and speed of lines do you use? Fastest is best. Also consider the capacity to handle multimedia transactions if that's your present need or future vision.

What other services can you provide? It would be simpler to one-stop shop.

Do you have access to my local telephone exchange? If not, every time you go online, you may incur a toll call.

any service provider before you make a decision about which one to use. Refer back to Chapter 6 for details on this table.

■ Cost-Effective Technology Ideas

There are other low cost—but more involved—ways to move into online selling quickly. Some small businesses have been extremely successful in managing their own menu of e-commerce system components. For example, a small business could decide to select services from a variety of providers:

- Design a site using Microsoft Corp.'s FrontPage 98 (about $149).
- Select a Web host, at an estimated cost of $20 per month.
- Customize programs with a CGI script.
- Handle order processing through a "shopping cart," probably via the Web host.
- Add a Secure Server ID to enable Secure Sockets Layer (SSL) transactions for credit card orders.
- Establish credit card accounts (about $1,000).

Caution. Check out your Web site yourself to make sure everything works the way it should. Do what your customers do:

☑ Try to access your Web site using keywords.

☑ Try out the site as if you were a first time visitor, and as if you were in a hurry to buy a specific item.

☑ Check out how long you have to wait—your customers will experience this, too.

☑ Work your way through your catalog as your typical shopper will.

☑ Place an order. Are you being asked to provide too much information?

☑ Repeat this process frequently to ensure that your system *really* works.

■ The Best Tools, Products, and Services

Typically, e-commerce systems for small- to medium-size businesses are composed of communication lines, required hardware, operating system software, custom software, and technical support. Today a growing number of entrepreneurial companies have attempted to simplify the transition to e-tailing through commerce packages. These combination packages offer turnkey e-commerce solutions that combine many or all of the different functions of customized sites:

- *Web graphic design tools* assist in the creation of illustrations and layouts, animation, and standard graphics.
- *Catalogs* are expensive components, with prices ranging from $1,000 for a basic catalog to $250,000 for the most sophisticated software.
- *Shopping carts,* which allow shoppers to gather products at a site and check out in one stop at the end of their "visit," simplify and speed up purchases.
- *Content management tools* help you identify customer preferences instantly, which enables the site to adjust content and presentation to individual customer needs.
- *Configurators* help Web site visitors select product combinations by presenting the user with a variety of buying options (including pricing information, product specifications, and product availability). The masters like Dell Computer and Cisco use configurators to help shoppers select and purchase highly complex equipment. Auto manufacturers and electronics companies are also dependent on configurators to let users play around with features and pricing combinations.

- *XML (Extensible Markup Language)* provides a standard way to describe electronic transactions and data so that companies can share data on the Web without using the same application software or databases.
- *Web site traffic analysis tools* provide your company with information about who's shopping, who's buying, and who's coming back. The market for these analytical tools is expected to grow from $21 million in 1998 to $2 billion by 2002, according to Forrester Research.

Network and Communications Solutions

Computer networks transfer data (including multimedia) between computers and across the Internet. Network communications take place over conventional leased lines: T1, T3, or ISDN lines. In Chapter 6, we also introduced LANs (local area networks) and WANs (wide area networks). Today, Virtual private networks (VPNs) are hot items. What's so great about VPNs? They are expected to save money. Internet VPNs theoretically reduce the cost of network communications compared to leased lines. The same equipment is required for either connection; the number of devices can differ (fewer devices for a VPN). VPNs can incur additional costs, however, for security. If high-speed encryption is needed, dedicated VPN devices are expensive. A VPN can

---

Figure 12.6   Examples of Technology Components

Web Servers   Servers are the backbone of the Internet, acting as central information services. Web servers store and retrieve HTML (hypertext markup language) and other Internet or intranet resources using HTTP (hypertext transfer protocol).
 Examples include Netscape SuiteSpot, Microsoft Internet Information Server, Roxen, Apache.

Web Server Platforms   The platform is the basis on which all other programs operate.
 Examples include Windows NT, Linux, SUN Solaris, DEC Unix.

Product Databases
 Examples include ODBC, Access, Personal Oracle, IBM DB/2, Sybase, Informix.

Merchandise Management Systems
 Examples include SAP R2/R3, Navision, Baan, PeopleSoft, IBM XAL, interact!

Online Payment Systems
 Examples include CyberCash, eCash, MilliCent, SET, and Mondex.

Security Technologies
 Examples include SSL (secured socket layer), SET (secured electronic transaction), and S-HTTP (secure Hypertext Transfer Protocol). See Chapter 10 for details on these and more.

provide secure communication, but reliability and quality of service should be checked out carefully. Some brief additional background on telecommunications follows.

Computer networks follow a standard architecture called OSI (open systems interconnection) that was defined in the 1980s by ISO (International Standards Organization), the same organization that standardized the hell out of factory production standards. The seven-layer OSI model is:

1. *Physical layer*—the cables, fiber optics cables, signal amplifiers (repeaters)
2. *Data layer*—data transfer, including error handling, sequencing, and other operations
3. *Network layer*—transmitting data packets over multiple channels. All the protocols are here—TCP/IP (Transmission control protocol/Internet protocol) has become a fundamental part of the Internet. This protocol covers the network layer, plus the remaining four layers.
4. *Transport layer*—communication links between applications running in different computers
5. *Session layer*—additional communication functions
6. *Presentation layer*—formatting, display, and editing
7. *Application layer*—communications services among user applications. EDI falls into this layer.

Now you have a few of the buzzwords that engineers throw around. Here's another important concept: ATM—not your automated teller machine, but asynchronous transfer mode—refers to the switching and multiplexing technology that transports data over existing LANs, WANs, and MANs (metropolitan area networks). ATM breaks all data into cells with 53 bytes for transport over a virtual path, allowing a more efficient and cost effective use of network bandwidth.

Big businesses commonly use computer networks, but small businesses are less likely to take on something so complex. However, mininetworks can help small businesses communicate faster and more efficiently. Save time, and you eventually save money. Of the 5.6 million small businesses that use PCs, about 78 percent have not installed a network. Today there are products that enable small businesses to build their networks in stages, growing as they need to. Building a network is not a do-it-yourself project.

The giants who configure the network infrastructure for the digital economy include Intel Corp., Cisco Systems, 3Com, Netscape Communications Corporation, Novell, and Microsoft Corporation, to name a few. Cisco and 3Com now offer hardware bundles that enable small businesses to network easily. Intel has formed a specialized small business networking division.

A network configuration could be as simple as three PCs communicating with a Pentium server and several printers. Following is a rundown of the components of a network for small businesses and some of the packages available today:

Server. Pentium II (or the new Pentium III) PCs can act as the server (and if the traffic volume is not too high, double as a PC for someone in the office), but the level of power required will depend on the number of PCs that will be connected. A 266MHz Pentium II PC could handle up to four PCs; a dedicated 300MHz for up to seven PCs; a 350MHz for up to 15 PCs—with extra memory and extra storage; and 400 MHz for 16 PCs and up.

Network operating system. The most popular software packages today are Microsoft Windows NT, Novell's IntranetWare, and Microsoft's BackOffice Small Business server.

Network hardware. An example is the Network Starter Kit from Linksys. Networks of five to seven PCs can consider 3Com's OfficeConnect Networking Kit. Larger networks (about eight or more PCs) also need network interface cards for each PC.

Communications server. InBusiness Internet Station from Intel and Micro Web100 from Cisco are two examples. Larger (about eight or more PCs) networks should shift to a "network switch," like Intel's InBusiness or Cisco's 1548 Micro Switch.

Host Companies and Internet Service Providers

For small businesses, the cost of running a simple commerce site can be reduced by using a service bureau (e.g., iCatCorp, Viaweb) or Internet access providers like AT&T Corp. that build, host, and maintain commerce sites for monthly fees.

Ultimate Web Host List (www.webhostlist.com) is a Web site that offers detailed information to anyone searching for a Web host provider free of charge. The Ultimate Web Host List gives a Top 25 Award to distinguish those hosts that offer reasonable pricing, multiple features, and great customer support. Following are descriptions of a few of their recent picks:

Hiway Technologies. Hiway, the Ultimate Web Host List number-one choice in October 1998, hosts over 100,000 customers with plans starting from $15.95 a month. E-commerce hosting starts at $34.95. They offer six T3 network connections and Cisco routers, the fastest equipment available. Your account and domain can be registered within hours, and they guarantee reliability.

Media3 Technologies. This company works with both large and small companies to help them establish a presence on the Web. Small business hosting plans start at $19.50 a month. Their hosting plans allow businesses to upgrade their site anytime and add features as needed. Turnkey electronic storefronts are offered, as well as a full suite of services to sell products and services online. Their partnerships include industry leaders IBM, CyberCash, Verisign, and Microsoft. With a Web hosting company like Media3, your company is on high speed servers, always available and monitored 24 hours a day, seven days a week.

HostPro (a division of NetLimited LLC). Also promising speedy, reliable service, and a wide array of features, HostPro rates start at $19.95 for standard features of 60 MB of Web space; 2,000 MB of traffic/month; and 12 e-mail accounts. All standard packages include free domain name registration, Unix and Microsoft NT hosting, Mircrosoft FrontPage 98 support, and more. Their most elaborate package at $49.95 a month expands to 100 MB of Web space; 3,000 MB traffic per month, and 20 e-mails. At this rate, users have a shopping cart, CyberCash, SSL, database support, complete statistical reports, and much more.

9NetAvenue. Offering Web site and e-commerce hosting, 9Net Avenue has a staff of multilingual technicians available 24 hours a day, seven days a week, who "cater to your Web site's every need." Onsite monitoring, full backup, and meticulous administration mean a lot to business owners who need to keep their eyes on their businesses. Their hosting plans start at $14.95 a month. For $99 a month, you can have a dedicated server with hardware. No downtime.

ValueWeb. Standard hosting with ValueWeb starts at $19.95 a month; commerce hosting is $49.95 a month. Standard packages offer everything you need to do business on the Web, including huge disk space, unlimited data transfer, shopping carts, CyberCash support, database support, and more. Security, speed, reliability, and backup are guaranteed.

Search Services and Portals

Created to help us maneuver through the Web, search services and portals have been motivated by economic incentives to assume a new role to support e-tail. Yahoo!; America Online; Lycos, Inc.; Excite, Inc.; AtHome Corp.; and InfoSeek Corp. are all in hot pursuit of online stores to add to their own malls. Yahoo! acquired ViaWeb, the online store creation software company, and charges store owners between $100 and $300 a month. Yahoo!Store has more than 1,100 merchants.

iMall. One of the most popular cybermalls, iMall offers secured commerce hosting that includes e-commerce solutions that they guarantee will provide you with millions of visitors. Millions. No kidding. A quick check on their methodology and you'll be inclined to believe they will deliver as promised. Their iStore package allows any merchant to build a complete e-commerce site in minutes. These sites are then automatically promoted on Yahoo!, Infoseek, AltaVista, Hot Bot, and Lycos. They also promise special promotions on Internet ad banners and radio spots. A second solution called "Bolt-on" adds e-commerce to any existing Web site, working with FrontPage, NetObjects Fusion, Netscape Composer, or any other design software. To use their secured commerce hosting, fees start at $39.95 a month.

Internet Software

Forrester predicts that the market for e-commerce software packages will increase by 3,000 percent in five years, from $121 million in 1997 to $3.8 billion by 2002. Software packages provide many of the features needed for e-commerce, including order and payment processing, back-office functions, database integration, and more. These packages eliminate the need to patch different e-commerce systems together. Prices for e-commerce software packages range from $1,000 to $250,000. Commerce suites take on the software programs that are needed for simple e-commerce operations and package them into turnkey solutions that work for small business. ICat Corp., for example, makes several e-commerce software products, including Electronic Commerce Suite. These products have become popular for their ease of use; but they become a problem when a company is ready to add additional functions.

At the high end of packaged commerce software are sites that handle heavy traffic. Packages that meet these needs include Open Market's Transact and One-to One by Broadvision, Inc. Less expensive products for small to medium-size businesses have better brand recognition, and range between $1,000 and $10,000. These include the following:

- IBM Corp.'s Net.Commerce
- Oracle Corp.'s Internet Commerce Server
- Microsoft's Site Server Commerce Edition
- Netscape Communications Corp.'s CommerceXpert
- iCat's Electronic Commerce Suite

Microsoft was the last to jump on board, announcing electronic commerce software products and services in March 1999. Microsoft's Biztalk is a new language designed to help draw different business practices and e-commerce technologies together via the Internet. Their approach should enable retail (as well as business-to-business) companies to configure e-commerce systems with a "Lego-block" approach. Microsoft also acquired Comparenet, a comparison-shopping Web site that added to the MSN Web portal. Their goal is to make it easier for small businesses to create an online store. Today the industry-standard to connect databases to the Internet is XML, so Biztalk may help Microsoft be "better late than never."

E-commerce solution providers offer a variety of packages that can make the transition to online sales simple and painless. Leaders in software technology include AT&T, IBM, Lotus, iCat, Harbinger, Open Market, and Pandesic. Following is a synopsis of offerings from a few leaders and up-and-coming companies.

Open Market ShopSite. ShopSite is an online store creation system of Open Market, Inc., a Burlington, Massachusetts software solutions company. ShopSite was designed for small businesses. It features help in setting up an online catalog, graphics, a "specials" page, easy indexing to be located by search engines, a complete shopping cart, and secure commerce functionality. An easy HTML forms–based interface and store setup wizard simplify additions and changes for the merchant. Packages are available to get any business up and running as an e-commerce site in little time, for under $1,000. Open Market offers several other software packages for larger companies.

WorldWide Merchant™. This company promotes a total e-commerce solution that allows consumer order tracking and order shipment tracking. They propose reduction of customer service costs, including personnel and 800 phone lines. They also include an online real-time order management system (so no e-mail or faxed orders), support of any Internet payment method, and shopping cart functions. As an extra feature, your Web site will be linked to any existing Web page. This total package to set up an Internet store is around $1,000. Your company can choose to add InterShipper™ to obtain shipping rates from several leading shipping companies for the best rates.

Primecom Interactive, Inc. This Illinois company, which recently received an infusion of funds from Colorocs Information Technologies, Inc., was formed to help grow small business in cyberspace. Their product, Primecom QuickSite, was designed for individuals who are not PC savvy, providing an all-in-one simple tool to sell online quickly and securely. Primecom Quick-Site Gold Edition sells for about $90, and Premier Edition for entry level companies sells for about $50. Primecom also offers monthly hosting services starting at $29.95 a month.

UPS. Yes, that one. UPS has an award-winning Web site that averages over 4 million hits each business day. UPS has created a strategy of working with "solution providers" to include UPS functions into their Web site programs. With the UPS component, customers can select the level of shipping urgency and track their own shipments. UPS Online Tracking provides timely information about specific packages 24 hours a day, seven days a week. Other services include secure delivery of electronic documents through to downloadable Internet tools. UPS also offers to help any business determine which company could offer the best solution to their transition to e-commerce.

Hitachi Computer Products Inc. Hitachi TradeLink makes it possible to add e-commerce without re-engineering your existing business systems. TradeLink is a modular software suite that adapts to any industry, product, or service. It is described as a "comprehensive, enterprise-class I-commerce solution."

Accrue Software. Accrue Software has been described as one of the major players in the market of high-end Web site traffic analysis tools. Accrue Insight 2.5 is the latest version of their traffic analysis software, which provides daily automated reports on traffic and ad performance. Accrue makes it possible to see exactly which parts of a Web site visitors go to. The information is available immediately, and can be automatically routed to Web site managers via e-mail. Managers can also select the information they would like to see, including an executive summary and graphics.

CyberCash, Inc. This Virginia company is the leader in moving money for e-commerce businesses, the most secure Internet payment solution. The CyberCash Cash Register includes a choice of Internet payments: credit card, checks, and cash. They handle SSL and SET security, with easy to implement solutions. With CyberCash, a merchant can concentrate on the many other details of getting the Web site up.

I/US Corporation. Their new Web service called JumpList provides link pages from your site to external sites. JumpList automates the process of exchanging reciprocal links with other sites, letting you add and manage your own links. A free version is available to get you started by going to JumpList.com. An advanced version called JumpList Deluxe, which offers extensive customizable features, is available for $30 per year. I/US is a Canadian company located in Ottawa.

Java and other programming languages. When Sun Microsystems released the Java programming language into the Internet, the game changed. Java is a platform-independent software environment. The best thing about most digital technology is that it is extremely flexible. Interoperability, or the ability to merge different vendor equipment with varying transmission and receiving technicalities, is improving. When new releases come out, there is less upheaval than in the past. Java begat Javascript. Predecessors Perl, C. C++ are still around. Most host companies will accommodate these languages as well as SSI and Python.

■ Maintenance and Product Support

The leading software providers proudly advertise that they are available 24 hours a day, seven days a week—many in a multilingual capacity—to help you. Take this very seriously. Most problems will occur when you least expect them, and a late-night call for help should be answered.

Maintenance on your system is as important as dealing with regular oil changes in your car, according to Joan Leavey. If you overlook maintenance because everything is running smoothly, you'll end up leading your site into a crisis. Regularly scheduled maintenance runs, during non-peak periods and before any anticipated surge in activity, can make a tremendous difference for your Web site.

Product support is a birthright of all system users—make sure you have that guarantee—at any time, for every product, with replacements so there's never downtime.

Crisis Management and Preventing Downtime

When Charles Schwab & Co.'s online brokerage went down in February 1999 just as the stock market opened, other Web-dependent companies surely felt an empathetic twinge of panic. No matter how large or small any e-commerce site is, performance can't be taken for granted. All components need to be rigorously tested, including every addition of new devices, software, and hardware. Backup procedures need to be in place, and brought into motion instantly. In the case of the Schwab failure, officials claimed that the system had been tested offline, but reality challenged it beyond the limits.

Reality is difficult to imitate for any company that can experience peaks. At best, systems can be tested through a series of simulations that attempt to mimic best through worst case scenarios. But just in case, the ability to move quickly into a backup plan is essential.

The bad news about testing is that it will make all system upgrades, additions, and changes take longer to implement. The bad news about not testing is that prayer alone won't work. For healthy, popular Web sites with a steadily growing population of users, the additional time and precision of testing pays off.

Dealing with Congestion

Web managers today seek 99.9 percent uptime. They know that if users have to deal with slow loading pages at a Web site, they'll leave rather than buy. Load balancers can give companies a competitive advantage by routing traffic, providing failover (instant backup in the event of a failure), and load balancing. Load balancers help systems handle peak traffic volumes by balancing data across multiple sites and servers, directing Web traffic to the nearest, most available server. These products are for the larger networks, the stuff of Fortune 1000 companies. Load balancers cost from $10,000 to $20,000. For corporations like the airlines and brokerage houses, this investment is well worth the cost. The market for Internet traffic management products is expected to grow to $800 million in 2002. Today Cisco is a significant market leader, with Radware, Inc., Alteon Networks, Inc., and F5 Labs Inc. following with smaller market shares.

13

Building Successful Net Partnerships

■ Potential Partners

Deb Zeyen of CBS New Media has played an integral role in the decisions about partnerships for CBS.com, and believes there is a recipe for strategic relationships. For CBS New Media, Zeyen says the partnership should make sense to the user, make sense to CBS.com as a way to reach out to new Internet users, and provide new revenue opportunities for their local affiliates. CBS New Media established partnerships with Sportsline.com, Marketwatch.com, and America Online for content and exposure and continues to work on new venues to give their site depth and breadth.

- *Make sense to the user.* "We think of ourselves as a direct extension of CBS," said Zeyen. "CBS is known for entertainment, sports, news, and money. I want to be sure I have content for each of these topics." Sportsline.com provides content for sports, and Marketwatch.com provides the material needed for money. News includes daily headlines, a wealth of current information, and health updates. "These sites are influenced by information that you would expect to find from CBS. We'll probably add a health site in the near future," Zeyen said.

- *Reach out to new Internet users.* The partnership formed with America Online provides CBS with access to AOL's 16 million (and counting) users. This partnership created a vehicle for distribution and for revenue. It also supplants a deal AOL had with ABC since 1997. "We give AOL eight slide shows a day on news so they don't have to create their own in-house news department," said Zeyen. CBS provides for AOL what their other partners provide for CBS. They engage in heavy cross-promotion. As a result, CBS now reaches a huge audience through AOL, including the younger demographic Internet users who were elusive for CBS in the past. According to Zeyen, "From our two perspectives, it's a win-win situation."
- *Create new revenue opportunities.* The Job Connection, like classified ads, is a way for local affiliates to tap into a resource supplemented with local information supported by local advertising revenue.

The formula for net partnerships forged by new or existing companies can be the key to success in the next millennium. A well-crafted partnership can be the single most critical factor to turn consistent but unremarkable growth into a meteoric rise to market leadership. Partnerships can follow a variety of formats, in which money, reputations, or both are put on the line. No matter what the financial deal points, however, experts agree that partners must have a shared vision.

■ Types of Partnerships

Partnerships may take the form of acquisition strategies, strategic alliances, virtual companies, distribution partners, creative partnerships, and industry alliances. Each structure serves a different purpose; all can achieve the goal of economic growth and corporate vitality.

Acquisition Strategies

The mantra today is "If you can't create it now, buy it." The speed of technological innovation leaves little room for second place. There are few silver medals in the Internet Olympics. If a business sets its strategic course in a direction where it is not already first to market, it is a far better thing to buy than to build. Yahoo! bought GeoCities, for example. Why build communities when someone else already has? America Online bought Netscape Communications Corporation, acquiring a more businesslike tone and software in the process.

Strategic Alliances

Strategic alliances can create synergy between compatible corporations. Ebay, the leading online trading community, and Netscape Communications Corporation, one of the largest Internet portals, moved into a strategic relationship in February 1999. Ebay had been a "distinguished provider" on Netscapes's Netcenter site, which was like dating. This agreement will allow Ebay greater exposure from targeted placements on the Netcenter homepage and from two bookmarks on Netscape Communicator, to name just a few of several key placements. This is like an engagement. A recent press release announced that "This relationship will continue to evolve over time to include additional advertising across the site and within the Netcenter Newsletter." That must be the marriage. What's in it for Netscape? All those dedicated Ebay consumers, checking out more than 1,000 categories of items up for auction over and over again.

Virtual Companies

Streamlined organizations with exceptional speed in getting new ideas and products into the marketplace are the trademarks of virtual companies. Virtual companies (also referred to as *virtual corporations*) can be a combination of strategic alliances and outsourcing relationships. *Internet Business* magazine identified Bluefly.com, a clothing marketing company, as a perfect example. Bluefly.com pulls together manufacturing, distribution, sales, customer service, shipping, and distribution under completely different roofs.

"By partnering with other companies for some processes," wrote Alan Kay, "companies such as Bluefly are able to stay lean and mean in the volatile land of online retail—and hopefully give established brands a run for their money."

Introducing the partners in this virtual company: Bluefly (developed overall procedures); On Demand Solutions (warehouses merchandise; fills customer orders, handles customer service); Kaufman Patricol Enterprises (Web site design); DIGEX (Web connections and site maintenance); United Parcel Service (shipping). Will this work? Bluefly is still a young company, and some experts warn of potential problems from outsourcing customer service, your link to future sales. Others say that virtual companies such as this are the business model of the future to get to market quickly.

Distribution Partners

When a product or service receives high level exposure and a host of companies provide distribution, it makes a grand entrance. When SNAP, the Internet portal from NBC and CNET, announced SNAP Cyclone, a collection of companies were on board from the start. SNAP Cyclone is a free Internet search service for high-speed users. Cyclone enhances video, audio, animation and communications for high-speed Internet connections. SNAP Cyclone was initially carried by GTE Internetworking, SBC Internet Services, Bell Atlantic Internet Solutions, Epoch Internet, JPSnet, DSLnetworks, Eastlink Cable, and Triax Telecommunications. Additional high-speed Internet access services were expected to be added to the list in the months to follow.

Creative Partnering

The role of content in getting customers to return to a Web site has been emphasized often in this book. Content is one of the most difficult components of a Web site for many e-tailers. Strategic relationships that merge commerce and content brains can result in highly creative, "sticky," sites. These arrangements, or deals, take different forms: equity investments, revenue sharing, content licensing, comarketing, or any combination of these practices.

Industry Alliances

A most significant gathering of industry giants resulted in a March 1999 announcement by IBM, Motorola, Sun Microsystems, Lucent, and ten other companies. Their joint mission was to create a new set of standards based on Sun's Java programming language to connect the next generation of smart devices. By combining forces, these giants challenged the dominant role of Microsoft.

A second announcement the same day by US West and Network Computer Inc. confirmed a schedule for trials of a new service called AT-TV. This service integrates the telephone, television, and Internet. Merge the resources, creativity, and financial power of the giants and the outcome can be the development of technology combinations that no one partner could create alone.

Affiliate Programs

Shifting focus from the mighty industry alliances to simpler partnerships within the scope of even very small companies, consider affiliate programs.

Affiliate programs bring an extended sales force into partnership with a business in another win-win situation. Affiliate programs offer commissions to individuals (or businesses) who help a company sell its products and services. Art.com, for example, pays a 15 percent commission on every product their affiliates sell for them. The process is simple. The Art.com Affiliate Program lets participants create a personal gallery; link to their home page; use their template holiday banners, search engine box, and gift certificates. For a limited time, they also offer a $20 credit bonus to be issued with the first commission check. Affiliates can also receive commissions on their own purchases.

■ Sponsors, Advertisers, and Others

The links that are created from one Web site to another become a form of partnership over time. As your business becomes more comfortable (and trusting) of Web partners, the relationships can be expanded. Some of the mega-alliances described in this chapter began as sponsorships or straightforward advertising arrangements.

As the shared vision of two enterprises becomes clear, and the benefits of forming an alliance outweigh the risks, the links become more permanent and profitable bonds.

CASE STUDIES ■

Examples of partnerships forming among Internet companies seem endless. The race to secure a stronghold as Internet players continues. Following is a partial list of alliances. These sometimes strange bedfellows have forged dynamic and profitable relationships between corporations and small businesses, traditional brand names and new media entrepreneurs, online and offline companies.

3Com and Microsoft. This team develops cobranded home networking products, paving the way for consumers to have easier access from personal computers to the Internet. They plan on developing the technology which will enable two or more family members to be on the Web simultaneously. The idea of connected PCs in the home seems like a vision of the future, but it's here today.

Innovative Holdings and Valu-Net. Innovative Holdings & Technologies, Inc., works with niche technology companies with growth potential. They own Global Sports Network, Inc., proponents of the "Total Sports Experience." Valu-Net is a leading marketing and technology company. Valu-Net has long-term relationships with leading ISPs and consumer marketing companies. They have the capacity to make Global Sports Network *the* brand name in sports information and e-commerce.

Dell and Amazon.com. These two pioneers of e-commerce comarket their products on joint Web sites. Amazon.com was the first company Dell linked to; Dell.com was the first computer company Amazon.com linked to. These two leaders have that "shared vision" thing in common. Both have an unprecedented customer appeal on the Internet; both were market leaders; both take particular pride in their Web site design and easy navigation; and they are also leaders in customer service.

***New York Times* with TheStreet.com.** The Times invested $15 million in TheStreet.com, an online source of financial information and investment news. TheStreet.com was perceived to be a good fit with the *New York Times* because of the mutual needs of their customer bases. Both sets of customers seek timely information to make investment decisions. While some sort of editorial relationship may eventually evolve, experts believe that the big benefit now is advertising and promotion. And by the way, the two company presidents were close friends who attended Springfield Township High School in Pennsylvania together. A few more criteria to add to "successful net partnerships": a track record of accomplishment, mutual respect, and long-term relationships. The rules that govern any successful partnership are magnified in the Web.

Lycos and USA Networks. Lycos, operator of the world's second largest search engine, expects to gain access to 20 million credit card holders as part of a deal with USA Networks' Home Shopping Network. Lycos will be able to target consumers directly with this arrangement.

14

The Global Challenge

■ Special Considerations of the Global Economy

The enhanced market research capabilities of the Internet and e-commerce provide powerful tools to enable even the smallest company to become a global enterprise. Online merchants can become exporters faster than ever. E-commerce is taking companies global that never thought of it before. With planning and research into market differences, your company can successfully expand to global markets. Almost any small business can increase their revenue by reaching out to new markets worldwide.

About 96 percent of the world's consumers live outside the United States. A large portion of this number are located in developing countries, where the spending on information technology is increasing at twice the global rate. E-commerce is the new frontier for small business. "The most exciting opportunities are emerging markets, especially in Latin America and Asia," said Diahann Lassus, 1998–1999 president of the National Association of Women Business Owners (NAWBO). "The challenge is to get in early enough to establish yourself but not so early that the costs are prohibitive." Any business that enters this global market on the crest of this wave of growth can expect to reap the benefits.

The European online market is the most rapidly growing international market today. The increase in European online shopping is most likely due to a combination of factors: the deregulation of telecommunications, the decreasing cost of online service subscriptions, and the increase in Web sites which are customized to the needs of individual European countries. The jump in online purchasing is encouraging. Europe's e-commerce revenues for music, books, software, and travel are expected to more than double every year through 2002. The Internet population in England alone more than doubled in one year. Frequency of Internet usage is also rising. Where typical users signed onto the Internet about once a week in 1997, users are now most likely to sign on daily.

To their credit, e-tailers have moved away from mass marketing to European nations and engaged in localized sales strategies. The first U.S. corporations to jump into global sales quickly learned that successful strategies at home were not guaranteed to work across the ocean. With quick revamping of sales efforts, market leaders created customized approaches geared to individual countries. Their efforts are paying off.

To date, not all businesses are equally confident in approaching the global marketplace. A Small Business Administration (SBA) report on exporting by small firms showed that more firms owned by men (2.2 percent) are involved in exporting than women-owned firms (1.1 percent). Only .8 percent of black-owned firms, 2.7 percent of Hispanic, and 2.3 percent of Asian and Native American firms are involved in exporting. The Department of Commerce is aggressively using information technology to target minority and women-owned companies for greater involvement in global markets. A program called Video Golden Key lets companies communicate with potential business partners overseas using real-time video on their computers. The program is targeted for the benefit of women and minority-owned enterprises. The Department of Commerce expects to expand this program to its domestic offices and over 150 U.S. embassy and consulate offices overseas over a two-year period. This desktop video conferencing is an inexpensive way to match buyers and sellers, show samples, and acquire counseling.

Any business that wants to make the move to expand from domestic to global sales is wise to consider the most significant differences between the U.S. and other markets before launching an international sales effort. Issues which will be addressed in this chapter include the following:

- Import/export laws
- International distribution
- Dealing with different currencies
- Currency conversion
- Language and cultural issues
- Customer contact
- Potential tax problems

Import/Export Laws

The U.S. does not allow some products to be exported, including several types of computer hardware and software. In addition, some categories of products require an export license in order to be sold outside of the U.S. The Export Administration Act of 1979 includes a list of products that require licenses. Export licenses are most likely to be required for technical goods and information. The U.S. grants two kinds of export licenses—general and individual. E-commerce businesses usually require a general license. Check with the U.S. Department of Commerce to see if you need an export license. The Bureau of Export Administration issues licenses. Contact information is listed in the Appendix.

Several U.S. government Web sites provide export help:

- www.ita.doc.gov/tic—the Trade Information Center, a clearinghouse of information on federal export assistance programs.
- www.stat.usa.gov—STAT-USA/Internet, a comprehensive collection of international market research, trade reports, and basic exporting information.
- www.cnewsusa.com—Commercial News USA, a public/private catalog/magazine that promotes American products and services in 152 countries.

The U.S. restricts trade with certain countries. The list of these countries is provided in the Export Administration Act.

Every country also has import laws, so it is important to check the regulations in the countries in which you plan to market. Products with high levels of cryptography are particularly sensitive. France, for example, does not allow this type of software to be imported; the U.S. restricts exports of the same type. Most countries have fixed prices for books, so online book discounts present another problem.

Most e-commerce ventures will export directly, so the merchant will be responsible for shipping, collecting payments, and providing customer service.

Some e-tailers may choose to make other arrangements using intermediaries such as shipping agents, export management companies, or export trading companies, but the trend is to eliminate dependency on these entities. In some situations, however, there will be no flexibility. Export trading companies are the only permitted route in Japan, for example.

International Distribution

Territories are a familiar concept for anyone who has ever worked in sales for a major corporation. Sales personnel have strictly defined geographic areas that they are responsible for, and all volume and commission credits from sales in that territory are awarded accordingly. No other salesperson will work that territory. At a global level, corporations have traditionally established agreements with distributors in specific countries that also affect how sales are handled. No other distributor will work that country. The Internet changes the rules of the game completely.

When geography disappears, the e-commerce business can sell virtually anywhere. However, if an international distributor has exclusive marketing and sales rights in a particular territory, there will be a conflict. If an e-tail business charges lower prices for the same products, the problems will be exacerbated.

Different Currencies

When 11 European countries adopted the euro as their common currency, analysts predicted that e-commerce would boom. The euro market has a population around 300 million worldwide. Denmark, Greece, Sweden, and the United Kingdom initially voted against the euro but are expected to come on board early in the millenium. All companies doing e-commerce business in Europe beginning in 1999 should be ready to accept payments in the euro.

The euro was introduced as an electronic currency only—no bank notes or coins until 2002. All electronic transactions are processed in euros: credit cards, debit cards, inter-bank transfers, checks, other. In January 2002, the old currency bank notes and coins will be removed and the new euro version will go into circulation. During the transition period, the 11 countries will move toward having just one currency again—the euro.

Trading in different European currencies has always involved multiple tasks and numerous risks. The euro simplifies the process for at least 11 currencies. The currencies may vary against the dollar, but not against one another. Using the euro, e-commerce risks are no greater than the risks incurred in domestic sales. But the euro only covers part of currency conversion. You still have the rest of the world to factor in.

Global e-commerce requires the ability to receive payment for products and services in any currency. Only a small portion of the total international market uses the U.S. dollar. Today American Express, MasterCard International, VISA International, and Diners Club are among the corporations that act as intermediaries. E-tailers can accept payment by credit card in the currency of the customer, and receive payment in the form of their own currency. The credit card companies can convert from one currency to another in almost every country in the world, whether the transaction takes place in person or over the Internet.

The early global Internet businesses have successfully used this method of credit card payment to establish a firm footing in countries that now have an increasing demand for their products. Virtual Vineyards, for example, sells a substantial volume of California wine in Japan.

Currency Conversion—on Demand

We know that online shoppers love to compare prices, as well as quality, when they browse. Comparison shopping on the Internet offers the potential to select from companies anywhere in the world. But how can you assess price structures when the currency of one online store differs from the currency of another?

As shoppers, we'd like to see the products we are interested in purchasing clearly displayed, described in our own language, and priced in our own currency. E-commerce companies who accommodate this need go a long way to facilitating sales. Unlike language, however, pricing changes. While a Web site design may include translation of product descriptions that are written once and revised when the product changes, prices fluctuate daily. As the value of one currency shifts relative to another, so do prices. Who performs the conversion in this case? Credit card associations will handle currency conversions for merchants at the time of purchase. However, they do not provide real-time updates on the exchange rate for their merchants on a daily basis. Nor do they translate this information into a product price list for every country an e-tail merchant markets to.

Major European banks, Japanese banks, Chase, and Citicorp already perform currency conversions daily. Companies like CyberCash work with the major international banks to provide this information to Internet merchants. For immediate currency conversions from any sources, check the Web site www.gnn.com/gbi.bin/gnn/currency.

Language and Cultural Issues

Consider creating different Web pages in the languages of the countries you market to. For products, the visual image is important and can alleviate many language differences. Services are a different story. Without a visual image, and with total dependence on language, services may be more difficult to present accurately. Translation and interpretation are critical and should be handled carefully. Social and cultural norms will also influence how customers in different countries respond to your marketing and sales efforts. Every member of an e-commerce business who will come into contact with customers should be educated and trained in the cultural dynamics that affect communication. As any successful domestic marketing effort labors to grasp the subtleties of each market niche, so should an international marketing effort emphasize depth of understanding of cultural differences.

"The most important goal in dealing with international cultures," according to Jim Foley, author of *The Global Entrepreneur: Taking Your Business International* (Dearborn, 1999), "is to build trust and respect in the relationship as well as flexibility in your business practices." There is a danger in making too many assumptions about any culture, no matter how often you have visited. Foley has found at least five potential areas of misunderstanding:

1. *Language.* Your translations need to be as accurate as possible. To test this, have your materials reverse-translated; that is, have your foreign language version translated into English and see if the meaning is still precise.
2. *Localization.* Use industry quotes from local magazines and newspapers, not just U.S. resources. Give your marketing materials a local flair.
3. *Color.* Be sensitive to the use of color as a symbol in different countries. Some colors have very strong connotations or associations that could be negative for your business.
4. *Gesture.* Watch out for American slang in hand signals that could be offensive in another culture.
5. *Role of females.* Not every nation has designated all beings equal, especially in clothing and work roles. Watch your use of models in catalogs (online and offline) and promotional materials and stay within cultural limits.

On the other hand, it isn't necessary to "neuter" your material so much that you are no longer identified as an American company. In many nations, buying American is itself a treat. "Just don't become the ugly American," cautions Foley. Or the ugly online American.

Remember also that shopping for many cultures is a social activity, with a clear distinction between shopping and buying. Shopping is a reason to dress up, stroll around, and meet friends. Can you recapture *this* cultural nuance on your Web site? What kind of community experience can you generate?

Customer Contact

After all that has been written about the importance of connecting with customers to establish long-term repeat sales, how can an e-commerce business replicate this overseas? Large corporations manage this through a physical presence worldwide. Levi Strauss & Co., for example, has more than 35 international branch offices. These branch offices establish a physical presence and facilitate personal contact for customer service (Figure 14.1). There is an obvious advantage over e-mail correspondence.

Companies that are not large enough to take the Levi approach and establish their own base in foreign countries can arrange for customer service functions to be handled through intermediaries. Virtually any small business can use their Web site to promote products and services, and a local staff to

Figure 14.1   Levi Strauss & Co. has branch offices all over the world to service its customers. The Web site makes it clear that all countries are not to be treated the same.

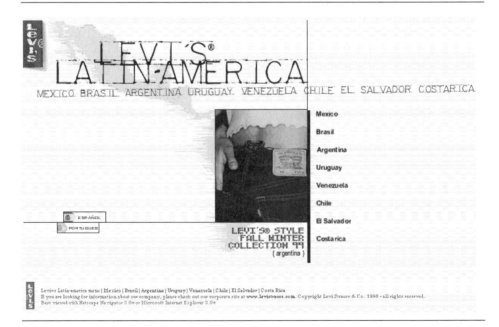

handle support. Perhaps this will be the future role of many international distributors—to provide product support and customer service in every country where business has a strong market.

Potential Tax Problems

Just like any traditional catalog company, U.S. online merchants are responsible for federal and state taxes based on the location in which their business operates. The same is true for international sales. Tax issues significantly differ from country to country, including value-added taxes. As a result, shipping even the most simple product from one place to another can be a complex operation. Calculating taxes is even worse.

To date there is no central list of this information to draw from. As a result, e-commerce merchants need to research the countries in which they will do business and insure that they are aware of all potential tax liabilities and fees.

■ The Internet Name and Address System

An international nonprofit corporation has been created to reform the Internet name and address system. This is a private-sector self-regulated organization charged with managing the system of names and numbers used to call up World Wide Web pages or send e-mail. The European Union, the international community, and the U.S. agree that this organization will handle decisions on how to govern the Internet. Trademark disputes regarding Internet names will be handled by the World Intellectual Property Organization.

■ European Markets

European online shopping revenues were $1.2 billion in 1998, out of a total $1.3 trillion in retail sales. Online shopping revenues from music, travel, books, and software sales in Germany, France, and the United Kingdom are projected to reach $3.3 billion by 2004, up from $68 million in 1997, according to Jupiter Communications and Forrester Research. European online advertising revenues are expected to reach $1.2 billion by 2002, up from $5.6 million in 1996.

Germany has been projected to be the best potential online market because of its large population (80 million), high level of Internet interest (8.4

million), and relatively strong economy. Only 11 percent of all German on-line users shopped online in 1997, but this number is projected to grow to 40 percent by 2002. And online stores are growing. More than 1,200 online stores sell books in Germany, and more books are sold per capita than in the United States.

In the United Kingdom, 14 percent of online users shopped online, but this number is expected to reach 40 percent in 2002. In France only 9 percent of the online users shopped online, but this number will reach 35 percent by 2002. In Italy there are over 2 million Internet users, with growth of more than 25 percent in a single year.

Political climates can and will influence the support for Internet business, as well as the restrictions various European governments place on the protection of information, such as personal financial data and personal information gathered on the Internet for data banks. Britain and France successfully pressured phone companies and Internet service providers to reduce costs, and in some places free Internet service is available.

E-tailers and major U.S. e-commerce players are locking up portals and creating alliances with the major European players to beat their competition, according to analysts. Affiliate programs are proclaimed by some e-commerce businesses as another way to gain a stronghold on the European market. IBM, Microsoft, and Cisco Systems are pushing e-commerce among their European customers. Amazon.com opened offices in Germany and Britain, while Barnes & Noble joined up with the German giant Bertelsmann A.G.

■ Pacific Rim Markets

The Pacific Cooperation Council has sponsored summits for Taiwan, China, Japan, and other Pacific Rim powers to seek a global framework for Internet business practices. Issues of primary concern include the choice of language and standards to use, privacy protocols, and other ethical considerations. Asia is expected to have the largest growth in computer purchases and Internet use globally, according to experts.

15

Visions of the Future

■ Projections from Industry Leaders

The annual Internet World Conference and Expo at the Jacob Javits Convention Center in New York City is not for the faint-hearted. A zillion people pace the floors and halls of the exhibition area and workshops for three consecutive days. Or it seems like that many people, because most attendees crowd around the Disney-like exhibits of the major players, like kids.

Major new media companies and the smallest consulting firms show off their hottest new services at these conferences, while sales reps distribute about a million mouse pads and refrigerator magnets. Okay, maybe a few thousand. But the show-stopper is usually Microsoft, set up right near a major convention center traffic artery, with a larger-than-life screen to simulate your computer terminal during regularly scheduled performances of Windows New Releases and their hottest new concepts. You can see the future and it is now.

"Imagine you're in your office," says the perky exhibit host (with nails too long ever to have struck a keyboard), *"and you*

decide to watch a bit of a basketball game." (Switch to full screen transmission of a playoff game, with sound and full television commentary.) *"You hear someone coming . . ."* (Switch playoff game to a very small window in the corner of your screen, lower volume, display an Excel spreadsheet.) *"Then you realize it's your boss."* (Remove television transmission window, cancel sound, display full screen of Excel spreadsheet. Basketball scores and highlights are displayed in a summary in a tiny box no bigger than a single cell. Not a sound but the clanking of industrious little fingers on a keyboard.) *"The boss leaves."* The game's back on, the volume's up. He scored. Yes!

But the future is not only in the office—it's also in the home. *"You're watching a documentary about dolphins with your kids."* (Looks like a nice Public Broadcasting type of special.) *"Want to know something else about their average size and weight?"* (Just ask for it, and a small interactive window appears on the screen. Enter your information request, and receive a response back in seconds.) *"Would you like to know more? Do you want to print a copy of this response?"* (Homework was never so easy, or fun. Before long, someone will have added, "Would you like to include your name, homeroom teacher, date, and anticipated grade on this report?")

■ Where Are We Headed?

Diahann Lassus, president of NAWBO and a partner in Lassus, Wherley & Associates, feels that e-commerce and the Internet in general will continue to change lives. "Easy access to information will raise the bar for education and access to knowledge," she said. "We'll be so connected, you'll be able to find *anything* online, which will shift our focus from how we find the information to how we *use* the information." Lassus feels that those who can analyze and interpret data will benefit the most. "You will have to add value."

New announcements about technology releases occur daily. Delivery of superfast, highly reliable Internet transmission never fails to turn heads. The Abilene Network announcement did just that. The opening demonstration showed remote surgery in which doctors collaborated over the network while hundreds of miles away from one another. The Abilene Network, a new national research network, links 37 universities today across 10,000 miles and will double. This network moves data 1,600 times faster than T1 lines. The Abilene Network was developed with an investment of $500 million in equipment and services from Qwest, Cisco Systems Inc., Nortel Networks, and Indiana University. It is one of several networks under development by the federal government and Internet 2 consortium, which is privately financed.

ABC National Television Sales Vice President, Research and Marketing Sales Development, Cathy Egan looks forward to the convergence of television, telephone, and Internet technologies. "Our company is well positioned to capitalize on the converging marketplace with the launch of the Go.com portal and the rich content that will be included from ABC and the Disney family of brands." One of the most important developments today to move us to the future, according to Egan, is the ability to be connected to the Internet all the time, without the need to sign on either by PC or TV.

CBS New Media vice president Deb Zeyen strongly feels that the Internet as we know it and television as we know it will converge. "When you watch TV, it will be interactive. And you won't have a lot of different equipment to deal with." How would this work in reality? Zeyen can envision it as flawlessly simple. "You could be watching the Grammys, and decide you would like to order the CD from a winner when it's announced. You will be able to order it right away from your television." The cable industry is supportive, and there are clear reasons to move ahead quickly. From a user's point of view, there is increased ease of use. From the cable companies' point of view, there is increased revenue. Think of the simplicity of it in your home: with cable connections to the Internet, you are always ready to be online, just as you are always cable-ready with your television set once you are a subscriber. There is no need to "sign on" and "sign off" when you have the direct cable connection.

■ Interviews with Trend Readers

Mark Bregman, general manager of IBM's pervasive computing division, reports that there will be a shift of focus toward a broader range of intelligent devices, and not all of these devices will be like computers. Bergman also predicts that washing machines and other home appliances will come with LCD panels and Web browsers. These appliances will be able to communicate with the Internet and with other home gadgets. Does this mean an Electrolux will automatically contact a neighborhood service center when we're out of vacuum cleaner bags and schedule a delivery? This is looking more and more likely.

■ The Ten-Year Forecast

Resistance to projecting beyond five years is amazingly strong. Ten digital years is like a lifetime away. The changes that occur within a two-year period are far greater when you're traveling at Internet speed than in the previous

decade. The changes are also more life-changing than many people anticipated. "If you had a crystal ball, what would you predict?" At the risk of looking foolish in retrospect, many experts dance around this question, lest ten
years from now should happen tomorrow.

APPENDIX

Sign Off—Resources

■ Where to Go for Help

Never have the resources for e-commerce development been as abundant as now. Virtually every major newspaper carries a weekly column related to the Internet, often focusing on e-commerce. Magazines and periodicals are available online and through most major retail distributors. And of course, the best resources are also available online, where information is updated regularly.

Virus Protection

The following Web sites have virus information online:

- www.zdnet.com. Tips for fighting viruses and current information about software and suppliers, from Ziff Davis
- www.symantec.com. From Symantec, which sells antivirus software
- www.clac.org. the Computer Incident Advisory Capability

- www.cert.org. The Computer Emergency Response Team at Carnegie Mellon University

Useful Business Web Sites

Online magazines and newsletters

- *NetCommerce* magazine: www.netcommercemag.com
- *Internet Business* magazine: www.ibizmag.com
- *Internet Week*: www.internetwk.com
- *E-Business Advisor:* www.advisor.com
- *ComputerWorld* E-commerce: www.computerworld.com/emmerce
- Ziff Davis Publications: www.zdnet.com
- Smallbiznet (The Edward Lowe Foundation): www.lowe.org
- *Inc.* Online: www.inc.com
- *Entrepreneur* magazine: www.entrepreneurmag.com
- Entrepreneurial Edge Online: www.edgeonline.com
- Income Opportunities Online: www.incomeops.com
- *Small Office Computing/Home Office Computing:* www.smalloffice.com
- *The Small Business Advisor:* www.isquare.com
- *The Small Business Journal:* www.tsbj.com
- *Home Business* magazine: www.homebusinessmag.com
- *Small Business News* Online: www.sbnpub.com
- *Fast Company:* www.fastcompany.com

General business information

- CEO Express: www.ceoexpress.com/
- *Business Week:* www.businessweek.com (check out quarterly e-business supplement)
- National Association of Women Business Owners (NAWBO): www.nawbo.org

Small business information

- National Small Business Development Centers (SBDC): www.smallbiz.suny.edu/roster.htm
- University of Scranton Electronic Commerce Resource Center: www.ecrc.uofs.edu
- Netscape Small Business: www.netscape.com/netcenter/smallbusiness
- Lycos Online Resources for Small Business: www.lycos.com/business

- Quicken Small Business Resources: www.quicken.com/small_business
- Ziff Davis Small Business Advisor: www.zdnet.com/smallbusiness/
- Winstar's Office.com: www.office.com
- SBA Women's Business Centers: www.onlinewbc.org/docs.starting/index.html
- Office of Women's Business Ownership: www.sbaonline.sba.gov/womeninbusiness
- Bell South Small Business: www.bellsouthcorp.com

Research sssistance

- *Thomas Register* (the manufacturer's directory): www.thomasregister.com
- Yahoo! (navigation service): www.yahoo.com
- Excite (search engine): www.excite.com
- InfoSeek (search engine): www.infoseek.com
- Jupiter Communications: www.jup.com
- DejaNews (search engine for Internet newsgroups): www.dejanews.com

■ Associations, Societies, and Institutes

Trade associations and general business associations can offer help in gathering marketing information, networking, gaining referrals for services in other parts of the country, finding potential partners for strategic alliances, and simply connecting in person rather than by the Internet once in a while. Here's your help in monitoring legislative and regulatory developments at the federal and state level.

Trade Associations

Advertising Mail Marketing Association
1333 F Street, NW, Suite 710
Washington, DC 20004-1108
202-347-0055

American Bankers Association
1120 Connecticut Avenue, NW
Washington, DC 20036
202-663-5000

American Electronics Association
1225 Eye Street, NW, Suite 950
Washington, DC 20005
202-682-9110

American Financial Services Association
919 18th Street, NW, Third Floor
Washington, DC 20006
202-296-5544

American Forest and Paper Association
1111 19th Street, NW, Suite 700
Washington, DC 20036
202-463-2700

American Health Care Association
1201 L Street, NW, Eighth Floor
Washington, DC 20005
202-842-4444

American Institute of Certified Public Accountants
1455 Pennsylvania Avenue, NW, Suite 400
Washington, DC 20004
202-737-6600

American Insurance Association
1130 Connecticut Avenue, NW, Suite 1000
Washington, DC 20036
202-828-7100

American Retail Federation
701 Pennsylvania Avenue, NW, Suite 710
Washington, DC 20004
202-783-7971

American Society of Travel Agents
1101 King Street
Alexandria, VA 22314
703-739-2782

American Trucking Association
430 First Street, SE
Washington, DC 20003
202-544-6245

Association of American Publishers
1718 Connecticut Avenue, NW, Suite 700
Washington, DC 20009
202-232-3335

Associated Builders and Contractors, Inc.
1300 North 17th Street
Arlington, VA 22209
703-812-2000

Associated General Contractors of America
1957 E Street, NW
Washington, DC 20006
202-393-2040

Automotive Parts and Accessories Association
4600 East-West Highway
Bethesda, MD 20814
301-654-6664

Automotive Service Association
P.O. Box 929
Bedford, TX 76095-0929
817-283-6205

Computer and Business Equipment Manufacturers Association
1250 Eye Street, NW, Suite 200
Washington, DC 20005
202-737-8888

Electronic Industries Association
2001 Pennsylvania Avenue, NW
Washington, DC 20006
202-457-4900

Food Marketing Institute
800 Connecticut Avenue, NW
Washington, DC 20006
202-452-8444

Independent Insurance Agents of America
412 First Street, SE, Suite 300
Washington, DC 20003
202-863-7000

Information Industry Association
555 New Jersey Avenue, NW, Suite 800
Washington, DC 20001
202-639-8262

International Association for Financial Planning
Two Concourse Parkway, Suite 800
Atlanta, GA 30328
404-395-1605

National Association of Convenience Stores
1605 King Street
Alexandria, VA 22314-2792
703-684-3600

National Association of Desktop Publishers
426 Old Boston Street
Topsfield, MA 01983
800-874-4113

National Association of Home Builders
1201 15th Street, NW
Washington, DC 20005
202-822-0200

National Association of REALTORS®
777 14th Street, NW
Washington, DC 20005
202-383-1000

National Association of Wholesaler-
Distributors
1725 K Street, NW, Suite 710
Washington, DC 20006
202-872-0885

National Lumber and Building
Materials Dealers Association
40 Ivy Street, SE
Washington, DC 20003
202-547-2230

National Restaurant Association
1200 17th Street, NW
Washington, DC 20036
202-331-5900

Printing Industries of America, Inc.
100 Dangerfield Road
Alexandria, VA 22314
703-519-8100

Travel Industry Association of America
1133 21st Street, NW
Washington, DC 20036
202-293-1433

■ Business Organizations

U.S. Chamber of Commerce
1615 H Street, NW
Washington, DC 20062
202-659-6000

Alliance of Independent Store Owners
and Professionals (AISOP)
3725 Multifoods Tower
Minneapolis, MN 55402
612-340-9855

American Entrepreneur Association
(AEA)
2392 Morse Avenue
Irvine, CA 92714
714-261-2325
800-421-2300—Membership information
(Note: AEA publishes *Entrepreneur.*)

Edward Lowe Foundation for
Entrepreneurship
P.O. Box 8
Cassopolis, MI 49031
616-445-4200/4244

Employee Benefit Research Institute
(EBRI)
2121 K Street, NW, Suite 600
Washington, DC 20037-1896
202-659-0670

National Association for the Self-
employed (NASE)
2121 Precinct Line Road
Hurst, TX 76054
800-232-6273

National Association of Small Business
Investment Companies (NASBIC)
1199 N. Fairfax Street, Suite 200
Alexandria, VA 22314

National Association of Manufacturers
(NAM)
1331 Pennsylvania Avenue, NW, Suite
1500
Washington, DC 20004-1780

National Business Association (NBA)
5025 Arapaho Road, Suite 515
Dallas, TX 75248
800-456-0440

National Federation of Independent Businesses (NFIB)
53 Century Boulevard, Suite 205
Nashville, TN 37214
615-872-5800

National Small Business United (NSBU)
1155 15th Street, NW, Suite 710
Washington, DC 20005
202-293-8830

Small Business Survival Committee (SBSC)
1320 18th Street, NW
Washington, DC 20036
202-785-0238

National Association for the Cottage Industry (NACI)
P.O. Box 14850
Chicago, IL 60614
312-472-8116

National Association of Home-Based Businesses (NAHBB)
10451 Mill Run Circle, Suite 400
Owings Mills, MD 21117
410-363-3698

■ National Resources

Online Export Resources

- Video Golden Key. Contact: Curt Cultice, U.S. Department of Commerce, 202-482-3809. This program was designed by the Department of Commerce to help companies communicate with potential business partners globally using real-time video on their computers. The kick-off program was a partnership with the South Dakota International Business Institute, and the goal is to replicate the program with additional partners.
- www.ita.doc.gov/tic. This is the site of the Trade Information Center, a clearinghouse of information on federal export assistance programs.
- www.stat.usa.gov. This, the site of STAT-USA/Internet, is a comprehensive collection of international market research, trade reports, and basic exporting information.
- www.cnewsusa.com. Commercial News USA. A public/private catalog/magazine that promotes American products and services in 152 countries.
- www.onlinewbc.org. Striving to be the International Women's Business site, this Web site offers a full range of business-related services to women in Spanish. Information includes marketing strategies, management techniques, credit, new technology, government contracts, business links, export opportunities, and more. Chat rooms and individual counseling are also available. Some information is offered in

French, Portuguese, German, and Italian. Future plans include Chinese, Japanese, and Russian.

- www.gnn.com/gbi.bin/gnn/currency. This site provides immediate currency conversions from any currency to another.

Small Business Administration (SBA)

The SBA serves small businesses directly through a wide variety of programs. Start-up business counseling includes business plan preparation, workshops, and individual counseling. The SBA offers publications on virtually all aspects of small business needs. Following are the main offices and functions of the SBA:

U.S. Small Business Administration (SBA)
409 Third Street, SW
Washington, DC 20416
800-827-5722

The SBA Small Business Answer Desk (800-827-5722) will provide information (by phone only) on specific issues as well as direct inquiries to the appropriate person or department.

SBA on the Internet

- Home page: www.sba.gov
- Gopher: gopher://gopher.sba.gov
- File transfer protocol: ftp://ftp.sba.gov
- Telnet: telnet://sbaonline.sba.gov
- U.S. Business Advisor: www.business.gov

SBA OnLine provides immediate access to information on SBA programs, SBA field offices, business development services, government contracting opportunities, and more by dialing the following:

- General access: 800-697-4636 (SBA and other government agency information, downloadable files)
- Additional information: 202-401-9600: Washington, D.C. area (toll charge varies by local service provider) or 900-943-4636 at a fee of 14 cents per minute (downloadable application software files, news groups, online searchable data banks)
- Tech Support: 202-205-6400

SBA Office of Economic Development
409 Third Street, SW, Suite 8200
Washington, DC 20416
202-205-6657

Office of Advocacy
409 Third Street, SW, Sixth Floor
Washington, DC 20416
202-205-6531

Veterans Affairs Office
409 Third Street, SW, Sixth Floor
Washington, DC 20416
202-205-6773

U.S. Department of Commerce (DOC)
14th Street (between Constitution Avenue and E Street, NW)
Washington, DC 20230
202-482-2000

Patents, Trademarks, and Copyrights

Patents. Patents give owners the right to exclude others from manufacturing, using, or selling an invention throughout the United States. If the invention is a process, a patent gives the owner the right to exclude others from using, selling, or importing into the United States products made by that process. Information on patents, including patent applications, is available by mail or calling 703-557-4636. A publication entitled *General Information Concerning Patents* is available from the Government Printing Office, Washington, DC, 20402. Call 202-783-3238 to order by phone or write to:
Patent and Trademark Office
U.S. Department of Commerce
Washington, DC 20231

Trademark. This is a unique symbol, design, name, slogan, or sound used in trade to distinguish the goods and services of one party from another. Registration is not necessary for trademark protection, but it does give the registrant priority. Other benefits include the right to use the registered trademark symbol with the mark. Trademarks are registered at the national level with the Patent and Trademark Office at the address cited earlier. A publication entitled *Basic Facts about Trademarks* is available by calling 703-557-4636.

Copyright registration. Registration is not necessary to claim copyright of an original literary, dramatic, musical, or artistic work. However, registration does provide certain benefits in the event of infringement. To order copyright forms, call 202-707-9100. Details on how to register a copyright can be obtained by writing to:
Copyright Office
Library of Congress
Washington, DC 20231
202-707-3000

■ Local Resources

National programs that have local offices throughout the United States include:

- Small Business Development Centers (SBDCs). The SBDCs coordinate federal, state, local, university, and private resources for counseling and training small business owners. Services include management and technical assistance and training, advice on marketing, finances, production, and organization.
- SBA Regional and District Offices
- Office of Export Assistance
- Department of Commerce and Economic Development

GLOSSARY

ActiveX A combination of existing technologies packaged by the Microsoft Corporation to enable interactive content on World Wide Web sites (WWW). ActiveX enables Web sites to use interaction, multimedia effects, and more to enhance the user's experience.

address Internet addresses are based on the IP protocol, using 32-bit code in the IP header for host addresses. Web URLs and e-mail addresses are text addresses that correlate to IP addresses.

ADSL (Asymmetrical digital subscriber line) A technique that uses advanced analog modulating technique to deliver high speed data over the telephone company cabling. Input speeds are higher than output speeds.

ANSI X 12 The American National Standards Institute (ANSI) X 12 committee. This committee was charged with the task of identifying a standard of transaction sets (somewhat like a programming language) that could be used in United States government, education, and industries like banking. The result was EDI (electronic data interchange). EDI standards address every bit of detail that could pass from one trading partner to another (product codes, descriptions, costs, company information, standard form information, etc.).

applet An application program written in Java to perform a specific function as part of a series of activities. Often distributed in attachments to Web documents.

ARPANet (Advanced Research Projects Agency Network) The precursor to the Internet. Developed in the late 60s and early 70s by the U.S. Department of Defense as an experiment in wide-area networking that would survive a nuclear war.

ASCII (American Standard Code for Information Exchange) The worldwide standard for the code numbers used by computers to represent all the upper- and lower-case letters, numbers, punctuation, etc. There are 128 standard ASCII codes, each of which can be represented by a seven-digit binary number.

asymmetric cryptography A cryptographic system in which encryption and decryption are performed using different keys. Also referred to as *public key encryption*.

automated clearing house (ACH) Nationwide electronic funds transfer systems that provide for clearance of electronic payments for participating financial institutions.

back-end processes Computing applications running and using data stored on large mainframe computers.

bandwidth The amount of information that can be sent through a connection, usually measured in bits per second. A full page of English text is about 16,000 bits. A fast modem can move about 15,000 bits in one second. Full-motion, full-screen video requires roughly 10,000,000 bits-per-second, depending on compression. Example: 56k line is a digital phone line connection (leased-line) capable of carrying 56,000 bits per second.

baud In common usage, the baud rate of a modem is the number of bits it can send or receive per second. Technically, baud is the number of times per second that the carrier signal shifts value. For example, a 1200 bit-per-second (bps) modem actually runs at 300 baud, but it moves 4 bps ($4 \times 300 = 1200$ bps).

bit (short for binary digit) The smallest unit of computerized data; a single digit number in base 2, either a 1 or a zero.

bps (bits per second) A measurement of how fast data is moved from one place to another. A 28.8 modem can move 28,800 bits per second.

bookmark A menu of URLs created by a user.

browser Software program that retrieves, displays, and prints information and HTML documents through the WWW. Popular browsers include Microsoft Internet Explorer, Netscape Navigator, and Mosaic.

bulletin board system (BBS) A computerized meeting and announcement system that allows people to carry on discussions, upload and download files, and make announcements which will be available to users not currently online.

byte A set of bits that represent a single character. Usually there are eight bits in a byte, but there can be more, depending on how the measurement is being made.

Certification Authority A trusted company or organization that will accept your public key, along with some proof of your identity, and serve as a repository of digital certificates. Others can request verification of your public key from a certification authority.

CGI (common gateway interface) A set of rules that describes how a Web server communicates with another piece of software on the same machine, and how the other piece of software (the CGI program) talks to the Web server. Any piece of software can be a CGI program if it handles input and output according to the CGI standard.

client A software program used to contact and obtain data from a server software program on another computer, often across a great distance. Each client program is designed to work with one or more specific kinds of server programs, and each server requires a specific kind of client. A Web browser is a specific kind of client.

cookie A piece of information on the Internet, sent by a Web server to a Web browser, that the browser software is expected to save and send back to the server whenever the browser makes additional requests from the server. Cookies are typically set to expire after a predetermined amount of time and are typically saved in memory until the browser software is closed down, at which time they may be saved to disk. Examples of cookie use include login or registration information, online shopping carts, or user surveys. When a server receives a request from the browser that includes a cookie, the server is able to use the information stored in the cookie for a variety of things such as to customize what is sent back to the user to track a particular user's requests.

cyberspace A term originated by author William Gibson in his novel *Neuromancer,* the word cyberspace is currently used to describe the whole range of information resources available through computer networks.

digital certificates An electronic document issued by a certification authority that is used to establish a company's identity by verifying its public key.

domain The unique name that identifies an Internet site.

EDI (electronic data interchange) The electronic exchange of business documents, such as purchase orders, invoice, quotes, etc. in a standardized form among a company's computers in different locations. Companies can communicate with their suppliers using EDI.

e-mail (electronic mail) Messages, usually text, sent from one person to another via computer. E-mail can also be sent to a large number of addresses on a mailing list.

ethernet A common method of networking computers in a LAN. Ethernet will handle about 10,000 bits per second and can be used with almost any kind of computer.

extranet An extended intranet that links two or more intranets together and makes information available to authorized members of the participating groups.

FAQs (frequently asked questions) Documents that list and answer the most common questions on a particular subject.

firewall A combination of hardware and software that separates a LAN into two or more parts for security purposes.

FTP (file transfer protocol) An Internet utility for storing and retrieving files. A common method of moving files between two Internet sites. FTP is a special way to log into another Internet site for the purpose of sending or receiving files. There are many Internet sites that have established publicly accessible stores of material that can be obtained using FTP by logging in using the account name anonymous. Thus these sites are called anonymous FTP servers.

gateway The technical meaning is a hardware or software setup that translates between dissimilar protocols. For example, Prodigy has a gateway that translates between its internal, proprietary e-mail format and Internet e-mail format. Also, *gateway* is sometimes used to describe any mechanism for providing access to another system.

gopher A method of making menus of material available over the Internet, Gopher is a client and server style program, which requires that the user have a gopher client program. Gopher has widely been supplanted by hypertext, also known as WWW (World Wide Web).

home page The main Web page for a business, organization, person, or the main page of a collection of Web pages.

host Any computer on a network that is a repository for services available to other computers on the network. It is quite common to have one host machine provide several services, such as WWW and USENET.

HTML (Hypertext Markup Language) The coding language used to create hypertext documents for use on the World Wide Web. In HTML you can specify that a block of text or a word is linked to another file on the Internet. HTML files are meant to be viewed using a World Wide Web client program such as Netscape Navigator or Microsoft Explorer.

HTTP (Hypertext Transport Protocol) The protocol for moving hypertext files across the Internet; requires an HTTP client program on one end and an HTTP server program on the other end. HTTP is the most important protocol used in the World Wide Web (WWW).

hypertext Any text that contains links to other documents. Words or phrases in the document that can be chosen by a reader and which cause another document to be retrieved and displayed.

internet The worldwide collection of interconnected networks which allows computers to communicate. The Internet consists of utilities which include the World Wide Web, usenet news, IRC, telnet, FTP, and e-mail.

intranet A private network inside a company or organization that uses the same kind of software that you would find on the public Internet, but it is for internal use only. For example, many companies have Web servers that are only available to employees.

IP number A unique number consisting of four parts separated by dots. Every machine that is on the Internet has a unique IP number. Most machines have one or more domain names, which are easier to remember.

ISDN (integrated services digital network) A way to move data over existing regular phone lines. It can provide speeds of roughly 128,000 bits per second over regular phone lines.

ISP (Internet service provider) An institution that provides access to the Internet in some form.

Java A programming language which allows for more advanced features on Web pages, such as drop-down menus, scrolling text, and moving graphics.

LAN (local area network) A computer network limited to the immediate area, usually the same building or floor of a building.

leased line A phone line that is rented for exclusive use from one location to another. The highest speed data connections require a leased line.

log in The act of entering into a computer system or the account name used to gain access to a computer system. Differs from a password in that it is not proprietary information.

megabyte A million bytes, a thousand kilobytes.

MIME (multipurpose Internet mail extensions) The standard for attaching nontext files to standard Internet mail messages. Nontext files include graphics, spreadsheets, formatted word-processor documents, sound files, etc. When nontext files are sent using the MIME standard, they are converted (encoded into text), although the resulting text is not really readable.

modem (MOdulator, DEModulator) A device connected to your computer and to your phone line that allows the computer to talk to other computers through the phone system.

Mosaic The first WWW browser that was available. Mosaic has been credited with making the Web accessible, subsequently increasing its popularity.

netiquette The etiquette on the Internet.

Netscape Navigator One of the most popular WWW browsers.

network Two or more computers which share resources; two or more networks connected are an internet.

newsgroup The name for discussion groups on USENET.

NIC (networked information center) Generally, any office that handles information for a network. One of these is the InterNIC, where new domain names are registered.

node A single computer connected to a network.

packet switching The method used to move data around on the Internet. In packet switching, all the data coming out of a machine is broken up into chunks. Each chunk has the address of where it came from and where it is going. This enables chunks of data from many different sources to commingle on the same lines and be sorted and directed to different routes by special machines along the way, enabling many users on the same data lines at the same time.

password A code used to gain access to a locked system.

POP (point of presence or post office protocol) A *point of presence* means a city or location to which a network can be connected, often with a dial-up phone: *post office protocol* refers to the way e-mail software gets mail from a mail server. E-mail software uses the POP account to get your mail.

port A place where information goes into and out of a computer. On the Internet, port refers to a number that is part of a URL, appearing after a colon, right after a domain name. Every service on an Internet server listens on a particular port number on that service. Most services have standard port numbers. Port also refers to translating a piece of software to bring it from one type of computer system to another. (A Windows program must be translated to run on Macintosh.)

posting A single message entered into a network communications system.

PPP (point-to-point protocol) A protocol that allows a computer to use a regular telephone line and a modem to make TCP/IP connections and thus be on the Internet. TCP/IP or Transmission Control Protocol/Internet Protocol is the suite of protocols that defines the Internet.

prefix The first part of the URL (uniform resource locator or address) which indicates the Internet utility being used.

router A special purpose computer (or software package) that handles the connection between two or more networks. Routers spend all their time looking at the destination addresses of the packets passing through them and deciding which route to send them on.

search engine Allows a user to find information on the Internet by typing in key words.

server A computer or a software package that provides a specific kind of service to client software running on other computers. The term can refer to a particular piece of software such as a WWW server, or to the machine on which the software is running. A single server machine could have several different server software packages running on it, providing many different services to clients on the network.

site The virtual location on the World Wide Web, usually made up of several Web pages and a home page, designated by a unique URL.

suffix The last part of the URL (uniform resource locator or address), which indicates the type of site being visited. Examples include *.com* for a commercial business, *.gov* for a government agency, *.edu* for an educational institution, *.org* for a nonprofit organization, *.net* for miscellaneous.

Telnet An Internet utility that allows a user to log on to a remote computer system.

URL (uniform resource locator) An address that allows direct access to an Internet site, consisting of a prefix, domain, and suffix. The prefix indicates the Internet utility being used, the domain is the unique name that identifies an Internet site, and the suffix indicates the type of site being visited.

usenet news An Internet utility made up of thousands of subject-oriented discussion groups known as newsgroups. Users can post messages to the group and read and reply to the messages as they wish. Usenet messages are archived at a remote site for a set period of time, rather than distributed via e-mail (as are listserv messages).

utility A portion of the Internet with a specific function and type of information.

World Wide Web An Internet utility made up of home pages with links to information such as information files maintained by the creator of the page or pages of related interest created by other people.

BIBLIOGRAPHY

Adam, Nabil R., Oktay Dogramaci, Aryya Gangopadhyay, and Yelena Yesha. *Electronic Commerce: Technical, Business, and Legal Issues.* New Jersey: Prentice Hall, 1999.

Cialdini, Robert B. *Influence: The Psychology of Persuasion.* New York: William Morrow & Co., 1993.

Downes, Larry, and Chunka Mui. *Unleashing the Killer App.* Boston: Harvard Business School Press, 1998.

Foley, James. *The Global Entrepreneur: Taking Your Business International.* Chicago: Dearborn, 1999.

Ghosh, Anup K. *E-Commerce Security.* New York: John Wiley & Sons, Inc., 1998.

Helmstetter, Greg. *Increasing Hits and Selling More on Your Web Site.* New York: John Wiley & Sons, Inc., 1997.

Janal, Daniel S. *101 Successful Businesses You Can Start on the Internet.* New York: Van Nostrand Reinhold, 1997.

Kosiur, David. *Understanding Electronic Commerce.* Redmond, Wash.: Microsoft Press, 1997.

McNeal, James U. *Kids as Customers: A Handbook of Marketing to Children.* New York: The Free Press, 1992.

Moore, Geoffrey A. *Inside the Tornado: Marketing Strategies from Silicon Valley's Cutting Edge.* New York: Harper Collins Business, 1995.

Moore, James F. *The Death of Competition.* New York: Harper Collins, 1996.

Pinson, Linda, and Jerry Jinnett. *Target Marketing.* 3d edition. Chicago: Upstart Publishing, 1996.

Reis, Al, and Jack Trout. *The 22 Immutable Laws of Marketing.* New York: Harper Business, 1993.

Ritchie, Karen. *Marketing to Generation X.* Boston: The Free Press, 1995.

Rossman, Marlene L. *Multi-Cultural Marketing.* New York: AMACOM, 1994.

Stein, Lincoln D. *Web Security: A Step-by-Step Reference Guide.* Reading, Mass.: Addison-Wesley Longman, Inc., 1998.

Treacy, Michael, and Fred Wiersema. *The Discipline of Market Leaders.* Reading, Mass.: Addison-Wesley, 1995.

INDEX